Helmet worn by Redskins QB Sammy Baugh, circa 1949.

Sports Illustrated

NFL QB

THE GREATEST POSITION IN SPORTS

Sports Illustrated

NFL QB

THE GREATEST POSITION IN SPORTS

CENTER STAGE

An aerial view from the Astrodome in 1968 captured the moment when the QB becomes the focus of everyone's attention as the Jets' Babe Parilli [15] took a snap against Houston.

Photograph by Chris Graythen/Getty Images

CONTENTS

GREG KELLY *Editor* / STEVEN HOFFMAN *Creative Director*
CRISTINA SCALET *Photo Editor* / KEVIN KERR *Copy Editor* / JOSH DENKIN *Designer*
STEFANIE KAUFMAN *Project Manager*

Classic QBs (from far left) Bobby Layne, Johnny Lujack and Sid Luckman of the Bears in 1948. | *Photograph by Hank Walker/Time Life Pictures/Getty Images*

Photograph by Neil Leifer

EYE OF THE STORM

The Steelers' Ben Roethlisberger battled
the elements and the Jaguars on the frigid
Heinz Field turf as Jacksonville handed
Pittsburgh its lone home loss of 2007.

4:11 FANTASY UPDATE

Photograph by Fred Vuich

Photograph by Walter Iooss Jr.

FOREWORD

BY BOOMER ESIASON

There are two WAYS TO LOOK AT THE QUARTERBACK'S job. One is that the entire franchise is going to be built around this one player, and he can camouflage whatever shortcomings his team might have. The other is that the entire franchise is going to be built around this one player, and whatever shortcomings he has, his team won't be able to camouflage them. And the view changes every week, depending on whether the team wins or loses.

That's the deal. When you are an NFL quarterback, you are the face of the franchise and even, in some places, the face of a city. Everybody is always watching you: the coaching staff, the ownership, the secretary in the front office; reporters, bloggers, sports radio yakkers; people in restaurants and at the grocery store. Your teammates, most of all. They watch the way you carry yourself. If you're sloppy, if you're late to meetings, if you seem unprepared, you're going to lose everybody's respect. The team is going to be a rudderless ship.

And yet, even though you are always the center of attention, quarterback is also the loneliest position in sports. It is most lonesome when you are facing adversity. Which is most of the time, when you think about it. When I got to the NFL, after the Bengals drafted me in 1984, I was trying to fool my teammates into thinking that I belonged. I was in so far over my head that I constantly wondered whether or not I could actually do the job. As a rookie, learning an NFL playbook is like trying to pick up a foreign language all at once, and as if your life depended on it. Which it might.

You have to learn entirely new personnel groups, formations, audibles, checks at the line of scrimmage. You also have to learn what everybody else is doing on a play at their position, because you have to be able to discuss it with them in short, five-second bursts. I would go over plays at home with my wife, like I was rehearsing lines for a movie. I would wake up at night with cold sweats. Long after everything clicked, which happened during my second year, I'd often drive right past my exit on the highway on my way home because I was thinking about how we were going to attack that week's defense. You always have to seem like you are in total control, even if you know you aren't. That is an isolating feeling.

When the team loses, you are the center of scorn, and that's also an incredibly lonely place. Never was more scorn heaped upon me than in 1987. The players went on strike early that season, and my Cincinnati teammates appointed me as union rep, figuring the team would never want to get rid of me. There I was, one of the highest-paid players in the league, sitting down in the middle of the road to block a bus carrying replacement players to the Bengals' facility. I looked like Public Enemy No. 1, insanely well-paid and yet looking for more (even if I didn't want more for myself).

Then the strike ended—and we stunk. We went 4–11. I was booed mercilessly. The fans wanted to run me out of the city. I remember going home after some of those games, lying on the couch, putting a cold towel on my forehead and drinking as much beer as I possibly could to try to forget how miserable I was. I was ready to put my house up for sale.

And just a year later, I got to experience the greatest highs the job can offer, when we made it to the Super Bowl. All the public wanted to hear was what I had to say. I was the same guy who went 4–11 the year before, but as the wins mounted, so did my popularity. I was honestly embarrassed when they handed me the league's regular-season MVP trophy that year. It's the ultimate team game. You can't do what you do without the guys around you. But outsized credit goes with the outsized blame.

And the funny thing was, I learned that it's still a lonely job even when things are going well. You spend so much of your time making sure that you're one of the guys, making sure the players around you know that you're all in with them. I would hang out in the locker room, arrange weekly dinners, have teammates over to my house. But even when you're one of the guys, you're something different too. All the great ones are like that: John Elway, Dan Marino, now Tom Brady, Peyton Manning, Drew Brees, Aaron Rodgers.

 N THE PAGES THAT FOLLOW IN THIS BEAUTIFUL BOOK, YOU WILL read about—and look at the most stunning photos ever taken of—the men who excelled at the most demanding job in sports. They are all part of a proud fraternity that bonds them with every quarterback who came before them, and every one who came after. They employed a variety of styles. There are the Golden Arms, the Bootleggers, the Tough Guys. There are the Chess Masters, and I am honored to be included in that category. Even though we all have different God-given skill sets, there are certain qualities that we all share. Leadership. Diligence. Toughness. Poise.

And because it's a complete look at the hardest job in sports, there are sections as well on the quarterbacks who fell flat, and who were knocked flat.

Probably the thing that unites all of us is that to be a great quarterback, most of all you have to never want to be anything else, from the day you first step into a huddle until the day you throw your last pass. I never did. I first played the position when I was 10, and I never played anything else until I retired from the NFL at age 36. And I never before or after experienced anything remotely close to what I did during those 27 years: the power, the excitement, the frustration. They were the most incredible feelings of my life. I think deep down, all the quarterbacks in the following pages would say the same thing. ∎

INTRODUCTION

BY TIM LAYDEN

On a field somewhere, little boys play football. They are wearing helmets and pads and oversized pants and jerseys, and coaches stand nearby with whistles at the ready. Or perhaps they are playing in shorts and T-shirts, with no coaches at all, just small kids with their dreams, on a field with no lines. They are in Florida or Texas or California; Pennsylvania or Ohio or Michigan. They mimic the grown-ups they worship on television, chasing each other along the grass, uncertain what do when the pursuit comes to an end. One of them holds the football. It is too big for his hands, too thick in the middle and too long from

Sammy Baugh of the Washington Redskins, in 1938. | *Photograph by Carl Mydans/Time Life Pictures/Getty Images*

SID LUCKMAN

Y.A. TITTLE

JOHNNY UNITAS

point to point. A baseball is so much simpler to grasp and to throw; a basketball so much more conventional in its symmetry. He cradles the football in the well of his palm and lets his skinny fingers lie across the strings the way he sees the grown-ups do. The ball is not gripped so much as it is balanced, like a piece of crystal on a waiter's serving tray. The boy raises the ball above his shoulder, steadying it with his other hand and looks out across the landscape in front of him where his friends run in straight lines and circles, waving their arms and beseeching that he throw it to them.

At last he releases the ball, sending it into the sky. The most amazing thing happens: The football corkscrews through the air in what can only be described as a spiral. Good lord, is there another sight in all of sports like a properly thrown football against an autumn sky? It is not a tight spiral; the tips of the ball wobble back and forth a little bit, but that happens on television too. In the distance the ball drops into a set of waiting arms and the receiver is wrestled to the ground by defenders. He jumps to his feet and he and his teammates run back and form a huddle around the passer. They are silent, awaiting his words. They are anxious, hoping he will throw them the ball next. He is their leader. He is the quarterback.

THERE IS NO POSITION LIKE IT IN ALL OF SPORTS. YOU CAN GATHER UP ALL the baseball pitchers and basketball point guards and hockey goalies. You can combine all the soccer strikers and tennis players and golfers and downhill racers and 100-meter sprinters. You can put all of them together and still they do not equal the quarterback. For it is the quarterback who commands the most complex and violent game on earth; it is the quarterback who brings order to the 22-man chaos, and it is he who decides when the action will commence and often when it will stop. It is he who is protected by the rules like no other player. It is he whom we watch, our eyes frozen on his form, our ears attuned to his signals. It is he who gets the money, the power and the girl. The quarterback is king, and the NFL quarterback is the king of kings.

He comes in all forms, as the following pages will show. He can be coolly elegant, like Joe Montana or a wild gunslinger like Brett Favre. He can have the intellectual brilliance of Peyton Manning or the exuberant athleticism of Steve Young. He can be drafted early, like Terry Bradshaw (and many others), or he can be drafted late, like Tom Brady, or not even drafted at all, like Kurt Warner. He can emerge from the black-and-white images of a bygone NFL like Sammy Baugh and Norm Van Brocklin; or he can help usher in the new era of the multiskilled athlete like Colin Kaepernick, Andrew Luck or Russell Wilson. He can famously love one woman, like Roger Staubach, or he can even more famously love many, like Joe Namath. His arm can be a quick-release cannon like Dan Marino's or a deadly accurate pop-gun like Drew Brees's. He can be big like Daunte Culpepper or small like Doug Flutie. He can stand still in the pocket like Dan Fouts or he can run around like Fran Tarkenton. He can be white, like almost all quarterbacks in the history of the game, or he can be black, like more with every passing season until, blessedly, it's nearly not worth mentioning. There is no template for the NFL quarterback except that he must lead and he must win.

The quarterback must arrive first at the office every morning and leave last at night. His work ethic will define the team's. He must be the one who watches videotape until his eyes are blurry and until the movements of the upcoming opponent are burned into his memory. He is the one who must know what every man does on every play. And when the ball is snapped, he is the one who must survey the length and breadth of the field, process the movements of multiple receivers and defenders and in only a second or two—while under siege from pass rushers intent on harm—determine where the ball must be thrown. Or he must run and slide, to gain yards but also preserve his valuable health. Then he must do it again and again, as plays crackle into his helmet receiver from a coach on the sideline.

His worth has become so outsized in the modern NFL that teams will regularly risk the future of the franchise to draft a college quarterback. Sometimes they'll package a bounty of draft picks just to move up one spot to select a savior who might turn into a Tom Brady, or a Peyton Manning or an Aaron Rodgers.

History says it's worth it. Sure, on rare occasions an NFL franchise has climbed all the way to the top of the mountain with a quarterback who was less than great, usually on the shoulders of a powerhouse running game or a dominant defense. The 1990 Giants won with backup Jeff Hostetler (after Phil Simms was injured) and the 2000 Ravens with Trent Dilfer; both had extraordinarily rugged defenses. The most overlooked example of this phenomenon is the 1985 Chicago Bears, whose defense overshadowed celebrity quarterback Jim McMahon's mediocrity. But far more often, teams have fallen short of a championship because their quarterback was less than great. Between Dilfer and Joe Flacco, the Ravens never had a quarterback to meet their defense halfway, including an aging Steve McNair, whom All-Pro linebacker Ray Lewis lobbied to join the team in 2006. The Rams went to Super Bowl XIV with Vince Ferragamo at quarterback because Bud Carson coordinated a strong defense and because they had a strong running game with Wendell Tyler. That wasn't enough to beat Bradshaw and the Steelers.

Without a great quarterback, every other employee of the franchise is endangered: The receivers, the offensive line, the head coach. The quarterback can win games that should be lost, yet he can also lose games that should be won. And that's never been more true than today. The modern NFL is a video game of receivers running unchecked into the secondary and defensive backs overmatched by rules changes that have steadily eroded their ability to provide coverage. In this league, it is the quarterback who holds the controller.

IT WAS NOT ALWAYS LIKE THIS. THE NFL THAT WAS BORN IN 1920 WAS A POOR STEPCHILD OF COLLEGE football, which was then one of the most popular sports in America. That early NFL shared with college football an aversion to frequently throwing the ball and remained firmly tethered to the deceptive and thoroughly ground-based single-wing formation that Pop Warner invented and installed in the early 20th century. In that formation, the center snap went to a player named the "tailback," who would usually run out of what's now called the shotgun formation. The "quarterback" was largely a blocker. Slowly, that changed, most dramatically with the introduction of the T formation, an innovation developed by University of Chicago coach Clark Shaughnessy in the late '30s. The T formation was the first offense that put the quarterback in a position to take a direct snap from center and it laid the groundwork for the so-called pro-style offenses that evolved through the next seven decades of the NFL. (George Halas and Chicago Bears QB Sid Luckman awakened the NFL by running the T formation and winning the '40 NFL title with a transcendent 73–0 win over the Washington Redskins.)

Yet the next evolutionary step was arguably the most significant in the early development of the passing game and the quarterback position. Founder and coach Paul Brown of the Cleveland Browns in the All-American Football Conference developed the first rudimentary "tree" of pass routes that required intricate coordination between the quarterback and his two primary receivers. For the first time, passes were being thrown not just to people, but to areas of the field; and quarterback Otto Graham was releasing the ball before receivers looked for

JOE NAMATH

JOE MONTANA

JOHN ELWAY

BRETT FAVRE

PEYTON MANNING

TOM BRADY

it, the precursor to anticipatory throwing that is now commonplace. It was primitive by modern standards, but Graham turned it into a transformative weapon. The Browns dominated the NFL in the early to mid-'50s, and Graham became the model for the next generation of quarterbacks.

Still, it wasn't until Dec. 28, 1958 that America truly fell under the spell of the power of the signal-caller. Late on that Sunday afternoon the Baltimore Colts defeated the New York Giants 23–17 to win the NFL championship at Yankee Stadium. That overtime thriller came to be called "The Greatest Game Ever Played," a designation that has endured not only for the drama, but also for its role in growing the NFL as a television product. In the game, the Colts' 25-year-old, crewcut quarterback, Johnny Unitas, masterfully led his team down the field to tie the game in regulation, completing one pass after another in the face of a waning clock and a punishing Giants' pass rush. His performance under such pressure—truly, the work of a field general—became the archetype for all future quarterbacks and for fans, a form of real-time drama unmatched anywhere else on their dial.

Six years after that game, the New York Jets drafted quarterback Joe Namath out of the University of Alabama and gave him a $427,000, four-year contract, an outlandish sum by the standards of the era. But it was Namath who took the quarterbacking baton from Unitas and ran with it into the next generation. He was many of the same things that Unitas was: cool under pressure, smart, strong-armed and tough. His surgical dissection of the heavily favored Colts in Super Bowl III ushered in the merger of the NFL and the AFL by proving that the upstart could compete with the established league.

But Namath was also something more—a celebrity. He could be seen long after dark with beautiful women in Manhattan nightclubs, and he even briefly owned a share in a local hotspot, until the NFL ordered him to divest because it was frequented by unsavory characters. He appeared in commercials that traded on his playboy image and rewarded him handsomely; he went to Hollywood and made movies and had his own TV show. He was in many ways the first true, larger-than-life quarterback.

Namath, too, was the prototype of the quarterbacks who played in the NFL from the late 1960s into the '70s. They were increasingly skilled, but the league still adhered to its running-game roots. Passing attacks were high on risk and low on precision. Quarterbacks such as Daryle Lamonica in Oakland, Sonny Jurgensen in Washington and Jim Hart in St. Louis were asked to throw bombs, convert third-and-long or execute a desperate two-minute drill to snatch victory from defeat. The most famous risk-reward quarterback of the '70s was Bradshaw, who led Pittsburgh to four Super Bowl titles.

But soon the game inexorably changed. In Cincinnati, a young Paul Brown assistant named Bill Walsh, who had learned the deep passing game from Al Davis in Oakland, lost his gifted rookie quarterback Greg Cook to a devastating shoulder injury and in his place acquired noodle-armed Virgil Carter. But Carter was nimble and smart, so Walsh developed a passing offense built on short, horizontal patterns that allowed Carter to read his receivers and steadily move the Bengals downfield. That attack was the foundation of the West Coast offense that Walsh would later install in San Francisco and which Joe Montana and Steve Young used to lead the 49ers to five Super Bowl titles.

Walsh's offense raised the bar for sophisticated passing systems, and it was spread across the NFL by acolytes like Mike Holmgren, Steve Mariucci and Jon Gruden. It demanded an expansion of the usual quarterback skill set. To play in the Walsh system, a man had to be quick and athletic in moving away from the center, capable of reading defenses while dropping back, making swift judgments on which receiver would be open and then delivering a perfectly placed pass. Montana was the ideal vessel for Walsh's brilliance, but a decade after Montana first took San Francisco to a Super Bowl title in 1981, Favre came into the NFL and would ride the West Coast offense under Holmgren to a place atop every career passing list in the NFL. He was both gunslinger and student, Namath mixed with Virgil Carter.

Almost concurrent with Walsh's system, Don Coryell used his exposure to a downfield passing game created by Sid Gillman with the Chargers of the 1960s (when Coryell was at San Diego State) and melded it with a complex series of medium-length pass routes to create what came to be known simply as the Coryell Offense. Fouts used it with Coryell's Chargers, Troy Aikman ran it with Jimmy Johnson's Cowboys and Kurt Warner played it with Dick Vermeil's Rams. Most of the moving parts in the modern passing game can be traced to either Walsh or Coryell. Suddenly NFL quarterbacks were managing a broad matrix of movement that made Graham's simple timing routes look like a game of schoolyard tag.

DREW BREES

THEN IT GOT EVEN MORE DIFFICULT FOR QUARTERBACKS. DEFENSES responded with ever more inscrutable systems that cleverly disguised which defenders might rush the passer and which ones might drop back into coverage. To combat the increasing complexity of defenses, coaches took play-calling out of the hands of quarterbacks. It had been one of the elements that made quarterbacks iconic; Unitas marching the Colts down the battered Yankee Stadium field while conjuring up the next call even as his receivers were being tackled. Instead, as the 1990s unfolded, all plays would be called by coaches. For many years, it was said that the last NFL quarterback to call his own plays was Jim Kelly, who took the Buffalo Bills to four Super Bowls while operating the K-Gun no-huddle offense.

But Kelly was not a dinosaur, he was a pioneer. Peyton Manning came into the NFL in 1998 and was followed two years later by Tom Brady. Together they would take the evolution of the position further, bringing to it a new level of cerebral activity. As Brady won three Super Bowls in the early 2000s and led the Patriots to an unbeaten regular season in 2007, and as Manning began chasing Favre's career records, the image of the quarterback as professor took hold. Defensive coordinators became fearful of attacking these future Hall of Famers because they could exploit any misplaced aggression and turn it into a touchdown. The new breed of chess master won games in the predawn hours of a Thursday, watching video in a darkened room at the team's practice facility. Brees followed in their footsteps and then Rodgers. Just as Kelly had done in Buffalo, they would call the game at the line of scrimmage with last-second adjustments.

AARON RODGERS

As the game rushed forward through the 2010s, and as Brady and Manning edged closer to their ultimate retirement from the game, a new generation of quarterbacks changed the job description again. There had always been quarterbacks who could escape from pressure and run with the ball: Tarkenton, Bobby Douglass, Randall Cunningham. Now here came players who were not only pure athletes—Kaepernick, Luck, Wilson—but who had also grown up watching the cerebral Brady and Manning. They brought a mixture of mind and movement to the position, a giant evolutionary step.

Yet even as the quarterback became a more complete creature, now a mix of intelligence and physical skill that his predecessors could not have imagined, the fundamental truth remains. He plies the most demanding trade in all of sports. For this he reaps the greatest rewards and suffers the most punishing critiques. He stands at the top of the hill, and he is alone. ∎

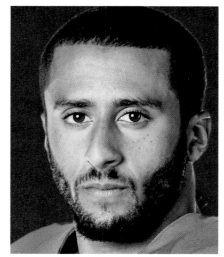

COLIN KAEPERNICK

Front row, left to right

Jim Ninowski, *Lions*

Fran Tarkenton, *Vikings*

Don Meredith, *Cowboys*

John Brodie, *49ers*

Sonny Jurgensen, *Eagles*

Y.A. Tittle, *Giants*

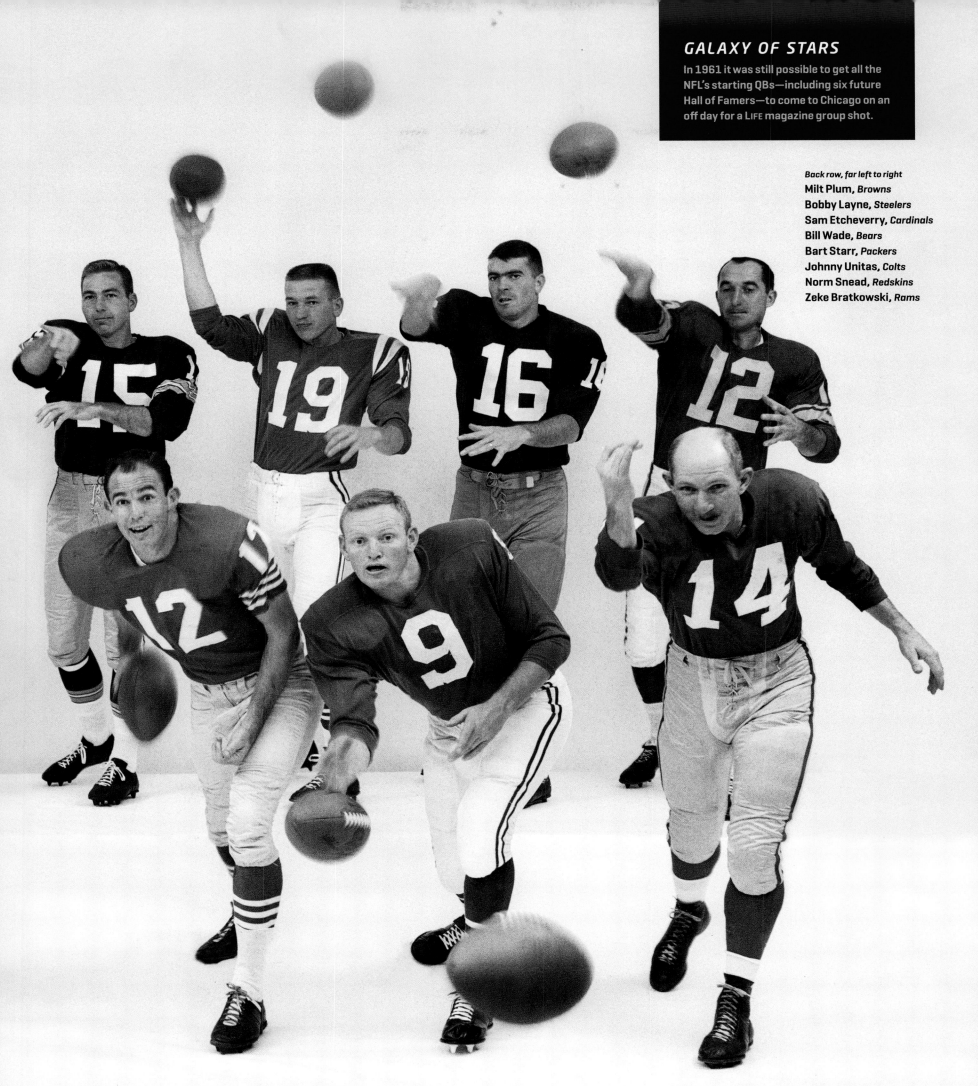

GALAXY OF STARS

In 1961 it was still possible to get all the NFL's starting QBs—including six future Hall of Famers—to come to Chicago on an off day for a LIFE magazine group shot.

Back row, far left to right
Milt Plum, *Browns*
Bobby Layne, *Steelers*
Sam Etcheverry, *Cardinals*
Bill Wade, *Bears*
Bart Starr, *Packers*
Johnny Unitas, *Colts*
Norm Snead, *Redskins*
Zeke Bratkowski, *Rams*

SNAP JUDGMENT

In the seconds before trench warfare broke
out between the Bears and the Packers
in 2012, Green Bay's Aaron Rodgers kept
a watchful eye on his left flank.

Photograph by John Biever

MIAMI MUDDER
Even with his feet on unsure turf while in the grasp of a Patriots defender, the Dolphins' Dan Marino was still an armed and dangerous threat.

Photograph by George Tiedemann/GT Images

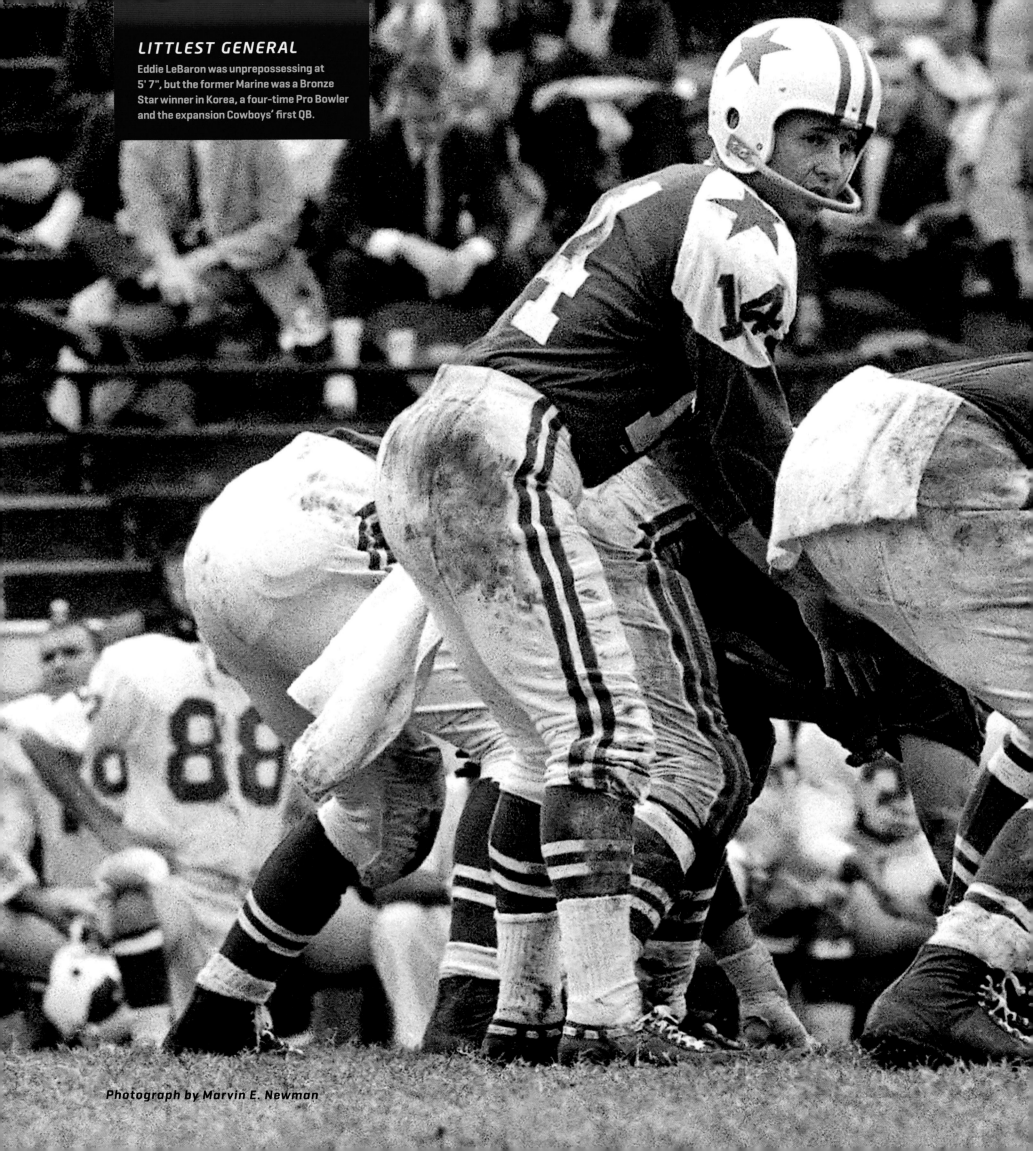

Photograph by Marvin E. Newman

Photograph by John Betancourt

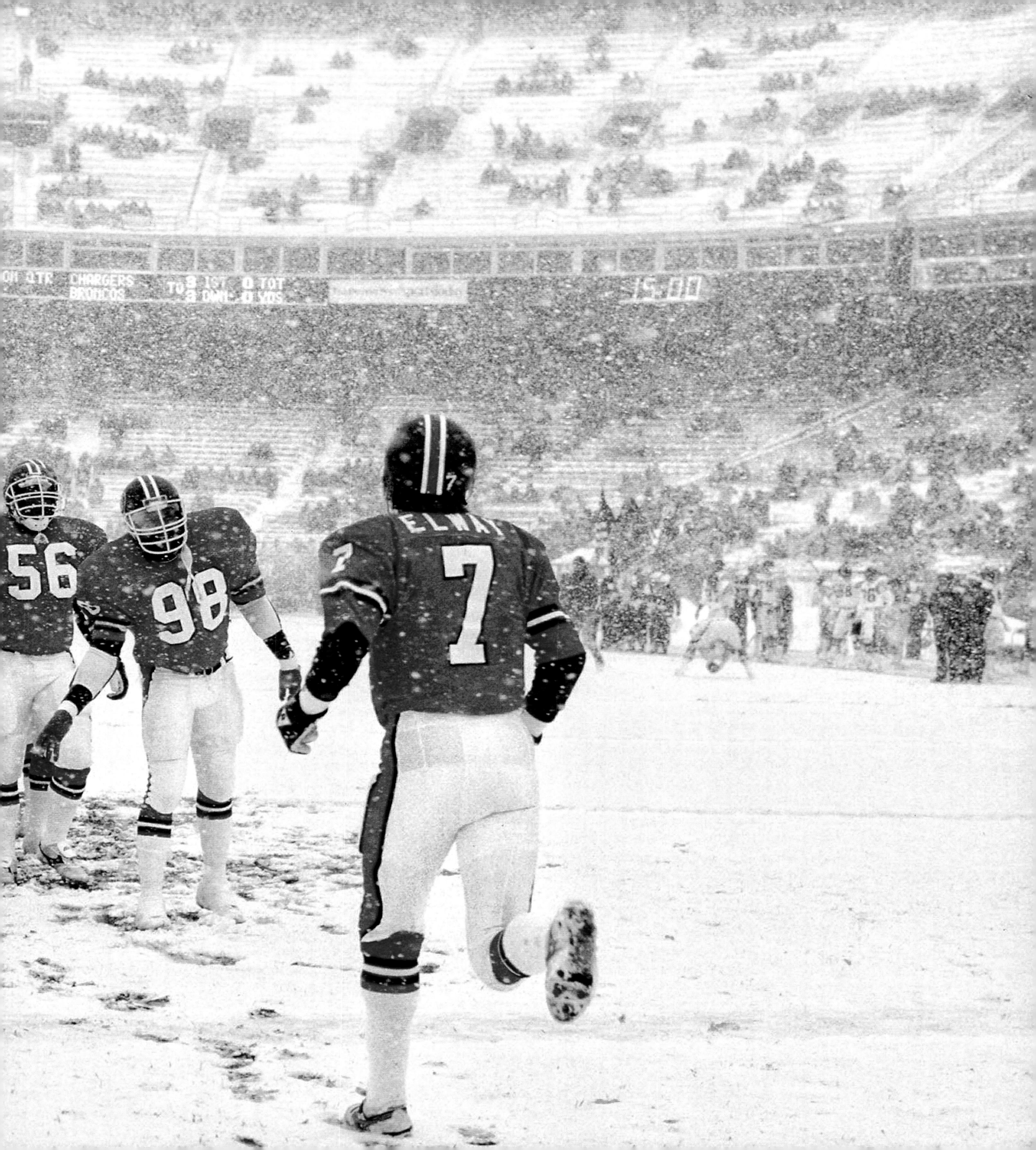
CHARGERS
BRONCOS
15:00
56
98
ELWAY
7

QBS ON
QBS

Fran Tarkenton
Hall of Fame, Class of 1986

Terry Bradshaw
Hall of Fame, Class of 1989

Dan Fouts
Hall of Fame, Class of 1993

Jim Kelly
Hall of Fame, Class of 2002

Troy Aikman
Hall of Fame, Class of 2006

Our blue-ribbon panel of Hall of Fame quarterbacks reveals the players they idolized as kids, admired as peers and ultimately judge as the Greatest of All Time

BY RICHARD DEITSCH

If you want TO KNOW ABOUT QUARTERBACKING, WHY NOT ASK THE BEST?

With that in mind, we convened some of the game's greatest to find out their thoughts on the position. Fran Tarkenton joined the NFL in 1961, Troy Aikman left it in 2000, and, in between, Terry Bradshaw, Dan Fouts and Jim Kelly were equally bright stars. Together they represent decades of playing and observing the game, and their opinions about the best and most underrated of their peers might surprise you.

Who was your quarterback idol growing up and why?

Dan Fouts

(Now an NFL analyst for CBS Sports):
"John Brodie was my idol because I was a ball boy with the Niners when my dad was their play-by-play announcer. I spent a lot of time with the Brode. We became friends and he persevered through some tough times in San Francisco and had a great career."

Fran Tarkenton

(Now a host for SiriusXM radio and an entrepreneur at tarkenton.com):
"Sammy Baugh. I lived in Washington, D.C., and like any kid I followed the local team, so the Redskins were my team. I thought he was a giant among giants. [Even] on losing teams, he did everything. He could throw, punt, just an iconic player. A lot of guys who played against him thought Sammy Baugh was the greatest quarterback who ever lived."

Terry Bradshaw

(Now a studio commentator on FOX NFL Sunday):
"I grew up loving and admiring Bart Starr. One of my highlights was in my rookie year playing against the Packers, I had a chance to run across the field and shake his hand. So cool. I've since had a chance to be with him at a couple of events and he's just a classy, classy man."

Jim Kelly

(His latest venture can be found at myfanclip.com, where a portion of the proceeds go to benefit the Hunter's Hope Foundation, one of his charities):
"This is a two-fold answer for me that I like to joke about: Terry Bradshaw was my idol on the field and Joe Namath was my idol off of it. And they both wore number 12."

Troy Aikman

(Now an NFL analyst for Fox Sports):
"When I was really young it was James Harris. I grew up in Southern California and he was with the Rams. But as I've gotten older, when people ask me this question, I say Vince Ferragamo. I keep very few autographed jerseys on my wall at home. I have four and Vince Ferragamo is one of them. I was a teenager in 1979 when he took the Rams to the Super Bowl and lost to Terry Bradshaw and the Steelers. My favorite quarterback of all time is Dan Marino, but he's not much older than me. I just loved the way he competed and the way he played the position. He was a fiery competitor and I liked everything about him."

You have the ball on your 20-yard line, two minutes left in the Super Bowl. Who is your choice of quarterbacks alltime to go for the win, and who is your choice among active quarterbacks?

Fouts: "Johnny Unitas. He was a teammate of my mine his last year and he would be my alltimer. He invented [the game-winning drive]. He did a lot of things before anyone else at the position. The rhythm passing, the timing routes, the five-step drop, the three-step drop, he perfected all of that. I'd think I'd go with Peyton Manning among the active quarterbacks. I like the weapons he has, but I just think Peyton would be my choice regardless."

Tarkenton: "Tough question. When you talk about situations like that I think of Johnny Unitas, Roger Staubach, Y.A. Tittle and Otto Graham. Those are the classics. But when we try to say who is the best, it is impossible. You have so many factors. What kind of team did they play on? What kind of organization? I can't say one guy. I could probably give you 20. Among active guys, the best players of this generation are Peyton Manning and Tom Brady. I'd take either one. There is no way to pick between them. But a third guy who does not get the recognition but has moved way up into their category is Drew Brees. Most people don't talk about him and they should. He is building a reputation of those two."

Bradshaw: "There are two guys I would hand the ball over to and if one of the guys were sick, the other guy could do it. One would be Roger Staubach and the other would be Tom Brady. Those would be my two guys. Now if I had to pick between one of those, then I'd pick Staubach, but they are pretty much even. Roger always made

From left: Clifton Boutelle/Getty Images; Heinz Kluetmeier; Focus on Sport/Getty Images; John Iacono; Peter Read Miller

something happen. He always brought his team back. He was amazing under pressure and he had this incredible athletic ability to get away from sacks and to be able to sprint and run around. He was scary, man. I loved watching him. I just marveled at how cool he was. He could throw that rock, man. He could sling it."

Kelly: "Alltime [and active], I'd say Tom Brady. When you watch him, he is flawless. Everything that you'd want your son to emulate as far as emotion, drop-back, everything, he has it."

Aikman: "I would say alltime would be Joe Montana, and I'd go with Tom Brady among those active. I think Joe Montana is the greatest quarterback to ever play. I didn't see Y.A. Tittle and Otto Graham and guys like that, but of the guys of the modern era that I got a chance to watch, Joe was the greatest. I saw him firsthand essentially do that in a Super

"AS A KID growing up in Southern California, my idol was Vince Ferragamo. I keep very few autographed jerseys on my wall at home—there are only four—and Vince Ferragamo is one of them."

—TROY AIKMAN

Bowl. With Tom, it's kind of the same thing. If it were not Tom, I'd probably say Peyton Manning today."

If you were running a team and had your pick of any quarterback today, who would you choose?

Fouts: "I'm not sure I'd pick an old guy. If I were starting a team today, I'd go with Andrew Luck. He already appears to play like a veteran and he has only played two seasons."

Tarkenton: "If I'm looking at the quarterback today, looking at his age, future and so forth, then I have to go with a young quarterback and that young quarterback would be Russell Wilson. People say I am prejudiced because he's my size. That's not it. What I like about him is that he is 5' 11" and a third-round pick, and they overlooked him because the NFL overlooks players if they are not a certain size at a certain position. If you are a 6-foot-or-under quarterback, which I was, which Y.A. Tittle was and Russell Wilson is, most of us don't get drafted in the first round because they think we are too short. But number 1, a quarterback has to be really smart, and Wilson is really smart.

The second thing they have to do is figure out how to play and how they do that is watch film, listen to coaches. The greatest quarterback coach cannot make a great player out of a guy who cannot figure it out. Russell Wilson was booked as a backup at best but Pete Carroll will tell you Russell Wilson had "It." He is smart and a terrific athlete, so he can use his legs, run the read-option and buy time and scramble. He plays safely so he is not jeopardizing himself. I could also argue Andrew Luck too. But when I look at the body of work of these young quarterbacks, I would want Russell Wilson. The great ones play consistently well every week, and I think Russell Wilson does that."

Bradshaw: "I would probably go with Tom Brady only because he has a history of winning Super Bowls and this is about winning Super Bowls. It's about the rings. I am not about stats or throwing for 50,000 yards. I'm about the rings and always will be. How many rings you have, jack? Oh, you don't have any? See ya. So Brady is my guy."

Kelly: "Tom Brady is one of the greatest to play the game but if I had to say one year, I'd choose Peyton Manning. Look at the way he runs a team, his smarts, he has everything that you want in a quarterback. So I'd take Peyton Manning and hope there is somebody behind him that will be able to learn from Peyton Manning's work ethic and what it takes to be a great quarterback from the neck up. There is nobody that works harder than Peyton. Frank Reich was his quarterback coach for a few years and he said to me, "Jim, you think we studied film? There is nobody like Peyton." So if I knew I had to have someone for one or two years, I'd take Peyton."

Aikman: "A couple of years ago I said Aaron Rodgers. Now he's played nine seasons. But he might have nine years left in him because I think guys can play until around 40, so I would probably still stick with him. But if it were not him, I'd go with Andrew Luck."

Who is the greatest of all time at quarterback, in your opinion and why?

Fouts: "Johnny Unitas. For all the reasons I mentioned before. For two decades he was considered the best and there were some great quarterbacks in those years, but hands-down all of them would say he was the best at that time. His longevity speaks to that."

Tarkenton: "People ask me that question and it is impossible. Now we want to measure quarterback on how many Super Bowls they won, right? You tell me a quarterback that played better than Dan Marino? Or Dan Fouts? Or Y.A. Tittle? There are none. So they take a backseat because they did not have the good fortune or good luck or right organization or right timing to win a Super Bowl? It's a B.S. category. What makes one quarterback better than another is how he performs week-in, week-out with the body of his career. He cannot control the drafting, the coaching, the defense, the special teams or the breaks. So it's a stupid thing to talk about. I crossed over a little with Y.A. Tittle, then I followed him and played against him and I will tell you that there is no quarterback in the history of the world that played better than Y.A. Tittle. He played on a lousy 49ers team in the '50s and comes to the Giants and they are in three championship games."

Bradshaw: "I have never [picked] a greatest of anything in all my life. You want me to pick one from Otto Graham to Sid Luckman to Slingin' Sammy Baugh, who I once met? He was spitting tobacco and cussing like a sailor and how cool was it to meet Sammy Baugh? There are guys I admire like Bert Jones and Kenny Anderson. Kenny Stabler was awesome. Roman Gabriel I loved. Johnny Unitas. But eras have changed. There were simple coverages back then. We go through progressions as decades move along so it is hard to say who is the best. You can do best of his time but the best ever? I don't even know how to categorize that."

Kelly: "That is tough one. I never saw Johnny Unitas play but I did speak to him many times and I have heard many people say he

"I WILL tell you that there is no quarterback in the history of the world who played better than Y.A. Tittle. He played on a lousy 49ers team, then came to the Giants and went to three championship games."

—FRAN TARKENTON

was one of the best. There is Joe Montana, of course, with all of his Super Bowls. It's almost unfair because Peyton Manning is a good friend of mine, Tom Brady is a good friend of mine, Joe Montana is a good friend, and so is Dan Marino and John Elway. For me, that would be a tough one. There are different eras of football, it is so tough to pick just one. It's hard not to take Dan Marino even though both of us will be labeled as quarterbacks that never won a Super Bowl. So maybe I'd say Marino, Brady, Montana, Manning and Elway. I really can't pick one."

Aikman: "Joe Montana. It just seems like people change their opinion on who is the greatest depending on who is playing at that time. Most of the time when people have these discussions, Otto Graham seems to be a guy who is oftentimes overlooked, but Joe, of the guys I have seen, there was nobody better. He was clutch when he had to be and he did things guys were not doing at that time. He was terrific."

Who is the most underrated quarterback of all time?

Fouts: "It's a tough question. There are a couple of guys I think who do not get enough credit for being great or among the greatest. One of them is Bart Starr. Nobody has won more NFL championships. Another one, even though he had talent around him, is Roger Staubach. Roger did not play as long as he could have because of his military commitment but you talk about a great quarterback, my God."

Tarkenton: "I think Y.A. Tittle was underrated. I think Dan Fouts was underrated. At the time they were not underrated, but

"THE BEST quarterback not in the Hall of Fame? Ken Anderson. He had that quick release and ran that West Coast offense. I remember he went 20 for 22 against us, and I'm thinking: Nobody goes 20 for 22 against us!"

—TERRY BRADSHAW

we don't talk about Dan Fouts and Y.A. Tittle. Dan Fouts was just great, phenomenal."

Bradshaw: "I have to bring up Philip Rivers. He is one of those guys in the mix. I loved Kenny Stabler. The Snake was smooth, man. Kenny Anderson was smooth too. If Bert Jones had not gotten hurt, there was nobody who could throw the ball like Bert Jones. He was an amazing athlete. And how can you not like Fran Tarkenton?"

Kelly: "Warren Moon had all the talent in the world, but I would say Phil Simms. He did well in the Super Bowl, played in a big city, and did a good job. I'd also say Boomer Esiason. He was a really good quarterback too."

Aikman: "I would go with Otto Graham because of the numbers of championships [seven], which is ridiculous. I read a book called *America's Game*, a historical perspective of football, and you read that and you just say, 'Wow, this guy was an amazing player.' In my era, I would probably say Phil Simms. I think he was a great player and if he had not gotten hurt in 1990—when Jeff Hostetler came on to win the Super Bowl—I think he would be in the Hall of Fame."

Who is the best quarterback who is not in the Hall of Fame but should be?

Fouts: "Ken Anderson. We had so many great battles. When Bill Walsh came to San Diego from Cincinnati, coaches would bring their tape and cut-ups, and Bill would put on Kenny for me to watch. I was like, 'Damn, that's not fair, Bill.' Early in his career he was such a dynamic runner as well as such an accurate passer. He was really talented."

Tarkenton: "I don't have a really good feel for this one but Kenny Anderson seems to have had a really good career and record."

Bradshaw: "Two of them right off the bat: First, Kenny Stabler. You play against Stabler and you did not sit down. He was like Staubach. He scared you to death. Nobody threw a comeback route better and nobody anticipated breaks of the receiver like Stabler. He had ice water in his veins. He was incredible. The other guy was Kenny Anderson. He had that quick, over-the-shoulder release and ran that West Coast offense. We did not know what the hell that was. I remember one time he went 20 for 22 against us and I'm thinking: Nobody can complete 20 of 22 against us. I'll tell you another guy who was pretty damn good and should be in the Hall of Fame: Brian Sipe. Go look him up."

Kelly: "Probably Phil Simms."

Aikman: "Kenny Stabler. He won a Super Bowl, he played in an AFC championship game and just won a lot of games. How do you define who is in the Hall of Fame and who is not? You can argue that in and of itself. But when you talk about the history of the sport, I think it's about: Does that guy have a place in that story, and I think Kenny Stabler does. The other guy I would say is Jim Plunkett. He was a multiple Super Bowl winner and, not that that is the end-all, but he is a guy who you could make a strong argument for."

What coach other than your own coach would you have loved to have played for and why?

Fouts: "Bill Walsh, because I had him for one year [as an offensive coordinator], and we had a great relationship. I was heartbroken when he was passed over for the job in San Diego. Ownership decided to keep Tommy Prothro instead. I took such huge strides under Bill. Things turned out O.K., though, because Don Coryell came along. I guess I played so crappy that they finally fired Prothro."

Tarkenton: "Bud Grant is my favorite coach of all time. I learned more from him than any other human being. But I played for Vince Lombardi, Tom Landry and Don Shula in Pro Bowls and I learned a ton from all three of them. I would have loved to have played for Lombardi or Landry or Shula. If I look at that group, I might put Shula at the top. He was such a great coach and a great personality."

Bradshaw: "Bum Phillips is number 1. Why? Because I think he would have understood me. I'm a Southern boy, a cattle guy, a cowboy-hat-wearing guy, his kind of guy. I think he would have been a guy I would have killed for. Who else? Don Coryell was a mad scientist. I had him at the Pro Bowl and I had to get someone to translate him. I remember Dan Fouts at the Pro Bowl saying, 'You are going to love this offense.' I said I don't think I can understand [Coryell]. He said just follow the arrows [in the playbook] and I lit it up just doing what Dan told me to do. I had no idea what I was doing, but I loved playing for Coryell. Also, I'd absolutely have loved to play for Bill Walsh and Tom Landry, too. I played for Don Shula [in a way] because I ran his offense under Chuck Noll or else he would be on this list too."

Kelly: "Of course everyone says Vince Lombardi. Even though I was a Bill, I always respected Don Shula. But I'd pick Mike Ditka. Blue-collar, tell it like it is, if I had to pick one, I'd probably say Ditka."

"JOHNNY UNITAS invented [the game-winning drive]. He did a lot of things before anyone else at the position: the rhythm passing, the timing routes, the five-step drop, the three-step drop. He perfected all of that."

—DAN FOUTS

Aikman: "I have a few. Vince Lombardi would be first. When they ask you who are the five people you would have at [a dream] dinner, he's always one. I'm a huge fan and would love to have played for him. The two most recent guys are Bill Parcells and Mike Holmgren. I like the toughness of Parcells. I got to know him when he was in Dallas, and I was a big fan when I was competing against him. I'm not sure we would have gotten along, though. I don't think he appreciated the forward pass as much as I would have liked. But I have enormous respect for him.

The other guy is Holmgren. I thought he was a great head coach, but I would have loved to have experienced what he was like as an offensive coordinator. He was in San Francisco with Joe Montana and then he was in Green Bay when I was competing against him, and they were throwing the ball with Brett [Favre] and doing things no one else was doing. It would have been a lot of fun to play in that offense. He's tough too, demanding. Those are the coaches I have always been drawn to." ∎

MEN WITH THE GOLD

EN ARMS

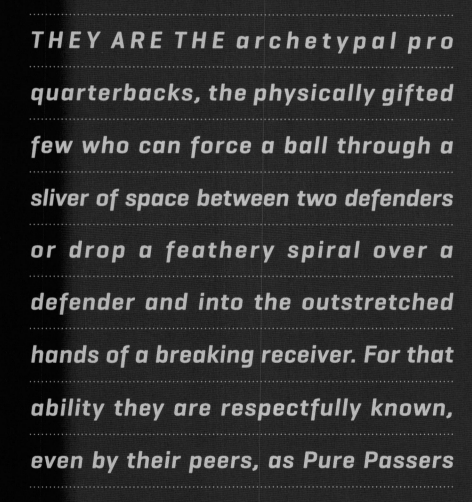

THEY ARE THE archetypal pro quarterbacks, the physically gifted few who can force a ball through a sliver of space between two defenders or drop a feathery spiral over a defender and into the outstretched hands of a breaking receiver. For that ability they are respectfully known, even by their peers, as Pure Passers

TROY AIKMAN The strength of his right arm carried Dallas on its greatest run ever, winning three Super Bowls in a four-year span, from 1993 to '96.

The Perfect Mix of Talent and Touch

BY TIM LAYDEN

The forward pass IS JUST A SLICE OF ATHLETIC MECHANICS, ROOTED IN fundamentals and techniques that are taught over and over to young football players from a very early age. It is the most significant game action in the most popular sport in the nation, and all quarterbacks who reach the NFL share some throwing traits. But for those who are hailed as the best pure passers, it's far more complicated, because completing a pass is just as much art as science.

Arm strength is part of it, but failed No. 1 pick JaMarcus Russell could throw a hole in the air, and he was nobody's idea of a pure passer. A passer has to have touch and timing, too. And like great art, you know it when you see it. Hall of Fame quarterback Dan Fouts can still recall being a rookie with the Chargers in 1973, and marveling at Johnny Unitas, his 40-year-old teammate, who was playing the last of his 18 seasons in the NFL and still delivering perfect spirals.

Almost everybody around football agrees that the guy who just might have been the most accurate passer in history was a pot-bellied, 5' 11" sidearm slinger. That was Sonny Jurgensen, who played 18 years for the Eagles and Redskins from 1957 to '74. Others will reach back into grainy history and pull up the name of Sammy Baugh as the best ever.

A pass is last contacted by the index finger of the throwing hand (much like a pitched baseball). A spiral is the goal, although not all quarterbacks throw a high percentage of spirals (Peyton Manning, most notably). Terry Bradshaw, who led the Steelers to four Super Bowl victories from 1975 to '80, put the index finger of his throwing hand very near the point of the ball. Troy Aikman, another Hall of Fame quarterback and winner of three Super Bowls from 1993 to '96 with the Cowboys, nearly ignored the laces, placing the knuckles at the top of his palm across the laces and his fingertips on bare leather. Drew Brees licks his fingers incessantly to strengthen his grip.

As the quarterback pulls away from the center and prepares to throw, he seeks an economy of tight movement while dropping back and looking downfield. Packers quarterback Aaron Rodgers is tight. Brees is tight. Joe Montana was the tightest of all. "Like a ballerina," says Mike Holmgren, who was his quarterbacks coach for three seasons with the 49ers under Bill Walsh. Meanwhile, Aikman pulled away from the center with terrific speed, giving him more time to survey the field.

But not every successful quarterback is so classic. One of the most iconic images in NFL history is that of Joe Namath, dropping back, holding the ball waist-high in his right hand, drifting back and then suddenly, every so briefly, patting the ball with his left hand as he brought it upward, almost as a trigger mechanism, before ripping it downfield. "Pulled it up and snapped it off his ear," says Bradshaw. "It was the coolest thing you could ever see." Most similar to Namath was Dan Marino, except he pulled the trigger after holding the ball high, with two gentle hands.

The quarterback's movement shifts dramatically at the back of the drop, like shifting a car from reverse to drive. His back foot hits and plants, he strides forward ("hitches") while moving the ball into position. Quarterback guru Steve Clarkson,

who has tutored scores of high school, college and NFL QBs, says no quarterback in history used his lower body more decisively in the throwing motion than John Elway. Brett Favre was spectacular when flushed *out* of the pocket.

Deliveries range from nine o'clock (Jurgensen, although not every time) to noon (Unitas). When he first came up with the Cowboys from 2003 to '05, Tony Romo would practice throwing from all manner of odd angles, trying to prepare himself to use varied release points during games. Perhaps no NFL quarterback has worked harder on his mechanics, but he's still not what's thought of as a pure passer.

Like deliveries, throwing mechanics vary. Kurt Warner, says former NFL quarterbacks coach Larry Kennan, "threw more effortlessly than anyone I every saw. He always looked like he was just playing catch." Former Ravens coach Brian Billick describes Warren Moon, whom he coached as an offensive coordinator with the Vikings, in similar terms. "On most of his passes," says Billick, "he was in perfect position to make the throw."

Big guns get the buzz. "After my senior year in college [at Indiana], I went to the combine," says Trent Green, an eighth-round pick in 1993, who spent 16 seasons as an NFL quarterback. "You get invited to the combine, you're pretty confident. You feel good about yourself and you just want to prove it. Everybody is that

way and you think everybody is good. Then Drew Bledsoe came out and his velocity was different, the spin on his ball was different and it was like, 'O.K., now I see why he's the No. 1 pick.'"

There remains a significant mythology surrounding Jeff George, who came out of Illinois in the spring of 1990 regarded as one of the most powerful throwers in the history of the game. Bert Jones, who played nine years for the Colts and one with the Rams from 1973 to '82, also had a high velocity arm. "Bert could get it wherever he needed to get it," says Archie Manning, who played in the same era as Jones. Favre's arm strength remains legendary.

The Bears' Jay Cutler is a flamethrower, but velocity alone isn't much more than a novelty. "It's fine to have a strong arm," says longtime coach and former NFL quarterback Zeke Bratkowski. "But lots of guys without real strong arms could make every throw. That's the difference between a thrower and a passer." It is the difference that separates the good from the great.

"Joe [Montana] had that ability," says Steve Young, Montana's Hall of Fame teammate. "Every football he threw had a message. There was no just throwing it and wishing it good luck."

A quarterback or a coach will tell you that the ultimate measure of a pass is not its meaning or its appearance, but simply whether it's completed. And that's fair. But the ultimate measure of the passer is much more elusive. ∎

Bledsoe wowed the other QBs at the '93 NFL combine and went on to play in four Pro Bowls. | *Photograph by Patrick Murphy-Racey*

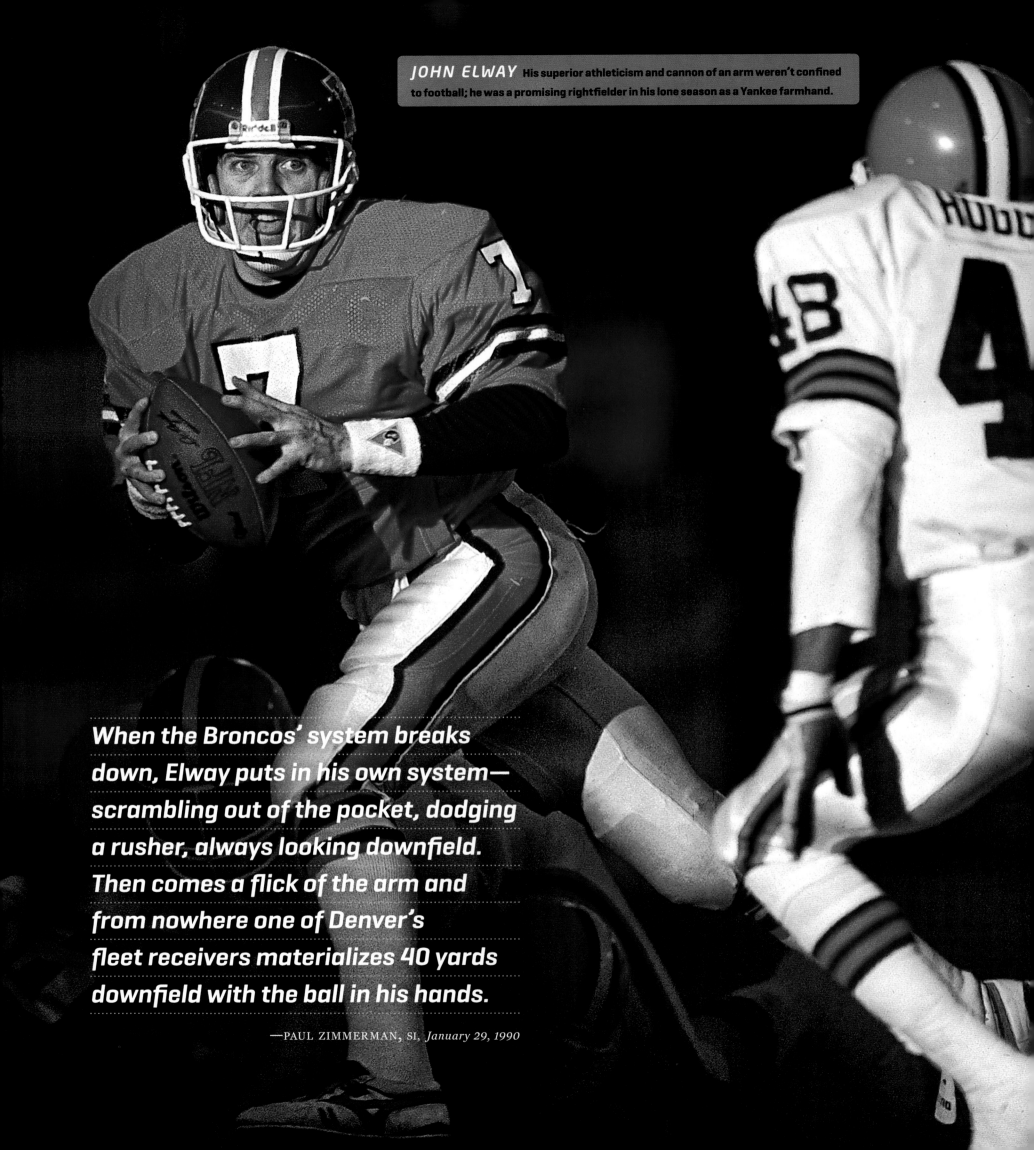

When the Broncos' system breaks down, Elway puts in his own system—scrambling out of the pocket, dodging a rusher, always looking downfield. Then comes a flick of the arm and from nowhere one of Denver's fleet receivers materializes 40 yards downfield with the ball in his hands.

—PAUL ZIMMERMAN, SI, *January 29, 1990*

BRETT FAVRE Despite playing much of his career in brutally cold weather, Favre passed for more yards (71,838) than any other quarterback in history.

ARMED FOR AN EPIC

WITH A SUPER BOWL SHOWDOWN AGAINST JOE MONTANA LOOMING IN JUST HIS SECOND SEASON, THE DOLPHINS' DAN MARINO WAS ALREADY DISPLAYING HIS CREDENTIALS AS PERHAPS THE GAME'S GREATEST PASSER

Excerpted from SPORTS ILLUSTRATED, *January 21, 1985* | BY PAUL ZIMMERMAN

T WAS MARCH OF 1978 AND THE NFL was meeting in Palm Springs, and the Competition Committee decided the game needed more passing, so it changed the rules and opened up the lanes. The members with foresight knew they were setting a time bomb, that out there, somewhere, was a young quarterback with a cannon for an arm and the guts to throw the ball anywhere. They didn't know where—Texas, California, Florida—but they knew he was waiting, and if their new rules would do what they were supposed to do, he would lift the art of throwing the football to a new level.

Actually, he was in western Pennsylvania, the Cradle of Quarterbacks, a lanky, gawky junior at Pittsburgh's Central Catholic High named Daniel Constantine Marino. In two seasons as the Miami Dolphins' quarterback, Marino has done everything the more prescient members of the Competition Committee expected. He is their monument. He has broken almost every passing record. And while Joe Montana and the San Francisco 49ers have won 17 of 18 games this season, Marino goes into Super Bowl XIX as *the* story. He has made these the burning questions of Sunday's game in Palo Alto: Can the 49ers stop him? Or control him? Or outscore him? Answer these and you'll have the answers to the Super Bowl. Everything else is window dressing.

Oh, Marino has been controlled on occasion—for a quarter, a half maybe. Then things seem to explode in what defensive coaches have come to call The Frenzy. The ball comes off Marino's hand like a rocket. The Marks Brothers, those two fine wideouts Mark Duper and Mark Clayton, start gobbling up yardage in huge chunks, 20-yard turn-ins, 30-yard fades, ups, goes. The defense drops off in double coverage and one of the tight ends, Joe Rose or Bruce Hardy, breaks one down the middle, or halfback Tony Nathan catches a little circle pass and races for 20 yards through a deserted zone. Everything is timed, everything delivered in rhythm in an incredibly short time and right on the money. The Frenzy is on and every drive produces a score. It's like an adding machine gone wild, and a tight game becomes a blowout.

Afterward you ask the defensive coach, "How do you stop Marino?" He'll tell you that the rush has to get to him . . . or you have to disrupt his rhythm . . . or your linebackers have to pop up in unexpected places. And then the coach will give a wan smile and say, "We sure as hell couldn't do it."

The silliest thing you hear is that someone's offense has to control the ball and keep Marino off the field. This is like facing a tennis player with a devastating serve and saying, "Well, I have to have a long service game myself to keep him from serving to me." Nope, you can't escape him.

Teams have noted the Dolphins' weakness against the run (4.71 yards per rush, the worst average in the NFL) and have come up with the obvious idea of grinding the ball on them and keeping Marino and the boys off the field. Fine, say the Dolphins, you take a long time on your drive, we'll take a short time, but you'd better not have any mishaps during your turn, such as a penalty or a three-yard loss, because you'll never catch up. "Our idea of a two-minute offense," says Marino's veteran backup, Don Strock, "is two scores."

Pittsburgh ran the ball very effectively at the Dolphins in the conference championship, winning the battle in the trenches. O.K., bring in the air force. It was a close game for a while, then late in the second quarter The Frenzy hit. Miami scored touchdowns on five straight possessions, and 14–10 Steelers became 45–21 Dolphins. The first three TD drives of The Frenzy were accomplished in 1:22, :33 and 1:48. Even scarier was the time it took Marino to get off his passes. Short, long, it didn't matter. Each pass completion was released from 1.4 to 2.65 seconds after Marino took the snap. They used to say that Joe Namath, who had the quickest release of his day, threw 2.2 to 2.7 routes on the quickies, but took longer for the deeper patterns. Consider this: On one Marino pass, a 24-yard TD on a fade pattern to Jimmy Cefalo that was called back, the ball was out of Marino's hand in 1.5 seconds.

"One-point-five seconds? That's incredible," says Tony Dungy, the Steelers' fine young defensive coordinator. "You know, it's almost a waste of time to blitz in a situation like that. I mean, you pull a stunt, like a deep loop, and you can get a guy coming in completely unblocked and he still can't reach the quarterback in 1.5 seconds.

Two classic Marino games stand out this year. Dallas, the masters of the blitz, managed to get rushers free up the middle against Marino, little guys mostly, safeties and nickel backs, so he stood up on tippytoes and threw over the blitz, flicking his wrist as if he were handling a flyswatter. When Marino was a schoolboy, his father taught him to throw the ball without bringing his hand behind his head and that flick technique paid off in a 28–21 Monday night victory.

In New England, the Patriots pressured Marino plenty. They forced him out of the pocket, which people have said is the key to stopping him. He can't scramble, they say, the way Montana can. He's a big guy who's got a bum left knee and is not that nimble. He sure was in Foxboro. He threw passes on the run, left or right. The Frenzy hit in the second quarter and a tight game became a 44–24 blowout.

Counting the playoffs, Marino has thrown for more than 400 yards five times this season. Marino tied the NFL record for touchdown passes in late November and by the end of the regular season he had 48 and had beaten it by 12. How do you stop him? "You play the best game you've ever played in your life," says George Seifert, the 49ers' defensive coordinator, "and make the right guesses—and pray." ∎

Marino would lose his only Super Bowl appearance, the sole stain on his illustrious legacy. | *Photograph by John Biever*

WARREN MOON He is sixth alltime in NFL passing yardage with 49,325 yards, even though he went undrafted and spent the first six years of his career in the CFL.

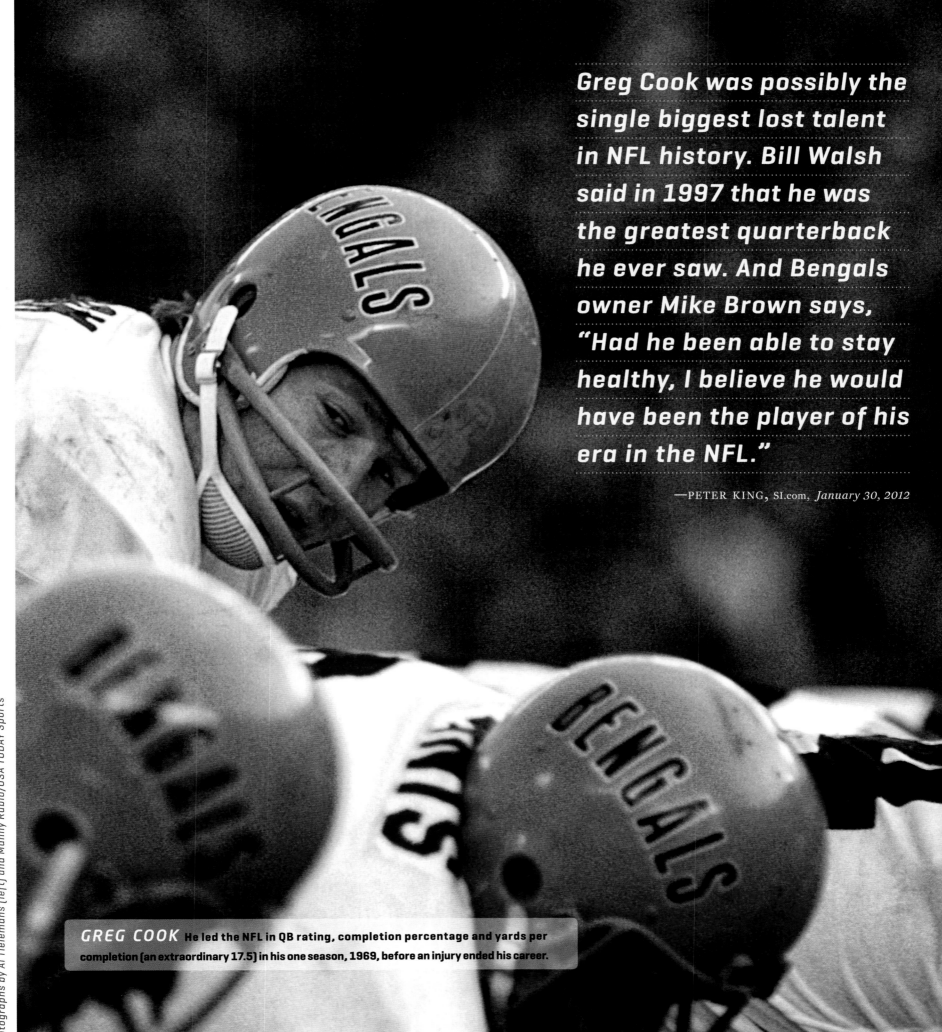

Greg Cook was possibly the single biggest lost talent in NFL history. Bill Walsh said in 1997 that he was the greatest quarterback he ever saw. And Bengals owner Mike Brown says, "Had he been able to stay healthy, I believe he would have been the player of his era in the NFL."

—PETER KING, SI.com, *January 30, 2012*

GREG COOK He led the NFL in QB rating, completion percentage and yards per completion (an extraordinary 17.5) in his one season, 1969, before an injury ended his career.

BALL   AT BA
STRIKE   OUT   IN

OTTO GRAHAM

IT'S A SHAME that pro football statistics don't compare very well across generations. Twelve-game, 14-game, 16-game seasons; bump-and-run, no bump-and-run; no roughing the quarterback. The result is that historic NFL figures aren't revered the same way as they are in baseball, for instance. That's too bad, because Otto Graham is a Ruthian figure, even if there is no eponymous adjective to celebrate him.

All Graham *(number 14, left)* ever did was win. He played 10 seasons with the Cleveland Browns—four in the old AAFC and six in the NFL, after the Browns were absorbed into the older league—and he played in the championship game *every* year of his career, winning seven. Oh, and he played one season of pro basketball with the Rochester Royals, and the Royals won the title. Yet when the subject is streaks, people think of DiMaggio.

Graham grew up in Waukegan, Ill., the son of two music teachers, and he went to Northwestern on a basketball schol-arship. In his first football game, as a sophomore in 1941, he returned a punt 93 yards for a touchdown. Three weeks later, he led Northwestern to an upset of Ohio State. The Buckeyes' coach, Paul Brown, would remember that performance and sign Graham to a pro contract while the quarterback was still serving in the military during World War II.

Graham was such a pure passer that he was known as Auto-matic Otto. "I could throw hard if I had to, I could lay it up soft, I could drill the sideline pass," he told SI in 1998. "We devel-oped the timed sideline attack, the comeback route where the receiver goes to the sideline, stops and comes back to the ball, with everything thrown on rhythm." Those were innovations which took place within an even larger change: plays called by the coach from the sideline. That would become the template upon which every modern football team runs.

The Browns' first game in the combined NFL came in 1950, against the defending champion Eagles. Most people were expecting a rout, and it was—only not the expected one. Cleveland crushed Philadelphia 35-10 as Graham threw for 346 yards and three touchdowns.

Graham would complete that magical season by throw-ing for 298 yards and four TDs to beat the Rams 30-28 in the title game. He'd eventually walk away from football on a high note, winning back-to-back NFL titles in 1954 and '55, both with performances that could be described as . . . Grahamian? Grahamic? In a more just world, there would be such an adjective.   — *Greg Kelly*

Photograph by Evan Peskin

QTR **HY** **HSN** **BALL ON** **DOWN** **TO GO** **TIME**
4 27 0 35 3 10 13 42

GEORGE BLANDA He may be best known for his longevity (a record 26 seasons at QB and kicker), but his passing led the Oilers to the first two AFL titles, in 1960 and '61.

ANDREW LUCK His classic drop-back ability made him the Colts' choice over Robert Griffin III with the top pick in 2012; the reward has been back-to-back playoff appearances.

ALL FOR ONE, ONE FOR ALL

IT TAKES TWO TO COMPLETE A PASS, AND FROM LAMBEAU FIELD BACK TO HIS HIGH SCHOOL IN CALIFORNIA, THE PACKERS' AARON RODGERS HAS MAINTAINED AN UNCANNY CONNECTION WITH HIS RECEIVERS

Excerpted from SPORTS ILLUSTRATED, *November 11, 2011* | BY TIM LAYDEN

HE FOOTBALL CONNECTS THEM. AARON Rodgers throws, and his receivers catch. It's that simple, but not simple at all. It's the culmination of endless practice repetitions and film study, a symbiosis of movement built on schematic design (but also on talent, instinct, trust and nerve) that ends with a pass spiraling tightly through the air into a waiting pair of hands. It happened late in the Packers' recent 33–27 win over the Vikings in the venerable Metrodome, when Rodgers hit 13-year veteran Donald Driver for a six-yard gain on second-and-12, the 711th catch of Driver's career. "Little *stick* route," says Driver. "Run down five yards, turn in or out, depending on where the defense is." (He shrugs as if to emphasize the routine nature of the play.)

"Base play in our offense," says Rodgers. "Trying to get half the [first-down yardage] back before third down." (He nods to affirm its simplicity.)

Shortly before that was a 15-yard completion to Jordy Nelson. And a little while before that, a 79-yard TD pass to Greg Jennings that Rodgers threw on a line while rolling to his right, and Jennings was so wide-open that he jogged in from the 40. Before that, 13 consecutive completions to start the game, including a first-quarter two-yard bullet to fullback John Kuhn just beyond the goal line. All day it looked easy, the way it has all season, as the Packers have won seven straight games.

If 2010 was the year in which Rodgers ascended to the top echelon of NFL quarterbacks, alongside Brady, Brees, Manning and Rivers, 2011 is the year in which Rodgers has become—at least for now—the best of them all. He has completed 71.5% of his passes (the single-season record is 70.9%, shared by Drew Brees in '09 and Ken Anderson in 1982) for 20 TDs (the league high) with just three interceptions (second lowest). He has averaged 9.9 yards per attempt, which, if sustained till the end of the season, would edge out Kurt Warner (2000) for the highest one-year average since 1956. Rodgers's passer rating of 125.7 is more than four points ahead of Peyton Manning's seven-year-old NFL one-season record.

Rodgers, 27, has been playing quarterback for 15 years, since he was a tiny eighth-grader in Chico, Calif. In that time he has completed approximately 2,000 passes to nearly 100 different receivers—and he says he remembers most of them. He can tell you that his first NFL connection went for no gain on a checkdown in garbage time of a 52–3 beatdown of the Saints in October 2005, his rookie year. It came on a play called H6 Flanker Pivot, and Rodgers was thinking before the call came in, *Please don't call Flanker Pivot*, because the fullback in the flat is always the only guy open on that play, and man, he just wanted to air one out. Vonta Leach caught that pass. Rodgers can tell you that one of the most important completions of his career came early in his first start at Cal, in the fifth game of the 2003 season, a Cover Two hole shot (between the corner and the safety) down the sideline against Illinois. "Gave me the confidence to make those throws," he says. The receiver was Jonathan Makonnen.

His receivers remember too. The guys from back home remember not just a little boy with a big wing but also a celebrity who hasn't forgotten his high school buddies and keeps their numbers in his cellphone. The ones from Cal remember a dorky kid who never got nervous, even in the tightest spots. The Packers remember a guy who showed uncommon grace while waiting for a legend to retire. *All* of them remember sore hands from fielding the Rodgers fastball. They're the ones who can draw the line from Green Bay back to Chico.

Before win number 7 this year in Minnesota, there was Super Bowl XLV in Dallas, a 31–25 win over the Steelers last Feb. 6, in which Rodgers threw for 304 yards and three touchdowns and was named the game's MVP. The first touchdown of the night came with 3:44 left in the first quarter, as the Packers faced third-and-one on the Pittsburgh 29-yard line. The play call into Rodgers's helmet was a screen pass. Nelson was to run a straight clear-out pattern to take the top off the Pittsburgh coverage and was categorically *not* to be thrown the ball.

Nelson arrived in Green Bay from Kansas State in 2008, the year Rodgers became the starter, and learned right away that a ball could come his way at any time, including when a screen pass was called in the Super Bowl. "We get up there, and Aaron signals me: tap to his helmet," says Nelson. "That means he's coming to me."

Rodgers recalls, "We needed a play to get us going. I liked the matchup, Jordy on [cornerback] William Gay. I do remember thinking at the top of my drop, I better make this one work." Besides the touchdown, Nelson caught eight other passes for a total of 140 yards.

Jennings came to Green Bay in 2006, a year after Rodgers. He caught 93 professional passes, all from Favre, before catching one from Rodgers. He has since caught 271. "He throws with velocity," says Jennings. "You turn, and the ball is going to be there. His deep ball is better than Brett's. His accuracy running outside the pocket is second to none, almost better than when he's in the pocket, which is almost impossible."

Before he became a star, Rodgers waited. Prior to playing at Cal, he had to spend a year at junior college. At Cal, he waited until the fifth game of his sophomore season before he got his first start. He waited, famously, in the NFL draft-day green room until the Packers took him with the 24th pick of the first round in 2005. He waited, quietly, for three seasons while Favre extended his Hall of Fame career before moving on to the Jets and Vikings. But he did not *just* wait. He also worked.

Every Wednesday, Thursday and Friday, Rodgers's job was to run the Packers' scout-team offense, mimicking the upcoming opponents' schemes, to prepare the Packers' defense. It's thankless work. The defense knows what's coming, and the scout-team offense is full of disgruntled players who think they should be starting or starters just helping out and making sure they don't get hurt. "But Aaron took every scout-team possession like it was the last possession of his life," says Driver.

"Those were my game reps," says Rodgers. "I tell [backup] Matt [Flynn] now, 'Scout team is a chance to work on things. Throw it into tight spots. Work on your look-offs. Do things you're not comfortable doing.' "

Rodgers's leadership grew in other ways. Says Ruvell Martin, a scout team receiver for four seasons, "The first day I'm in the locker room [in 2005], Aaron walks over to me and says, 'Hey, I'm Aaron, what's your number?' He punches my number into his phone. Then on my birthday he sees me in the locker room and says, 'Happy birthday, man.' Aaron gets everybody's number, looks up their birthday and then sets an alarm on his phone so that he wishes them happy birthday. Pretty cool that he cares about people like that."

Before a 2007 game at Kansas City, Martin was made inactive, and instead of going out early to throw with Rodgers, as he usually did, he sulked in the locker room. "Right before the game," he says, "Aaron came up to me and said, 'Why didn't you come and throw with me?' I told him I was inactive, and he got upset. He said, 'I throw with you every week, when we both know I'm not going to get in the game. You're inactive one game and you can't throw with me?' I thought, Wow, this is not all about me. This is about the team. And Aaron brought that to my attention."

Throughout Rodgers's apprenticeship and even through his rocky ascension in 2008 (the Packers went 6–10 in their first year post-Favre), he never complained. Every day that he remained on the high road, he earned more respect from his teammates. "He bottled everything up and just performed at a high level when he got the chance," says Jennings. "It was impressive. I mean, he got booed in training camp just because he wasn't Brett. And he just took it. I don't know if I could have done that."

Talent helps smooth any transition. James Jones was a third-round draft choice in 2007 and caught balls from both Favre and Rodgers every day. "He was making throws in practice that Brett was not making," says Jones. "I know Brett was older then. But Aaron was throwing no-look passes, deep balls on a string. I had never seen throws like that."

And they were all hard. "He never turns it off," says Martin. "He just smokes it. If you just stand across from him and let him laser balls at you, it is not fun, O.K.? You've got to create some motion, moving side to side, anything to take your mind off the sting that's coming at you."

Shaun Bodiford, a former junior-college teammate, also attests to Rodgers's arm strength. Early in summer practices, the two were playing catch, and Bodiford noticed the zip on Rodgers's ball. "I tell Aaron, 'Hey, you've got a pretty good arm,' " he says. "Then he tells me, 'Watch this.' And he starts throwing these 15-yard passes, with a tight spiral, *underhanded.* Then he does the same thing behind his back. Next time I saw the coach I said, 'Hey, I think this guy should be starting.' "

Before long he was. Bodiford, who would later play parts of two seasons with five NFL teams, remembers one game in which he was supposed to run a shallow dig route. Instead he ran a deeper post, stole a pass intended for another receiver and ran in for a touchdown. He remembers Rodgers finding him on the sideline and saying, "Hey, Shaun, awesome catch. Next time run the right route."

The memories are vivid, and Rodgers keeps the distance small between his ordinary past and his outsized present. Dane Baxter, one of his old high school receivers, asked him for tickets to a Packers game two years ago, and Rodgers not only provided the seats but also invited Baxter and a friend to stay at his Green Bay home. Rodgers and another high school receiver, Ryan Gulbrandsen, remain close, battling frequently on the golf course during off-seasons. They all watch him play on Sundays, silently connecting the dots from back then to right now. ∎

Rodgers ended up setting the NFL record for passer rating (122.5) in 2011. | *Photograph by Bill Frakes*

SONNY JURGENSEN He had a paunch and a love for the D.C. nightlife, but SPORTS ILLUSTRATED called him "the best natural passer in the NFL" in 1969.

JIM KELLY He terrorized the NFL in the early '90s, taking Buffalo to four straight Super Bowls as one of the last QBs to call his own plays in the Bills' no-huddle offense.

His first 13 months on the job have been the stuff of myth. Warner, the 1999 league and Super Bowl MVP, has passed for 6,300 yards and 55 touchdowns, completed 66.9% of his attempts and put up a 112.4 passer rating, all NFL bests for a quarterback over his first 21 regular-season starts.

—PETER KING, SI, *October 9, 2000*

KURT WARNER An undrafted free agent, he went from the Arena League to NFL MVP with a Rams offense that would become known as the Greatest Show on Turf.

BOOT

SOME RUN WITH purpose, some—with poor pass protection—just run for dear life, and for their trouble almost all are criticized for not being pure pocket passers. But mobile, scrambling quarterbacks electrify the fans and terrorize opposing defenses by adding an entertaining improvisational element to the game

FRAN TARKENTON Defenders wanted to dismember the man, but for all his scrambling he still only missed 15 starts in 18 seasons.

LEGGERS

Photograph by Walter Iooss Jr.

Scramblers, Gamblers And Ramblers

BY JENNY VRENTAS

Perhaps no quarterback LOVED RUNNING THE BALL AS MUCH AS Roger Staubach, who was in high school in Cincinnati the first time he went around left end and tore off about 70 yards for a touchdown. He looked back and saw how angry and demoralized the opposing defense was, and he never forgot it. He was still running almost two decades later, as a two-time Super Bowl champion quarterback for the Cowboys. And yet, as integral to Dallas's success as

his running ability was, it still made his legendary coach, Tom Landry, uncomfortable.

"Even at the end of my career, after 11 years [in the NFL], we'd be watching film, and coach Landry would say, 'You're gonna learn someday,' " Staubach says. "I said, 'Well, coach, I'll be retiring pretty soon.' "

The number of quarterbacks who can do more than just throw the football has grown exponentially since the heyday of Roger the Dodger in the 1970s, and of Frantic Fran Tarkenton before him. The 49ers' Steve Young and the Broncos' John Elway channeled their athleticism into Hall of Fame careers; Randall Cunningham on the Eagles and Michael Vick on the Falcons took mobility to a new level. In today's NFL, a whole new generation of quarterbacks—the Panthers' Cam Newton, the Niners' Colin Kaepernick, the Redskins' Robert Griffin III, Super Bowl XLVIII champion Russell Wilson of the Seahawks and even Andrew Luck of the Colts—has brought dual skill sets from college and chalked up multiple postseason appearances in just a few years. But still, even with all that success challenging the assumption that the most desirable quarterbacks are pocket passers, there's still a lingering discomfort in the NFL that Landry felt some 35 years ago.

Tarkenton recalls being "ridiculed and trashed" for his habit of scrambling, but, to him, it was also a necessity: He began

his career the same year as the expansion Minnesota Vikings, in 1961, and with a shaky offensive line in front of him, he felt his best chance to make a play was to get out of the pocket and buy time to throw. "And that was [considered] freakish," Tarkenton says. "In my era, if quarterbacks ever got out of the pocket, it was sacrilege." Staubach's approach was a bit different. He focused on running forward to get first downs, just as he had done at the Naval Academy before he joined the NFL in 1969, after serving a four-year military commitment which included a tour of duty in Vietnam.

Each bootlegging quarterback has his own style. The Bears' Bobby Douglass was a better runner than a passer; his 968 rushing yards in 1972 were a long-standing record for quarterbacks until Vick broke the 1,000-yard mark with the Falcons in 2006. (Vick holds the career record for a QB as well, with 5,857 yards.) Elway's legacy was built upon his unusually strong arm, but his mobility allowed him to locate receivers deep downfield and complicate an opponent's pass rush. Young had great speed, enough that his Super Bowl XXIX MVP performance also included finishing as the game's leading rusher.

Mobile quarterbacks hold a place in the past, present and future of the NFL for a simple reason: Defenses hate to chase around a quarterback. And even when the quarterback isn't running, defenses hate the threat that he could. Harnessing this advantage has driven many offensive innovations in the NFL. The 1975 Cowboys popularized the shotgun formation, and Staubach says one of the reasons Landry installed it was so that Staubach would have a better view of running lanes. Now, all these years later, Kaepernick has brought the run-friendly pistol formation to the 49ers. And the latest read-option craze, finally bubbling up from the college ranks, works on the notion that if the quarterback is a runner, the defense no longer has a man advantage.

But mobility comes with risk. The thought of the most important player on a team exposing himself to injury on runs gave Landry, and every coach since, pause. Landry's fears were realized in a 1972 exhibition game, when Staubach tried to run over Rams linebacker Marlin McKeever, and ended up with a separated shoulder that sidelined him for two-thirds of the season. "People said, 'Well, that's the end of his running career.' But it really wasn't," Staubach says. He learned to run smarter. And he got a pair of bigger shoulder pads.

More recently, Griffin's torn knee ligaments during his rookie year in 2012 reignited the durability debate around the subject of mobile quarterbacks. Yes, better athletes are needed at quarterback now because defenders are bigger, faster and stronger, but when the quarterbacks run, they're exposed to tremendous hits from those bigger, faster and stronger defenders. The toll on RGIII and the Redskins has been painful. In his stunning debut season, he threw for 3,200 yards and ran for 815 more, with seven rushing touchdowns, as he led Washington to its first playoff berth in five seasons. Even after his knee injury, which he aggravated during the 2012 playoffs, he still threw for 3,203 yards last season, but he ran for just 489 yards and for no touchdowns. The team finished with a record of 3–13 and coach Mike Shanahan was quickly fired. That's a sobering thought for every other coach in the league, and it remains to be seen how Griffin will adjust going forward.

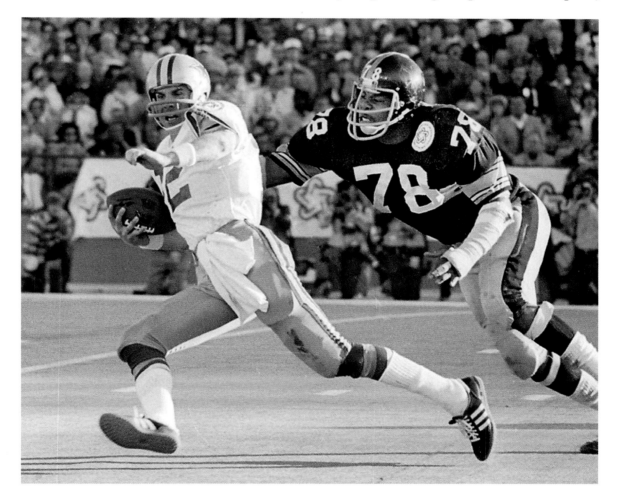

Elway was a case study of a player evolving over time. Early on, he recalls, his athleticism "is kind of what carried me." But later in his 16-year pro career, he became more of a pocket passer. His body was less able to take hits and with a better aptitude for dissecting defenses, he didn't have to run so much. Tarkenton, too, scrambled less after age 30, and barely at all after tearing an anterior cruciate ligament in his knee in 1976 (an injury which at the time was not diagnosed). Both stand out in the record books as passers, ranking in the top 10 in career passing yards.

The truth is that dual-threat quarterbacks also have a dual legacy: They are among the most exciting players to watch in football, and they also have historically been dogged by questions. Staubach was on stage with RGIII at an event to honor the military early in 2014, and Staubach marveled over the young Washington quarterback's speed, teasing that he would have averaged at least 10 yards per carry if he had been able to run that fast. He's also watched Kaepernick lead San Francisco to Super Bowl XLVII, and Wilson's Seattle Seahawks win Super Bowl XLVIII, but it seems Landry's displeasure is still echoing in his head when Staubach says almost apologetically, "It shows that running is not all bad." ∎

DOUG FLUTIE Written off as too small at 5'10", the 285th pick in the '85 draft lasted 21 pro seasons, thanks to his knack for escaping pressure and making plays.

STEVE YOUNG Despite four seasons as Joe Montana's backup, he rushed for
more yards (4,239) than every quarterback but Michael Vick and Randall Cunningham.

SEVEN UP

AFTER THREE EMPTY TRIPS TO THE SUPER BOWL, JOHN ELWAY FINALLY BROKE THROUGH WITH AN UPSET VICTORY OVER THE PACKERS, THANKS IN LARGE PART TO A MEMORABLY GUTSY RUN

Excerpted from SPORTS ILLUSTRATED, *February 2, 1998* | BY MICHAEL SILVER

HE SPENT 15 YEARS PUSHING THE physical limits of football, making jaws drop and decorating highlight clips with bursts of brilliance. Then, with one fearless thrust of his 37-year-old body late in the third quarter of Super Bowl XXXII, John Elway finally lifted himself and the Denver Broncos to the top. In the greatest Super Bowl ever, the pivotal moment, fittingly, belonged to one of the NFL's alltime greats.

For all the importance of coach Mike Shanahan's dazzling game plan, of running back Terrell Davis's MVP performance and of the game-ending stand by Denver's oft-slighted defense, it was Elway, with his self-described "three-inch vertical leap," who elevated himself into immortality and his franchise into the realm of champions with the Broncos' 31–24 upset of the Green Bay Packers on Sunday.

The play said everything about the defiant Broncos and their unlikely march to the title: With the game tied at 17 and Denver facing third-and-six at the Green Bay 12, Elway dropped back to pass, found no open receivers and took off down the middle of the field. He darted right and was met near the first-down marker by Packers strong safety LeRoy Butler, who ducked his head and prepared to unload on the quarterback. Elway took to the air, and Butler's hit spun him around so that he came down feet-forward as he was absorbing another shot from defensive back Mike Prior.

When Elway hit the ground at the four, an adrenaline rush surged through the Broncos. Denver scored two plays later, and though the Packers came back to tie the score again, Green Bay was a depleted team fighting a losing battle against an opponent that had been re-charged. When the Broncos launched their game-winning drive from the Packers' 49 with 3:27 left, it was like watching a battle of the bands between Pearl Jam and the Kingston Trio. "When Elway, instead of running out-of-bounds, turned it up and got spun around like a helicopter, it energized us beyond belief," Denver defensive lineman Mike Lodish said after the game. Added Shannon Sharpe, the Broncos' All-Pro tight end, "When I saw him do that and then get up pumping his fist, I said, 'It's on.' That's when I was sure we were going to win."

Though only an infinitesimal slice of the earth's football-viewing population believed Denver would dethrone Green Bay, the Broncos carried a confidence into this game that belied their station as a double-digit underdog. More than two hours after the game, as Shanahan rode from the stadium in a stretch limousine with Denver owner Pat Bowlen and their families, the third-year Broncos coach raised his champagne glass and said, without being brash, "This was just the way we planned it."

While the AFC's 13-year Super Bowl losing streak and Denver's 0–4 record in the big game helped convince many experts that a Green Bay blowout was inevitable, Shanahan saw no cause for panic. As early as eight days before the game, he began telling people he trusted that the Broncos were poised for victory, saying to one reporter, "Just between you and me, we're going to win the game."

History will show that this was Elway's week of glory. Sure, his stats were wimpy. He threw for only 123 yards, didn't complete a pass to a wideout until Ed McCaffrey's 36-yard catch-and-run midway through the third quarter and blew a chance to build on a seven-point lead by throwing an end zone interception to free safety Eugene Robinson with 11 seconds left in the third quarter. But Elway carried the day with his poise. "That was the ultimate win, there's no question," he said. "There have been a lot of things that go along with losing three Super Bowls and playing for 14 years and being labeled as a guy who has never been on a winning Super Bowl team."

This time Elway was as steady as the jets that buzzed the stadium during his introduction. He dismissed the Robinson interception from his mind immediately, and when he strutted onto the field with 3:27 left, the score tied at 24 and the ball on the Green Bay 49, he was in control and confident. "I looked at John before he took the field, and he had this huge smile on his face," Jeff Lewis, Denver's third-string quarterback, said after the game. "You could see it in his eyes; he was ready. It was one of those times you just have to stop yourself and watch the best quarterback ever do his thing."

It helped that the Broncos' offensive line, despite being the league's lightest, had worn down the Packers defenders—particularly mammoth nosetackle Gilbert Brown, who was being moved around like a giant beanbag chair. "He was lying down out there," Denver center Tom Nalen said of Brown. "We thought he was hurt. But he was just tired." Tired of watching Davis whiz past him, no doubt. Still, it was Elway's game to pull out, a chance for the quarterback with the most victories in NFL history to win the big one, finally. Put some points on the board, have them hold up, and all would be forgiven and forgotten.

On his biggest pass of the game, Elway made a perfect delivery, throwing a quick toss to fullback Howard Griffith that went for 23 yards and gave Denver a first-and-goal at the eight with two minutes remaining. That set up Davis's winning one-yard touchdown run, which the Pack conceded on a second-down play with 1:45 left in a futile attempt to get the ball back with enough time to win. (Mistakenly thinking it was first down, Packers coach Mike Holmgren, with only two timeouts left, feared the Broncos might run down the clock and kick a field goal in the closing seconds.)

"John makes mistakes; he is human after all," Broncos receiver Rod Smith would say later. "But you never see fear in his eyes. He's like a linebacker with a good arm." ∎

Elway's mobility helped make him a part of NFL nobility. | *Photograph by Peter Read Miller*

MICHAEL VICK The QB rushing record-holder for a single-season (1,039 yards) and career (5,857), he was unstoppable—until he ran up against the law.

In addition to adding an extra dimension with his legs, Kaepernick brings more of an in-your-face edge to the 49ers than Alex Smith ever did. Even when silent, Kap exudes a nonverbal, athletic swag that has energized and electrified the team.

—AUSTIN MURPHY, SI, *January 21, 2013*

COLIN KAEPERNICK In his first year as a starter, he had the best rushing game ever by a QB (181 yards), in a 2013 playoff victory over the Packers.

TOBIN ROTE

MOST OF THE early quarterbacking stars of the NFL —guys like Sammy Baugh, Otto Graham and Sid Luckman—could run with the ball. They had started out as single-wing halfbacks, after all. It was only after George Halas and the Bears popularized the T formation in the '40s that quarterbacks began throwing with any regularity. But the underappreciated Tobin Rote *(number 1)* would become the very model of a mobile quarterback when he joined Green Bay in 1950.

He was the Packers' second-round pick that year, after a very successful college career at Rice, where he led the Owls to a Southwest Conference title as a senior. But Green Bay wasn't known as Titletown then, and he never finished better than 6–6 there because he played on teams with some of the most pitiful defenses in franchise history.

For that reason, he often had to be the whole show in Green Bay. In 1951 he was the eighth-leading rusher in the league, with 523 yards. In '54, he led the NFL in pass attempts and completions (while also rushing for 301 yards). Two years later he led the NFL in passing TDs and yards, but he also had 11 rushing touchdowns, more than all but one other player in the league, Bears running back Rick Casares. His coach, Lisle Blackbourn, said of Rote, "When he's hot, he's positively the greatest of them all, and when he's cold, well. . . ."

The arrival of Bart Starr in 1956 allowed the Packers to deal Rote (a cousin of Giants star Kyle Rote) to the Lions the following year. With a better team around him, he showed what he could really do. Subbing for an injured Bobby Layne in the playoffs, he rallied the Lions from 21 points down to beat the 49ers in what was then the greatest playoff comeback ever. Then in the title game he threw for four TDs and ran for another as Detroit swamped the Browns 59–14. He remains the last Lions QB to ever win a championship game.

As a footnote, he would later lead the San Diego Chargers to an AFL title, in 1963, making him the only quarterback to win season-ending title games in both leagues. That victory sparked talk of a showdown with the NFL winner, three years before the first Super Bowl. An SI cover that December featured Rote and boldly predicted: A COMING WORLD SERIES: AFL VS. NFL.

Rote retired in 1966 with 3,128 rushing yards, then the highest total ever for a quarterback, and he still ranks eighth alltime, despite playing 12-game seasons for much of his career and spending three years in the CFL.   —G.K.

CAM NEWTON In his first season in Carolina in 2011, he set an NFL mark for QBs with 14 rushing TDs while gaining 706 yards on the ground.

BOBBY DOUGLASS In 10 seasons he threw just 36 TD passes and 64 picks, but his 968 rushing yards (in 14 games) for the Bears in 1972 stood as a QB record for 34 years.

The Bears quarterback this season will be either Jack Concannon or Bobby Douglass. Concannon would make a good receiver and Douglass is a natural to be the Bears' starting fullback. However, they insist on playing quarterback.

—SI, *September 20, 1971*

HE'S FRANTASTIC

FRAN TARKENTON WAS OFTEN MALIGNED FOR HIS SCRAMBLING AND FOR NEVER WINNING A CHAMPIONSHIP, BUT THE NUMBERS DIDN'T LIE AS HE CLOSED IN ON THE CAREER PASSING RECORDS OF JOHNNY UNITAS

Excerpted from SPORTS ILLUSTRATED, *November 10, 1975* | BY DAN JENKINS

E THROWS FOOTBALLS AT A MATTRESS in his attic, he eats chili before a game, he says what he thinks, and a lot of people do not like the fact that he sometimes runs into remote corners of neighboring states before he connects on another touchdown pass for the Minnesota Vikings. But Fran Tarkenton *is*, and Fran Tarkenton *does*, and whether any of the old-timers are going to be able to stomach it or not, Fran Tarkenton is on the verge of proving that he might be the greatest professional quarterback who ever drew back an arm.

Yeah, yeah, yeah. Baugh. Graham. Unitas. All that stuff. But Fran Tarkenton looks better right now in his 15th season than ever before. His Vikings are the only undefeated team in the NFL, and he is getting ready in the next 15 or 20 minutes to break every meaningful record available to a passer. And he still hasn't come close to being seriously injured, despite those journeys into the unknown. Also, he hasn't always benefited from brilliant receivers, and he calls his own plays, and he can see the whole field better than anyone, and he has an amazing touch, and he can throw long and short and medium, and he's a leader, and he doesn't panic, and he can make things happen. But mainly he is going to own all these passing records, and the critics can just shut up.

The fact is, whether you like a scrambler or not, and whether or not you like a guy who throws a lot to his backs, and whether you don't accept a guy who has "never won the big one," Fran Tarkenton is going to become the alltime, lifetime career passer, and you will be able to look it up.

One not so unimportant by-product of what Tarkenton is up to these days is the effect all this is having on the Vikings. When last seen, they were 7–0 with the best and most confident club coach Bud Grant has put together and looking very much like one of the Super Bowl entries.

Last Sunday the Vikings went into what figured to be their usual physical battle with the Packers, and all Tarkenton did was have the best day he has had all year, and by doing so, kept the Vikings rolling along with a 28–17 victory. Tarkenton did it like this: He hit the first seven passes he threw, he hit 11 of the first 12, 16 of the first 18, and so on like that to finish up with 24 completions out of 30 attempts, for 285 yards and three touchdowns.

It all goes back to his toys in the attic. "In the off-season," Fran says, "I get on my knees and throw 20 or 30 balls a day at a mattress." But you don't scramble on your knees, Fran. "I scramble to keep from getting tackled." But people don't like for you to scramble, Fran. "People like Johnny Unitas," he says.

It isn't easy to get Tarkenton to talk about Tarkenton until he has talked about the Vikings, who have only become a consistently fine team since he escaped from the New York Giants penal colony and returned to them. First, therefore, we must hear about the Vikings.

It may come as a surprise to most people, but the Vikings have subtly turned into a young team. There are still antiques around, like the defensive ends Carl Eller and Jim Marshall and the linebackers Roy Winston and Wally Hilgenberg, a safety, Paul Krause, and the center, Mick Tingelhoff. Their continued presence is what keeps the average age of the squad at 26.5 years, which is not high compared to, say, the Washington Redskins.

But look who is gone—Gary Larsen, Milt Sunde, Grady Alderman, Bill Brown, Oscar Reed and Mike Eischeid, all of them retired, waived, traded or simply not signed. Meanwhile, the new Vikings are being raved about by the older Vikings, and some of them are causing their elders to perform with a vigor defying their years.

The youth of the Vikings centers around five or six guys. In the backfield, for example, there is the combination of Brent McClanahan-Ed Marinaro to go along with Chuck Foreman. McClanahan will be what Dave Osborn was, only swifter, and Marinaro is a fine receiver. Foreman, of course, is the first breakaway threat in Minnesota since the emigrants.

Earlier last week, after a Vikings practice, as he sat in Eddie Webster's Peanut Bar near the stadium, cracking shells, Tarkenton spoke of all the reasons why these Vikings are so improved over the team that disappointed so many people in the last two Super Bowls. "Depth alone makes us better," Tarkenton said. "I think my arm is healthy. It wasn't last year. John Ward makes us better at guard. Doug Sutherland has developed as a first-rate member of the front four and can stand right up there with Alan Page. Bobby Bryant is back in the secondary. That's a big, big thing. Jim Marshall played all last season with pneumonia. McClanahan and Marinaro. We've got the six best linebackers in football. Depth. You can't say enough about depth."

Nor can you ever say enough about Fran Tarkenton. He retains an enthusiasm for the game that is unmatched among quarterbacks. For a man in his 15th season, you would expect him to show some signs of wear or scars of battle, or perhaps even a jadedness in his attitude, but he is as vibrant as ever.

"I'm a fan as much as anything," he said. "I really love the game. I love to follow it as much as play it. I wanted to be a football player from the time I can remember. Playing a touch game in an alley with just two kids when I was five years old, I knew I wanted to play football." And he has never been too badly injured to be able to play.

"I stay in shape, if that's part of the reason," he said. "Probably it's luck. I'm physically strong. I have strong legs. Maybe that's helped. Stand-up quarterbacks have stood in the pocket and gotten hurt. I've scrambled, and I haven't. I never scrambled with any design. I was trying to complete a pass, to move the team. But it's interesting. The old-timers have never accepted me as a good quarterback because I've run out of the pocket too often. All that does is amuse me."

They are not going to accept Tarkenton breaking all of those records that belong to Unitas, either, but he is surely going to break them, and in fewer seasons, and when he does, he will have done it playing on some far worse teams than Unitas ever did, and throwing to receivers who are never likely to take their places alongside Raymond Berry and Lenny Moore.

The two major records for a quarterback to covet are career touchdown passes and career completions. Unitas holds those records. In his 18 seasons he completed 290 touchdown passes and his lifetime total of completions is 2,830.

When Tarkenton left the field last Sunday his lifetime completions came to 2,781. Tarkenton needs only to hit Foreman or Jim Lash or John Gilliam for an average of eight catches a game over the second half of the regular season, and the record will be his.

As for touchdown passes, which might be the equivalent of home run hitting, Tarkenton now needs only 11 to surpass Unitas after he got his 12th, 13th and 14th of the season Sunday. If you consider that Tarkenton is going to play on a while longer, the world can surely look forward to his becoming the first man to throw 300 lifetime touchdown passes.

So why won't anybody name a candy bar after him?

"People don't like to admit that football teams get better every year," Fran said. "I promise you that athletes today are far superior to what they used to be. There were great players in every era, of course, but the linemen weren't what they are now. Guys today work out the year around. They go to health clubs instead of beer taverns. They're bigger and faster. They're smarter. You don't see linemen with fat bellies anymore."

But what about quarterbacks?

"I think Unitas was the best," Fran said. "But he didn't see the zones and subtle defenses we see. He got a lot of one-on-one coverage. He didn't see the pass rush we see."

Tarkenton said he would take Oakland's Ken Stabler for his ability to move a team, simple as that. Also for the variety of balls he can throw. He likes the unselfishness of Bob Griese at Miami. "We may never know how great Griese is because he plays behind the greatest offensive line ever, and he only has to throw 10 passes a game."

He said if you wanted the most tenacious, competitive guy around, you might come up with Billy Kilmer at Washington. "He'll wobble one in there somehow," Tarkenton said. For courage, what about Joe Namath? "Courage," he said, "and the ability to lay the 25-yard ball in there."

And how would history remember Fran Tarkenton, inasmuch as it is going to downplay the records?

"I'd like to be thought of as a good one," he said. "I hate to think I won't be unless I win a Super Bowl. You know, this team could win a Super Bowl, but I don't know that I would have made a bigger contribution to football by being a part of it than I did a couple of seasons in New York when we went 9–5 and 7–7 with no football players."

Happiness for a quarterback, naturally, is having yourself surrounded by receivers like Gilliam and tight end Stu Voigt and backs like Foreman and Marinaro who can also catch the ball. Against the Packers,

Tarkenton's ability to find these people when he needed them was the principal thing that kept the Vikings undefeated.

At the risk of sounding repetitious, having Tarkenton is like having a coach on the field. As Minnesota's offensive coordinator, Jerry Burns, says, "Certainly nobody today has seen more than Fran has. When we set up a game plan, I suggest what I think the running game ought to be, but Fran knows as much as anyone about what will work with the passing game. We manage to put together something that he's comfortable with."

When Tarkenton had his ritual bowl of chili the night before the game at Chili John's in beautiful downtown Green Bay, he couldn't help but dwell on how he might feast on the young Packers secondary. Some say that feasting on the current Packers is easier than feasting at Chili John's and Tarkenton proved as much on Sunday.

It would not be fair to suggest the victory was an easy one. The Vikings had to come from behind twice, from 10–7 and 17–14, but it never seemed that they were not in control. Receivers were open everywhere, and especially when Tarkenton needed them to be.

His three touchdown passes were of an assortment that only Tarkenton, perhaps, could have thrown today. The first was a play-action to the right where he zinged one in from five yards to Voigt. The second was a drop-back, a floater over the head of the defender into the arms of Gilliam in the end zone. And the third was a typical old-fashioned Tarkenton scramble. Running around, bringing the stadium to its feet, and then, as only a man with a still-good arm can do, firing one for 10 yards to Foreman, who caught it just on the line, inundated by people in green shirts.

And so Fran Tarkenton and the Vikings press on, wondering if they can finally do it all. "Getting through the playoffs is the hardest part," he claimed. "That's where the real pressure is. We've gone into two Super Bowls now, and we've lost our edge both times. Maybe it's because there's two weeks between the conference championship and the Super Bowl, I don't know. Maybe that's why there's never really been a great Super Bowl game." Tarkenton would like one more opportunity to do something about all that. ∎

RANDALL CUNNINGHAM Perhaps the greatest combo ever of a big arm and strong legs, he ran for more yards (942) than all but eight running backs in 1990.

Photographs by Peter Read Miller (left) and Rod Mar

RUSSELL WILSON A judicious scrambler, he ran for more than 1,000 yards while starting every game of his first two NFL seasons and leading Seattle to a title.

STEVE MCNAIR He threw well enough to be known as Air McNair, but his legs helped carry him to three Pro Bowls, a co-MVP and the Titans' only Super Bowl.

Photograph by Al Tielemans

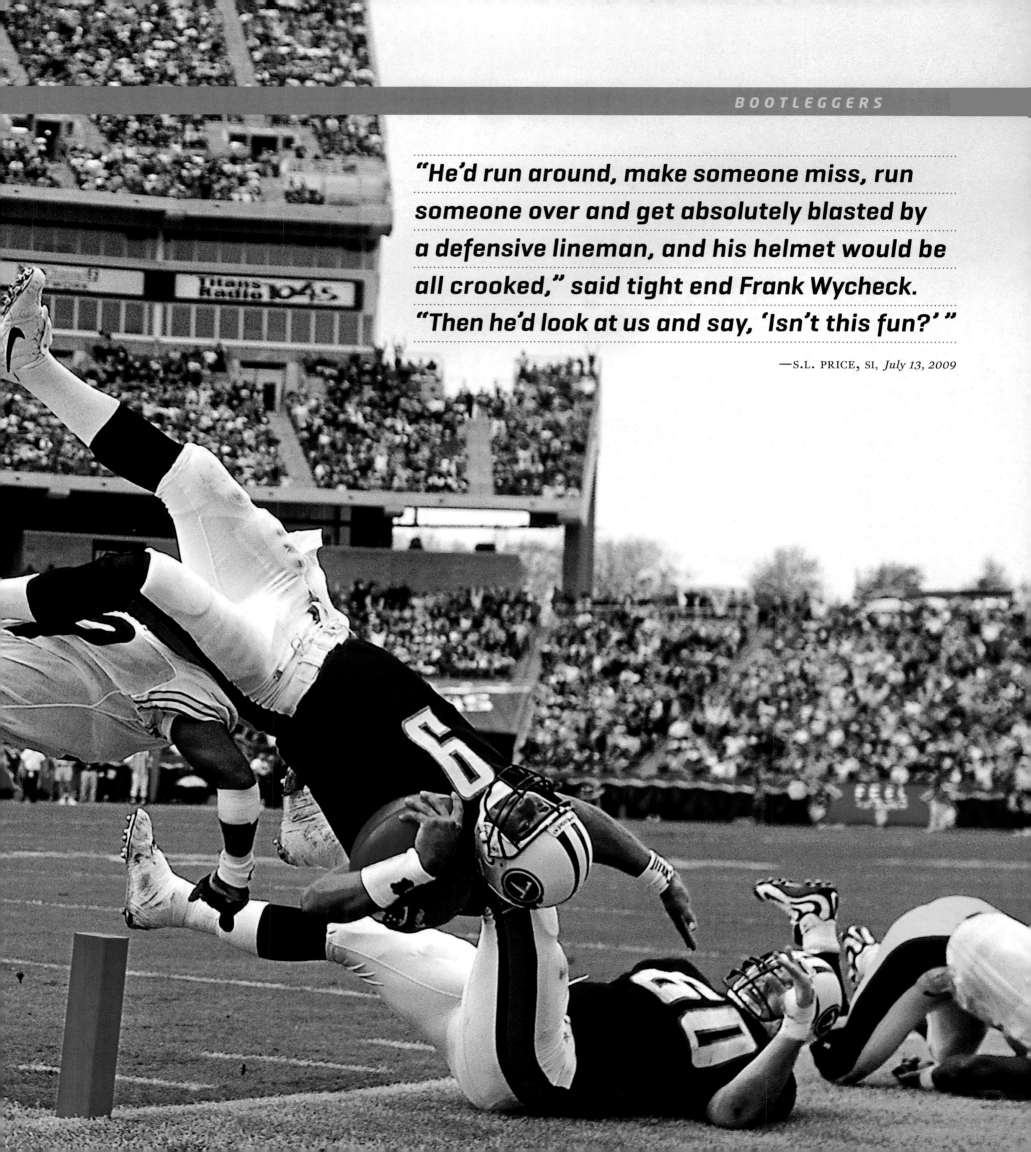

"He'd run around, make someone miss, run someone over and get absolutely blasted by a defensive lineman, and his helmet would be all crooked," said tight end Frank Wycheck. "Then he'd look at us and say, 'Isn't this fun?'"

—S.L. PRICE, SI, *July 13, 2009*

BOMB

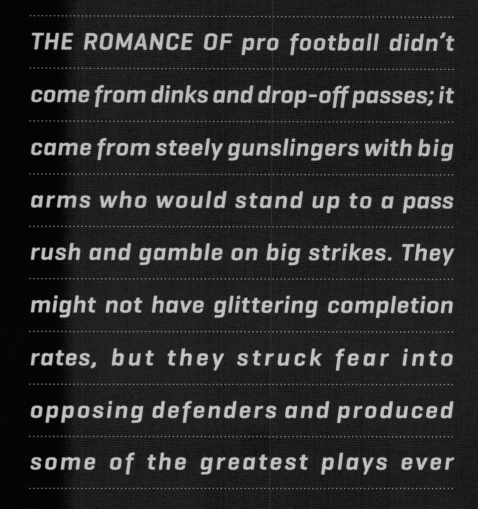

THE ROMANCE OF pro football didn't come from dinks and drop-off passes; it came from steely gunslingers with big arms who would stand up to a pass rush and gamble on big strikes. They might not have glittering completion rates, but they struck fear into opposing defenders and produced some of the greatest plays ever

DARYLE LAMONICA The Mad Bomber led Oakland to Super Bowl II and, at 66-16-6, has the second-best winning percentage ever, behind Otto Graham.

THROWERS

Photograph by Walter Iooss Jr.

Where Have You Gone, Daryle Lamonica?

BY MARK MRAVIC

There is nothing MORE BEAUTIFUL IN FOOTBALL, AND MAYBE IN ALL of sports, than a long, arcing pass that nestles into the outstretched arms of a wide receiver, running in stride just beyond a flailing defensive back and into the end zone. What is the root of its appeal? Why do we love the long ball? Some of it surely lies in the play's uncertainty. The moment when the ball hangs in mid-air is pregnant with possibility. The ball may drop harmlessly to earth, leaving us

to shrug or moan, and move on. Or it may fall into those waiting hands, and the potential becomes actual. The dream is made real, and nothing in football is more satisfying.

There was a time when the long ball ruled football. The pro game's first four decades were ground-bound; only four quarterbacks who played primarily before 1960—Otto Graham, Bobby Layne, Y.A. Tittle and Norm Van Brocklin—averaged more than 20 passes per game for their careers. But those '50s stars were the forerunners of a revolution that began in earnest in 1960 with the launch of the American Football League. Fueled by the sophisticated passing strategies of Chargers coach Sid Gillman and his protégé Al Davis in Oakland, the upstart league was an air show from the outset. Whereas the brute power of the Packers' running game and of Cleveland's Jim Brown characterized the NFL establishment in the '60s, the AFL let it all hang out. John Hadl and Jack Kemp, Daryle Lamonica and Joe Namath, the defining figures of the new league, were strong-armed quarterbacks who were free to let fly.

The new offensive strategy, exemplified by Davis's "vertical game" in Oakland, wasn't just a matter of heave-and-hope. Sophisticated pass patterns relied on precise timing of routes and a quick release by the quarterback. But make no mistake, the goal was to get the ball downfield fast. Lamonica was perhaps the greatest exemplar of that philosophy. A Notre

Dame grad who had languished as a backup in Buffalo, he was liberated when Davis stole him in a trade in 1967. That year Lamonica led the league with 30 touchdown passes, wideout Fred Bilentikoff led the AFL with 21.9 yards per reception, and Billy Cannon, the Raiders' tight end, was third in the league with 19.7 yards per catch. Also new to the team that season was explosive wide receiver Warren Wells, who would become Lamonica's favorite deep target, averaging a preposterous 26.8 yards on 47 receptions in 1969. He still has the highest per-reception average in NFL history, at 23.1 yards.

This focus on yards per catch has a purpose. Nowadays it's more fashionable to judge a quarterback by his completion percentage and yards per attempt, which are good measures of quarterback efficiency. But efficiency, moving the chains with short, precise strikes, wasn't at a premium in the long-ball era. Distance was. For that, yards per completion is a better measure, and the long-ball era is reflected in the stats: Of the top 40 quarterbacks in yards per completion in NFL history, only four—Jay Schroeder, Terry Bradshaw, Doug Williams and Craig Morton—played after 1980.

The trade-off for all that long passing, of course, was accuracy. The top QBs from the '60s and '70s rarely completed more than 55% of their passes. By contrast, the *worst* percentage among starters in 2013 was that put up by the Jets' Geno Smith at 55.8.

So was it really so romantic, the era of the long ball? Joe Namath is remembered for one game against the Colts in 1972 in which he averaged an astonishing 45.6 yards per completion, an alltime NFL high. But he completed just five passes that day; he missed on 11 of his 16 attempts.

In the 2010s, a 60% completion rate is the mark of an elite quarterback. In the long-ball era, that rate was unheard of. No quarterback who took a snap before 1979 completed better than 60% of his passes over his career. Among the quarterbacks with 1,500 career attempts who connected on fewer than half their passes are AFL heroes Lamonica, Kemp, George Blanda, Tom Flores and Babe Parilli.

And many of their misses were the worst kind. Namath threw 47 more interceptions than he did touchdowns over his career. Kemp, Hadl and Parilli also had more picks than TDs. And their deep-ball successors in the '70s—Jim Plunkett, Dan Pastorini, Archie Manning—fared about the same. The "efficiency" numbers of some of the top QBs in the '60s and '70s wouldn't merit a sniff from an NFL team these days.

That's because the game changed dramatically in 1978 with the introduction of the so-called Mel Blount Rule, which limited the amount of contact a defender could have with a receiver. Strategy shifted radically in favor of the passing game. Bill Walsh fine-tuned Gillman's West Coast offense to take advantage of the new opportunities, and his success with Joe Montana in San Francisco defused the bomb.

Think about two of the most memorable touchdown passes in NFL history. In Super Bowl XIV in January 1980, the Steelers trailed the Rams 19–17 in the fourth quarter. Bradshaw, facing third-and-eight at his own 27, dropped back and heaved a deep pass down the middle of the field, where a streaking John Stallworth caught the ball over the desperate reach of Rod Perry and took it in for the clinching score. Facing a similar scenario in the Super Bowl nine years later, Montana completed eight of nine passes with methodical precision, culminating in a 10-yard toss over the middle to John Taylor. Bradshaw had beaten the Rams with one killing stroke. Montana defeated the Bengals with a thousand cuts.

Of course the long ball didn't disappear altogether from the game after 1977. It's there in the arsenal of the great quarterbacks, and always will be. Dan Fouts could chuck it, and so could Dan Marino. Doug Williams won a Super Bowl for the Redskins with a jaw-dropping display of deep passing. Troy Aikman-to-Michael Irvin and Jim Kelly-to-Andre Reed were trademarks of the early '90s. And it's not as if Peyton Manning, Tom Brady, Aaron Rodgers and Drew Brees can't launch it long when they want.

But something has been lost in football's turn toward precision, its reliance on route trees and passing progressions, dinks and dunks. No one waxes poetic over the perfect bubble screen or back-shoulder throw. So go ahead and let it fly. A bomb can be a beautiful thing. ∎

Lamonica (with coach John Madden) completed only half of his career passes, but averaged 14.9 yards a reception. | *Photograph by Rod Hanna/USA TODAY Sports*

What was it his favorite receiver, Roger Carr,
had said? "Hey, this guy can unload one
70 yards anytime he likes and hit a dime."

—ROBERT F. JONES, SI, *November 15, 1976*

BERT JONES The Ruston Rifle, whom Bill Belichick called the best pure passer he
ever saw, was done in by a career-altering shoulder injury in 1978, his sixth season.

TERRY BRADSHAW Standing in for an extra count may have cost him cosmetically, but his big throws to Lynn Swann and John Stallworth made the Steelers fearsome.

TONY ROMO His rise from undrafted free agent to celebrity QB came in large part from making big plays; the knock on him is a propensity for just as big interceptions.

FRANK RYAN Probably the only NFL QB ever who had a PhD in mathematics and could pass from one end zone to the other, he once said, "I was meant to throw the long ball."

IN THE EYE OF THE STORM

JIM PLUNKETT WENT THROUGH SOME EPIC UPS AND DOWNS BEFORE HE FINALLY FOUND A HOME IN THE VERTICAL PASSING GAME OF THE OAKLAND RAIDERS AND BECAME A SUPER BOWL MVP

Excerpted from SPORTS ILLUSTRATED, *September 7, 1981* | BY RICK TELANDER

 T ALL COMES DOWN TO PERSPECTIVE, really, to understanding and angle. Thus, seen through the screen of Jim Plunkett's kitchen door, Harry, the Japanese gardener, seems to be harvesting a bumper crop of lemons. But the lemons aren't for squeezing or selling. The "harvest" isn't what it appears to be.

The Mediterranean fruit fly may have spread to Atherton, Calif., which is 25 miles southeast of San Francisco, and the lemons could be infested with Medfly eggs. Plunkett's lemons will soon join the other sacks of fruit lining the curbs of his fashionable neighborhood, to be carted off and buried by National Guardsmen. Later, a huge swath of land in the Santa Clara Valley will be sprayed from the air with Malathion.

Viewed from outside, Plunkett, seated heavily at the kitchen table, could be assumed to be mourning the loss of his lemons, or at least brooding about the coming dousing with the insecticide, which some of the local residents fear may be harmful to humans. But no, Plunkett's thoughts are far beyond fruit and politics.

"There was a baseball player at USC a while ago, a really good pitcher," he says, watching Harry reach for a high cluster. "He was great, a sure thing. But after school he bounced around in the minors, and he never made it to the big leagues. One day they found him on the pitcher's mound at SC's Bovard Field with his diploma and an NCAA baseball award with him. He'd shot himself."

Jim Plunkett, dark-haired, dark-eyed, gap-toothed but appealing at age 33, drums his fingers on the table. There was a time when he was down low enough to at least view at eye level the netherworld which could give rise to such an idea.

"A few years ago I was very depressed too," he says. "In 1978, after the 49ers cut me. But then I started to get things in perspective. I realized that a home life and the company of friends and your family are very important things. That doesn't mean the game becomes less important. When you throw an interception, the team loses, and it kills you for a while. But that's good because it shows what the game means to you. But then you've got to let it go. You've got to bounce back."

It's illuminating to point out that whenever Jim Plunkett speaks of his own comeback—from Whipped Dog to Super Bowl Hero—it's clear as he talks that he isn't certain he *has* come back. Coming back means having first gone somewhere else and he's not sure that he left at all.

"People think I went from being a bad quarterback to being a good one," he says now. "I didn't. I've always been a good quarterback. It's just like when O.J. [Simpson] first went to Buffalo. Everybody said he was a failure, but he just didn't have a team that could let him do what he could do best. Or like at L.A. now—they're good enough it doesn't

matter who the quarterback is. It's the *situation* that has changed. My career wouldn't have had all these peaks and valleys if I'd been with Oakland for 10 years. You know who I feel for? I feel for Archie Manning. He's a nice guy and a hell of a quarterback, and if he'd been with Pittsburgh all along and Bradshaw had been with the Saints, Archie would be the star and Pittsburgh still would have won those Super Bowls. It's the team you're with that matters."

Plunkett's chance came on Oct. 12 of last year. The Raiders were 2–3 and heading nowhere. San Diego was in first place in the AFC West. Dan Pastorini, Oakland's first-string quarterback, had broken a leg the week before, and rookie quarterback Marc Wilson was too green to send in. That left the Raiders with Plunkett, the shell-shocked vet who hadn't started a game in 2½ years, who in 1978 had been picked off the NFL scrap heap by the Raiders when no other team wanted him. Called gun-shy, paranoid, conservative, damaged and finished at times during the previous five years, Plunkett seemed to be on a permanent R&R program at Oakland, a plan designed by managing general partner Al Davis that seemed to have little purpose other than to soothe the player's psychic and bodily wounds before a quiet release into civilian life.

But Plunkett performed masterfully against San Diego, completing 11 of 14 passes. One pass went for a touchdown and Plunkett threw no interceptions as the Raiders won 38–24. With Plunkett in charge Oakland won its next five games and 12 of its next 14, including the AFC championship rematch against San Diego. Plunkett threw deep, he threw short, he ran for critical first downs, he was on a roll.

And then, two weeks after the San Diego win, Plunkett was sitting in the Super Bowl locker room in New Orleans, victorious, the champion of the world, the Most Valuable Player of the game with 13 completions in 21 attempts for 261 yards, no interceptions and three touchdowns (including a Super Bowl record 80-yarder to Kenny King) in the Raiders' 27–10 victory over Philadelphia.

"I'll never forget it," says a reporter who was there. "He looked grim, almost haunted. He was just sitting there with all these people around, and I actually felt sorry for him."

Plunkett doesn't like publicity, but more than that he doesn't like being singled out for praise after a team effort. He could never convince people of his certainty that he was the same, that he was "just playing with better people."

"I'm happy," he told the newsmen finally, weakly. "Believe me. I'm just not very good at showing how I feel."

Part of the problem, if it can be called that, is that Plunkett has always had his past crowding him. Just for a moment imagine you're a college sports information director and Plunkett is on your team. Could there be a simpler job? Your star quarterback, 6' 3", 204 pounds, redshirted his sophomore year after recovering from suspected cancer, now as a senior leads the team to a Rose Bowl victory over heavily favored Ohio State and is named the game's MVP. It's the first time in 19 years that your school has even been to a postseason game.

A first team All-America, the quarterback is named the 1970 collegiate player of the year by nearly everyone who dispenses such honors. He wins the Heisman Trophy. Moreover, the bright young man (a B student in political science) is the son of impoverished Mexican-American parents. The father, who worked at a newsstand in the San Jose post office and was legally blind, died in the young man's junior year. The mother, blind since she fell ill at age 20, cannot work. To help support the family (there are two older sisters), the quarterback has worked long hours as a grocery sacker, a construction laborer, an odd-job man. Though the quarterback lives on campus in a jock fraternity house, he visits his mother most weekends at her home in San Jose, walking with her and describing clouds and colors to her.

Plunkett's senior season, 1970, was called the Year of the Quarterback. Manning, Dan Pastorini, Rex Kern, Joe Theismann, Scott Hunter, Ken Anderson, Chuck Hixson and Lynn Dickey all were seniors enjoying fine seasons. Competition for the Heisman was unusually fierce, with

certain schools running pushy campaigns on behalf of their candidates. At Stanford, however, the hype was subdued.

"We could have made it maudlin, a real carnival, using a family situation like that," says Stanford associate athletic director Gary Cavalli, who worked in the sports information office then. "But we kept it very low-key, because we knew the kind of guy Jim was and it was only fair to him."

One thing is certain: If your life appears to be a cliché, its truth is obscured. For example, Plunkett's childhood is always described as "deprived." It probably was hard and certainly it was odd—his college coach, John Ralston, remembers visiting the household and seeing Mr. Plunkett with his face six inches away from the TV screen, complaining that he couldn't see anything—but deprived it may not have been.

Plunkett himself has always claimed that his childhood was "wonderful," that it gave him strength and pleasure. Jack Ditz, a San Francisco housebuilder who became a sort of big brother to Plunkett after Jim's father died, believes him. "Sure, the house was small," Ditz says. "But

the love was there. People always say, 'Isn't it remarkable that Jim was able to rise above the problem of two blind parents?' But isn't it obvious that those parents were the reason he rose in the first place?"

PLUNKETT WAS THE FIRST PLAYER TAKEN IN THE 1971 NFL draft, by New England. That first season Plunkett played well, guiding the Patriots on every single offensive down (an NFL first) and throwing for 19 touchdowns, the third-most ever by a rookie. The team finished 6–8, its best record in five years, and Plunkett was named rookie of the year.

Shortly after that, though, reality set in. The Pats were, in truth, a bad team, and they began to play that way. Plunkett was sacked, battered, trampled. His interceptions went up, his effectiveness down.

In 1973 Chuck Fairbanks replaced John Mazur as New England's head coach. Direct from the University of Oklahoma. Fairbanks had notions of putting some Sooner-style option plays into the Patriots' attack, with Plunkett leading the way. Two knee and three left-shoulder operations later, Plunkett was a changed man.

He had become jumpy and tentative on the field, partly hobbled, sometimes ducking blows that never came. He had been humbled, NFL-style. In 1976 he was traded, at his request, to San Francisco. The 49ers gave up a lot—three No. 1 draft picks, a No. 2 and backup quarterback Tom Owen—but Plunkett was back home in the Bay Area, the scene of his greatest triumphs, and he would surely lead the team to victory. "I really thought I was going to be the savior," Plunkett says, "but all I did was put more pressure on myself. San Francisco was by far the worst experience of my life. It felt like the whole world was falling in on me." The 49ers were an uneven team, with spotty pass protection, and Plunkett played erratically. With each sack, each hurried or missed pass, he felt more intimidated, more afraid, more unworthy.

By 1978 Plunkett was disoriented. After completing no passes in 11 attempts in a 31–14 preseason loss to Oakland, he was released. Joe Thomas, the GM who made the final decision, explained that the club was looking for a younger quarterback, one who threw "the intermediate game" better. The Raiders, the last refuge of lost souls, signed Plunkett a few days later, but not before making him face the final indignity of performing in a rookie-style tryout.

Everybody in the NFL needs something to believe in (Jesus is popular for many reasons, not the least of which is His assumed compassion for those subject to bad reads), and Plunkett is no exception there. But what he believes in is Stanford University.

Stanford was good to him at the beginning when things were tough—when he was a pimply-faced, crewcut mope wandering the campus with his head down (from neck surgery). Stanford was where things fell into place, where beauty and enlightenment were offered even to a poor kid like Plunkett, where athletes could be jocks but read books too. And it was, in fact, the Stanford-like conditions on the Raiders last year that enabled Plunkett to accomplish what he did.

There was no pressure on him. None. Pastorini's leg was broken, not bruised, and he wouldn't be back. Marc Wilson barely knew the plays, and Plunkett had been studying them for nearly three years. The fans didn't expect anything from Plunkett. Nor did the writers. Only Plunkett expected something. And he had a thousand outs.

And there was the Oakland offensive system, which, like Stanford's, was perfect for Plunkett's skills: straight drop-back, minimal dumping to backs, emphasis on hitting the receivers on longer routes. By design, Oakland quarterbacks get a long time to throw, up to a second more than the passers on some clubs, which is a direct function of the team's massive and skilled offensive line.

For Plunkett, a tall, over-the-top long-ball artist, hiding behind that wall gave him a feeling of confidence he hadn't known before in the pros. "I could see the confidence growing each day," says his coach, Tom Flores, "just in the way he practiced, the way he responded in meetings. A man who's lost his confidence plays conservatively. But Jim was calling audibles, taking command, going deep, looking for the big play." ∎

No one has ever questioned George's physical abilities. It is the rest of the package that has left people shaking their heads. "He has so much talent it's scary," says Jets GM Dick Steinberg. But in four years with the Colts, he never came close to realizing his potential.

—JILL LIEBER, SI, *August 16, 1994*

Photographs by Ronald C. Modra [left] and Damian Strohmeyer

JEFF GEORGE His 81-yard strike at a workout wowed scouts and made him the top pick in 1990, but his personality wore out his welcome in five cities.

ARNIE HERBER

THE NFL DID NOT START KEEPING INDIVIDUAL PASSING statistics until 1932, but the year they began, Arnie Herber led the league in both yardage (639) and touchdowns (9). He threw 101 times in 14 games for the Green Bay Packers that year (or about what Aaron Rodgers might attempt in three games nowadays) and completed 37, but his lasting contribution was what he did with the deep ball. "Herber revolutionized the game," coaching great George Allen wrote in 1982. "He was the first outstanding long passer, way ahead of his time."

Not bad for a local kid who went to Green Bay West High and was actually working as a handyman in the team clubhouse before he got a chance to try out for Curly Lambeau. He impressed the Packers' coach enough that he was added to the roster as a 20-year-old rookie. He ended up in the Pro Football Hall of Fame after playing 11 seasons with the Pack and winning four NFL titles.

The ball was rounder then and harder to throw than the modern ball, but with opposing defenders bunched at the line to stop the run, Herber would surprise teams again and again by throwing deep. He led the league in passing for a second time in 1934, and the following year became even more dangerous when wideout Don Hutson joined the Packers. Herber (number 38, at far right) and Hutson (14, with ball) quickly formed the first truly great passer-receiver combo in NFL history, and they paved the way for QBs like Sammy Baugh and Otto Graham to take passing to a new level.

Herber was so accurate with the long ball that in 1937 a Hollywood crew filmed him as part of a short called *Pigskin Championship*. A three-square-foot pane of glass was suspended from a goal post and Herber was set up at the 50-yard line to try to break it. Thinking it might take the better part of the day, the director had not yet turned on his camera when Herber calmly shattered it on his first try. Not a problem. Another pane was hung and Herber broke that with his second throw.

Herber would retire after the 1940 season, but when the war made players scarce he came back four years later and spent two seasons with the Giants. He'll always be most closely identified however with the Packers and Hutson, who said of his quarterback, "In Arnie Herber, Green Bay had by far the best passer in the league and one of the greatest long passers that ever played. He was a honey." —G.K.

Thought too small to stick in the NFL, the quarterback from Division III Occidental College caught on with the AFL Chargers in 1960. His gunslinging ways—he was a scrambler who could throw the ball 90 yards—were a perfect fit for the wide-open, progressive league.

—MARK BECHTEL, SI, *December 28, 2009*

JACK KEMP Before entering politics, he played nine seasons in the AFL, was an All-Star seven times, and went to five championship games, with two titles.

JOE NAMATH His playboy image can overshadow his ability, but Joe Willie could get down and dirty; in 1967, he was the first QB to throw for 4,000 yards, and in only 14 games.

KILLER GIANTS

DEEP-THROWING PHIL SIMMS SILENCED HIS CRITICS AND TURNED IN PERHAPS THE GREATEST BIG-GAME PERFORMANCE EVER BY A QUARTERBACK AS THE GIANTS ROUTED DENVER IN SUPER BOWL XXI

Excerpted from SPORTS ILLUSTRATED, *February 2, 1987* | BY PAUL ZIMMERMAN

 OMEWHERE INSIDE THE MIND OF EVERY quarterback there's a 22-for-25 day, a day when every pass has eyes and every decision is correct. And for a showcase there's a bright, sunlit stadium with more than a half century of tradition, a place like, well, the Rose Bowl. There are 101,063 people in the stands to watch, and about 2,000 writers and broadcasters to tell people about it, and some 130 million Americans gathered around their TV sets to see what has been called the Ultimate Game.

That's where the fantasy usually stays, inside, because nobody ever goes 22 for 25 in a game like the Super Bowl, not in this high-powered era with sophisticated defenses featuring shifting zones and blitzes and mixed coverages. But let's say there's a quarterback who deserves this mythical kind of day, a quarterback who has spent eight years in the NFL being hammered by adversity and injury, who has heard the boos of the New York fans for as long as he can remember, a quarterback like the Giants' Phil Simms.

On Sunday, Simms got even. The Giants crushed the Denver Broncos 39–20 in Super Bowl XXI, and Simms, the game's MVP, personally carved them up with the best percentage passing day in Super Bowl history—in any NFL championship game ever, for that matter.

You say someone must have gotten the name wrong, that Simms is a downfield passer, a low-percentage guy. Well, you have a point. He was below .500 for the two postseason wins, and that's not easy when you're beating people by scores like 49–3 and 17–0. Fourteen NFL passers had higher percentages than Simms this season. A day like 22 for 25 is for the dinkers, the dump-off artists, not the serious gunners like Simms. But there it was. The guy was simply amazing.

"He quarterbacked as good a game as ever has been played," said the Giants' head coach, Bill Parcells.

"Technically as close to a perfect game as I've seen a quarterback have," said the Giants' offensive coach, Ron Erhardt.

The guys on the same assembly line as Simms, the ones who work with him every day, said they had a hunch he might have a surprise like this cooked up for the Broncos. They said it started more than a week before the Super Bowl. "We came back to practice on Thursday," said Bart Oates, the center. "We had a lackluster, mediocre practice. The next day coach Parcells kind of got on us. He said, 'I expected a low-key practice, but this won't do. You've got to pick it up.'

"Phil was phenomenal in that Friday practice. He hit everything he threw. Parcells said, 'Hey, this is too much. Save something for the game.' Phil had this strange sort of a glow. It was like he was in a perfect biorhythm stage or something."

So the Giants came out to Pasadena, where every writer's pregame angle was Bronco quarterback John Elway versus the ferocious New York defense. There was a solid week of that stuff, but the Giants smiled to themselves because they knew that their own guy was getting himself ready for the game of his life.

When Sunday finally came around, Elway was magnificent in the first half, dodging a defense that had been geared especially to contain him, going deep downfield off scrambles—54 yards to Vance Johnson, 31 yards to Steve Watson. In five possessions he brought his team into scoring position four times. But there was little to show on the scoreboard for his performance, and anyway the Giants weren't overly worried. "Everyone's pretty frisky there in the first quarter, including Elway," Parcells would later say. "I talked to our defensive guys before the game and told them not to worry about him getting completions early and making plays. Keep wearing them down. Just don't let the receivers turn into runners. After a while, we'll make some plays."

Reality arrived in the third quarter, when the Giants set off the biggest one-half offensive explosion in Super Bowl history. Simms was literally perfect, going 10 for 10 in the second half. New York scored four TDs and a field goal on its first five possessions. Simms was finding all his receivers—short, long, primary, secondary, it didn't matter.

The real turning point came with the Giants' opening drive in the third quarter, when backup quarterback Jeff Rutledge shifted out of punt formation to sneak two yards for a first down on a fourth-down play at the Giants' 46. Simms made the gamble pay off five plays later by hitting tight end Mark Bavaro for a 13-yard touchdown against double coverage. "I probably should not have thrown it, but I saw this little opening," Simms said.

He got his longest completion of the day, 44 yards to Phil McConkey, off a flea-flicker that set up the Giants' second touchdown of the second half. Later, Simms found Stacy Robinson for 36 yards, laying the ball perfectly in the hole in the double zone, on the way to the third touchdown of the half.

In the final minutes of the game, linebacker Harry Carson gave Parcells his usual Gatorade bath, and even Simms got a drenching, ice water this time, with tackle Brad Benson and Oates doing the honors.

"I think it was very appropriate to cool the guy down," Oates said, "as hot as he was in the game."

The Giants are young. Only seven players on the 45-man roster have reached their 30th birthday. If you're thinking dynasty, though, remember that the Bears were a young team when they won the Super Bowl last year. Strange things can happen to a club during a season.

But right now the Giants are on top for the first time since 1956. They have made all the stops—dismay and hope and glory, you name it, they have been there. And so has Phil Simms. ∎

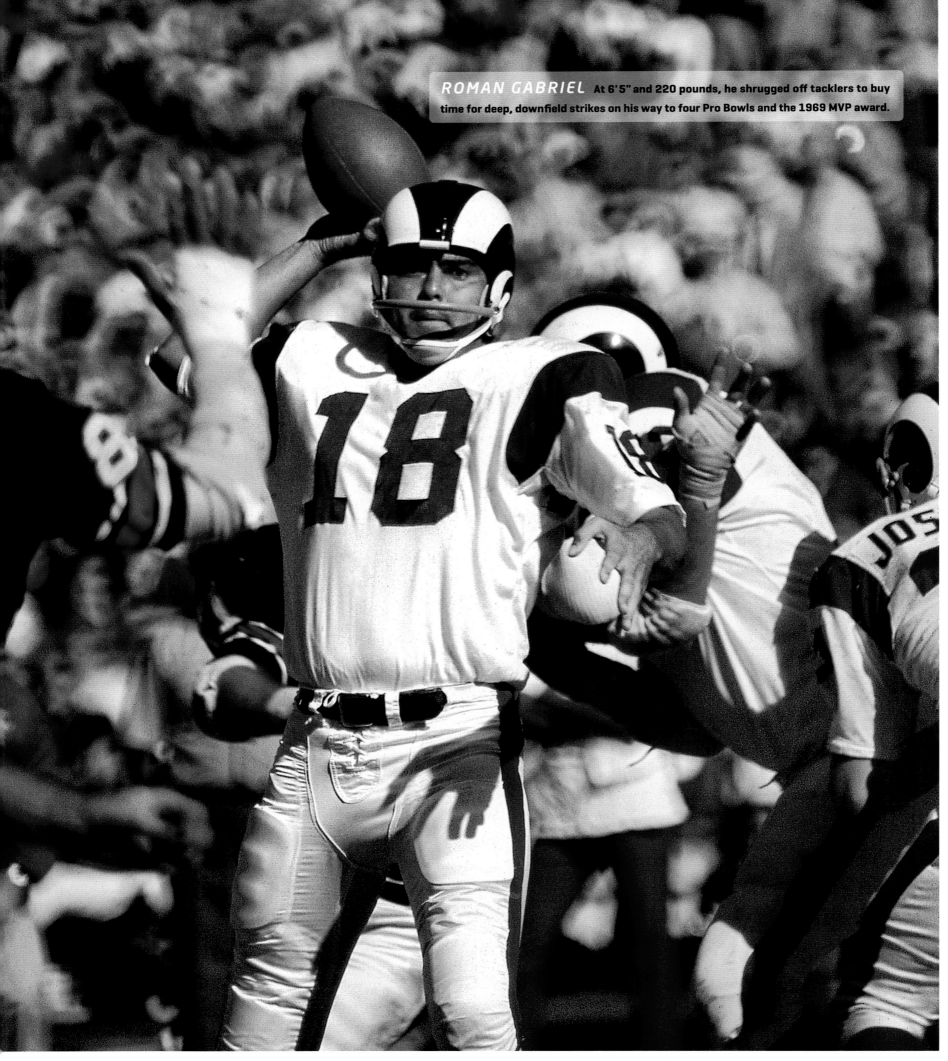

ROMAN GABRIEL At 6'5" and 220 pounds, he shrugged off tacklers to buy time for deep, downfield strikes on his way to four Pro Bowls and the 1969 MVP award.

JOHN HADL The Chargers' combination of Hadl to Lance Alworth in the
'60s helped establish the AFL as a wild and entertaining alternative to the NFL.

NORM VAN BROCKLIN The Dutchman, a nine-time Pro Bowler in 12 seasons, famously platooned with Bob Waterfield on the Rams before winning a title in Philly.

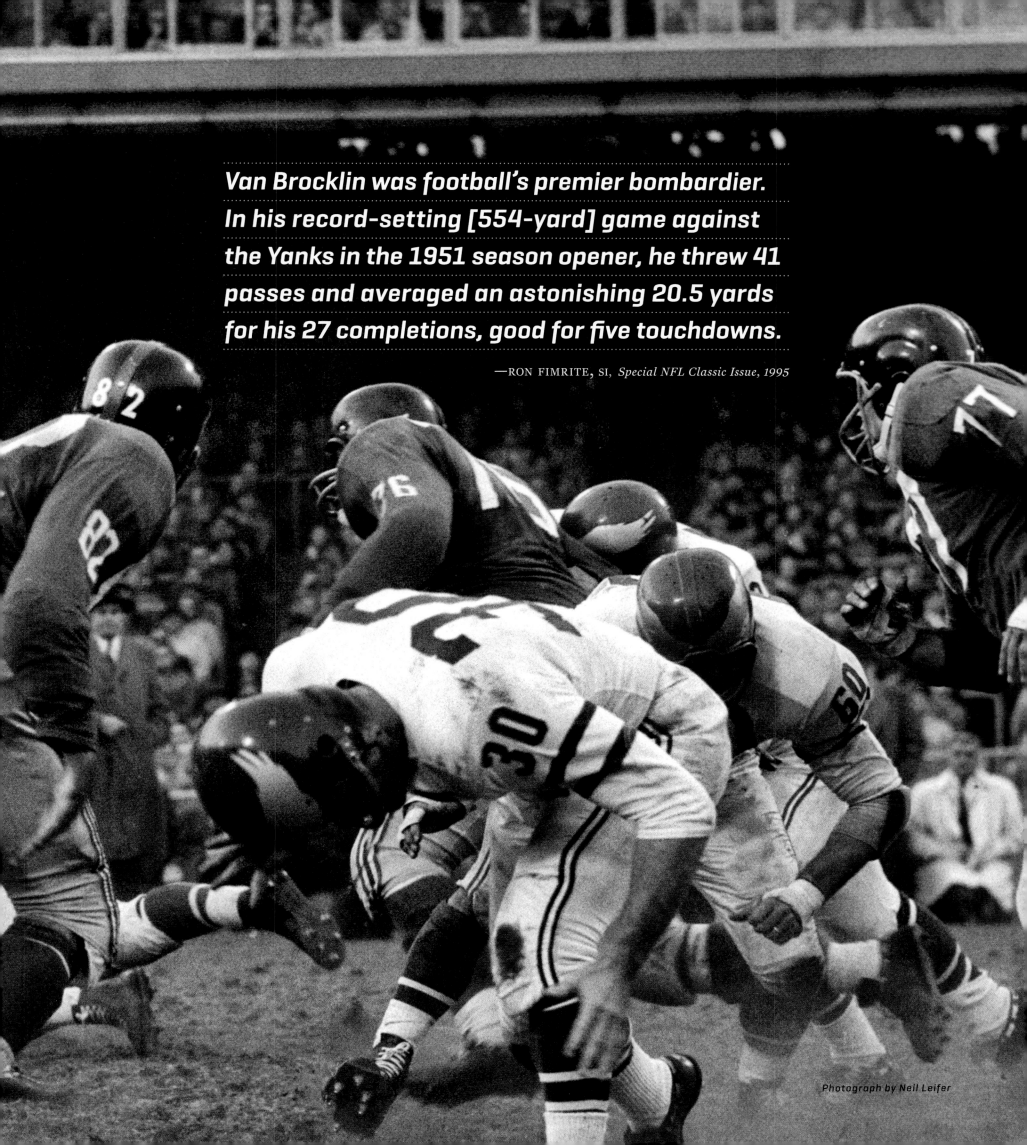

Van Brocklin was football's premier bombardier. In his record-setting [554-yard] game against the Yanks in the 1951 season opener, he threw 41 passes and averaged an astonishing 20.5 yards for his 27 completions, good for five touchdowns.

—RON FIMRITE, SI, *Special NFL Classic Issue, 1995*

ALMOST BY DEFINITION, anyone who plays quarterback in the NFL is tough. But then there are the toughest of the breed. They may not throw a perfect spiral or display the best form, but they are some of the most colorful players the game has known. They're the ones who will play through hell— and inspire others to follow them

BRETT FAVRE Played with ankle and knee sprains, a separated shoulder, even a broken thumb during 321 straight starts, 94 more than the next best QB.

TOUGH

GUYS

The Bloodied But Unbowed

BY STEVE RUSHIN

Tough can be GOOD ("TOUGH AS NAILS") AND TOUGH CAN BE BAD ("TOUGH luck") and tough can be good and bad at the same time ("tough love"). Tough can cut both ways— or can't be cut at all, in the case of a tough steak—leaving us with a serious question: Is tough a compliment ("He's one tough SOB") or a pejorative ("What are you, a tough guy?") or something in between? This ambiguity is at the heart of football tough guys, who have long been praised for

playing through pain and lately—given all we now know about the concussed brain and chronic traumatic encephalopathy— criticized for wantonly abusing their bodies.

Those players most deeply acquainted with professional football's theater of pain are NFL quarterbacks, who were once collectively described—by pain-inflicting Hall of Famer Warren Sapp—as the "piñatas of sports." Of these piñatas, Packers quarterback Brett Favre was renowned as especially tough, resistant to the assaults of men like Sapp, who once hit Favre so hard that officials on the field were scanning the tunnels for an ambulance even as the defensive tackle was bearing down on Favre from the blind side.

But Favre remained very much alive after Sapp's epic hit. Only the play was blown dead, after which Favre instantly popped to his feet and shouted at Sapp: "Is that the hardest you can hit you [everloving] [sissy]?"

Favre's pain threshold was off the (hospital) charts, so fans and journalists naturally projected that quality onto his interior life as well. When his father died in 2003, and the next night Favre played in a *Monday Night Football* game against the Raiders—and threw for 399 yards and four touchdowns in a 41–7 win—he appeared to possess a superhuman capacity to absorb physical *and* emotional pain.

That he struggled with addiction to painkillers was un-

derstandable, because few players had quite so much pain to kill—kill being a word often linked to the word quarterback, homicide apparently being the first motive of an NFL defensive lineman when the ball is snapped. "The name of the game is 'Kill the Quarterback,'" Joe Namath has said many times, most recently in 2014, when he acknowledged his own brain damage from multiple concussions. And while quarterbacks in the modern era are often seen as overprotected—coddled is a word that comes up often, spoken mostly by men who never played quarterback in the NFL—they weren't protected at all for most of the game's history.

Bobby Layne played smash-mouth football when mouths could still be comprehensively smashed: The Lions and Steelers quarterback was among the last players to wear a face mask. He didn't wear pads in his pants so as not to inhibit his running. What's more, Layne frequently played hungover, so that his toughness took on a kind of Rat Pack grandeur in that decade—the '50s—when going on stage buzzed or hungover was looked on as a badge of manliness.

Colts lineman Art Donovan claimed to have smelled booze on Layne's breath at the bottom of a pile and asked the quarterback, one tough guy to another: "Were you drinking last night?" To which Layne replied, "I had a couple at *halftime*."

Layne would eventually accept the minimal protection of a

single-bar face mask, which in turn would become the tough-guy hallmark of Billy Kilmer, who was badly injured in a car wreck in 1962 when he fell asleep at the wheel and ended up in San Francisco Bay. Kilmer suffered a compound fracture to his right tibia, and he nearly lost his entire foot after an infection set in. During his rehab he worked in the terrible heat of his father's dry-cleaning business. Pressing pants in Pomona—now there's a title for a memoir—Kilmer vowed that he would not do that for the rest of his life. And so this trial by fire, this trial by dry-cleaning steam press, steeled him to all manner of future assaults that he would suffer in the NFL.

Although Kilmer was always called hard-nosed, it was not literally true, as Giants defensive end Jack Gregory demonstrated in 1976, when Kilmer was 37 and the last quarterback in the NFL to still wear a single-bar face mask. Down 17–12, Kilmer had led the Redskins to midfield when Gregory landed on him (as one game story put it) "like a baby grand piano." Kilmer's nose was shattered and gashed and he exited the game, bleeding, replaced by the younger Joe Theismann, whose own career would come to a gruesome end against the Giants nine years later. Theismann lasted one play, overthrowing a receiver, after which Kilmer returned to throw the game-winning touchdown pass with 40 seconds on the clock.

Which isn't to say that tough guys always win. On the contrary, in the second game of his 17th season, Giants quarterback Y.A. Tittle was hit by John Baker, the Steelers 6' 7", 280-pound defensive end, immediately after throwing a pass. Tittle was concussed on the play, and cartilage in his rib cage was torn, a physical toll captured that day in photographs of the quarterback after the hit—on his knees, bleeding, his helmet behind him like a guillotined head—as the pass was intercepted and returned for a TD.

The quarterback had grown up in East Texas with the name Yelberton Abraham Tittle, which might have hardened him at an early age. He obstinately declined to sit out the next game, though he was barely released from the hospital in time, and he played out the rest of the 2-10-2 season, the last of his Hall of Fame career. He was 38 years old.

But then quarterback toughness doesn't die, or even fade away. Like any good QB, it keeps on throwing—haymakers, in the case of Joe Kapp. In 2011, the 73-year-old Kapp, late of the Vikings and Patriots and the CFL, attended a luncheon in Vancouver. There, on a dais, Kapp was seated near his longtime nemesis, Angelo Mosca, the 74-year-old former defensive tackle for the Hamilton Tiger-Cats and longtime practitioner of that game Namath called "Kill the Quarterback."

As an apparent peace offering, Kapp gallantly tried to give Mosca a sprig of flowers. Mosca blithely declined by deflecting them with his hand. Kapp hit him with the flowers and Mosca returned the blow with his cane. As the fists began to fly, the truth of what Norman Mailer once said became unmistakable: Tough guys don't dance, not even at 73. ∎

A huge Steelers hit left Tittle concussed and—in his mind, maybe worse—intercepted for a TD. | *Photograph by Dozier Mobley/AP*

"The quarterbacks I admire most are the tough, hard-living guys who don't know how to quit. We've got a lot of that spirit on the Raiders."

—KEN STABLER TO ROBERT F. JONES, SI, *September 19, 1977*

KEN STABLER After injuring a ligament in his twice-operated-on left knee, the Snake played on one leg while leading the Raiders to the 1978 AFC title game.

DAN FOUTS He often paid for the extra time he needed to throw long; Bill Walsh once said, "I'm not sure anyone is as tough as him standing up to the rush."

A MAN OF MACHISMO

IN A FIRST-PERSON STORY AFTER LEADING THE VIKINGS TO THE
SUPER BOWL, JOE KAPP DESCRIBED THE CULTURAL ROOTS OF HIS
REPUTATION AS ONE OF THE TOUGHEST QUARTERBACKS EVER

Excerpted from SPORTS ILLUSTRATED, *July 20, 1970* | BY JOE KAPP WITH JACK OLSEN

OOTBALL IS A KIDS' GAME, INVENTED TO give a lot of people a lot of fun. The minute a player loses sight of that fact, he's in trouble. By having fun I don't mean goosing each other and telling dirty jokes in the huddle. I mean doing your absolute best and enjoying it, because if you're doing your best you will be enjoying it. You don't always have control of whether you win or lose, but you do have control of your own effort and your own mind. If you can get enough ballplayers on your own club thinking this way, you can win anything.

I haven't missed many football games in my life, going all the way back to high school—like most pros, I've played with cracked ribs and a punctured lung and a torn knee and separated shoulder and half a dozen other injuries—and I've also never missed a postgame party. I've never missed the fun.

I've known players who get a little injury and rush off to the hospital and don't make the party. Bull! Not me. I never missed one and I never intend to miss one. You play out there together and you win or lose together, and after the game you should party together.

Of course there are certain players who will tell you that I never miss a party, period, and if they want to spread that propaganda, it's all right with me—mostly because it's true. I'm aware of my own reputation, and I enjoy it. I've been called "one half of a collision looking for the other." The adjectives you usually read about me are "unstylish," "brutal," "unrelenting" and sometimes "dumb." (That's when we lose; when we win, I'm a "great genius.") People take one look at the scars on my face and they assume that I spend most of my off-hours prowling around looking for fights, when the truth is that the fights are prowling around looking for me, and sometimes they find me. I think of myself as a gentle, fun-loving, peaceful person, but you can be all these things and still get in fights—especially if you don't back down, and I try not to. You won't see me running out-of-bounds to avoid a little physical contact with a line-backer, and you won't see me ducking out the window when somebody wants to tangle. So I've been known to get in an occasional tête-à-tête.

Maybe this goes back to my Chicano childhood and machismo. Machismo means manliness, a willingness to act like a man, and if a kid didn't have machismo in the polyglot neighborhoods of the San Fernando and Salinas valleys in California, where I grew up, he had it tough. When I was little I saw guys lying in their own blood at the corner of Mission Boulevard and Hollister Street in San Fernando. Sometimes the Mexicans would fight the Anglos; sometimes it would be the Mexicans and the blacks from Pacoima. They had gang fights going all the time and even an occasional shootout or knifing.

In the fifth grade a bigger kid called me "a dirty Mexican," and at first I didn't challenge him. But when I got home I brooded on what he had said. So I went back and found him. I didn't win the fight, but I got in some licks. That was machismo, not backing down.

I went to the University of California on an athletic scholarship, mostly for my basketball, but if you have never heard of me in that connection, you may be excused. I led the Pacific Coast Conference quarterbacks in rushing my senior year and was named to the *Look* All-America team, and so, of course, all I had to do was sit back and wait for the pro offers to roll in.

Nothing rolled. I was the 13th pick of the Washington Redskins, but they never contacted me, and I wound up signing with the Calgary Stampeders in the Canadian Football League. The ink was hardly dry on the contract before I got into the battle that produced these scars on my face. I've never told the whole story before, but now I'm telling it to nip off some of the sillier versions that have been circulating.

It was a hot, humid night during the training season, and most of the Stampeders were sitting around drinking beer. We'd had the annual rookie show earlier and nobody felt like going to bed, and around 1 a.m. I walked into a room where the guys were talking. Without warning, a big linebacker broke a quart bottle of beer across my jaw and raked it across my throat. We started to tangle, but there was so much blood spurting around the room that the other guys jumped in and broke it up. A couple of players took me to the trainer's room, and when the trainer answered the door all sleepy and red-eyed, he took one look at me and fainted. At the hospital they gave me 100 stitches, and the doctors said that the broken glass had missed my jugular by about half an inch.

I never missed a game in Canada. I played the exhibition game the week after my 100 stitches. I started and finished a game when my knee was twisted and torn. Later on the doctors took out bone chips and torn cartilage and everything else. One of them said that he couldn't believe so much matter could come out of one man's knee and they predicted that I would never play again. When the next season started, I was out there. Too dumb to know better, I guess!

After the 1963 season I picked up the nickname "El Cid." Football players go to the movies often, and I go more often than most, and we had all seen *El Cid* and that great scene where they strap Charlton Heston into the saddle so that he can lead the Spanish into battle and scare the hell out of the enemy, even though he's dead. Right after that I was dressing for a game and easing my uniform around all my injuries. One finger was dislocated and taped to the next one. One knee and both ankles were taped. I had bruised ribs and they were taped, and my shoulder was taped up because of a slight separation. Our captain, Norm Fieldgate, looked at me and said, "Hey, it's El Cid!" I took that as a compliment. I liked my reputation as a guy who finished the games he started, and I still do. ∎

Kapp proved he could take a hit—and dish one out—in his 12 flinty seasons in the CFL and NFL. | *Photograph by Neil Leifer*

JIM MCMAHON A charismatic leader, he routinely played with a right elbow so sore he couldn't comb his hair and once tried to play with a lacerated kidney.

Photographs by Peter Read Miller (left) and John Biever

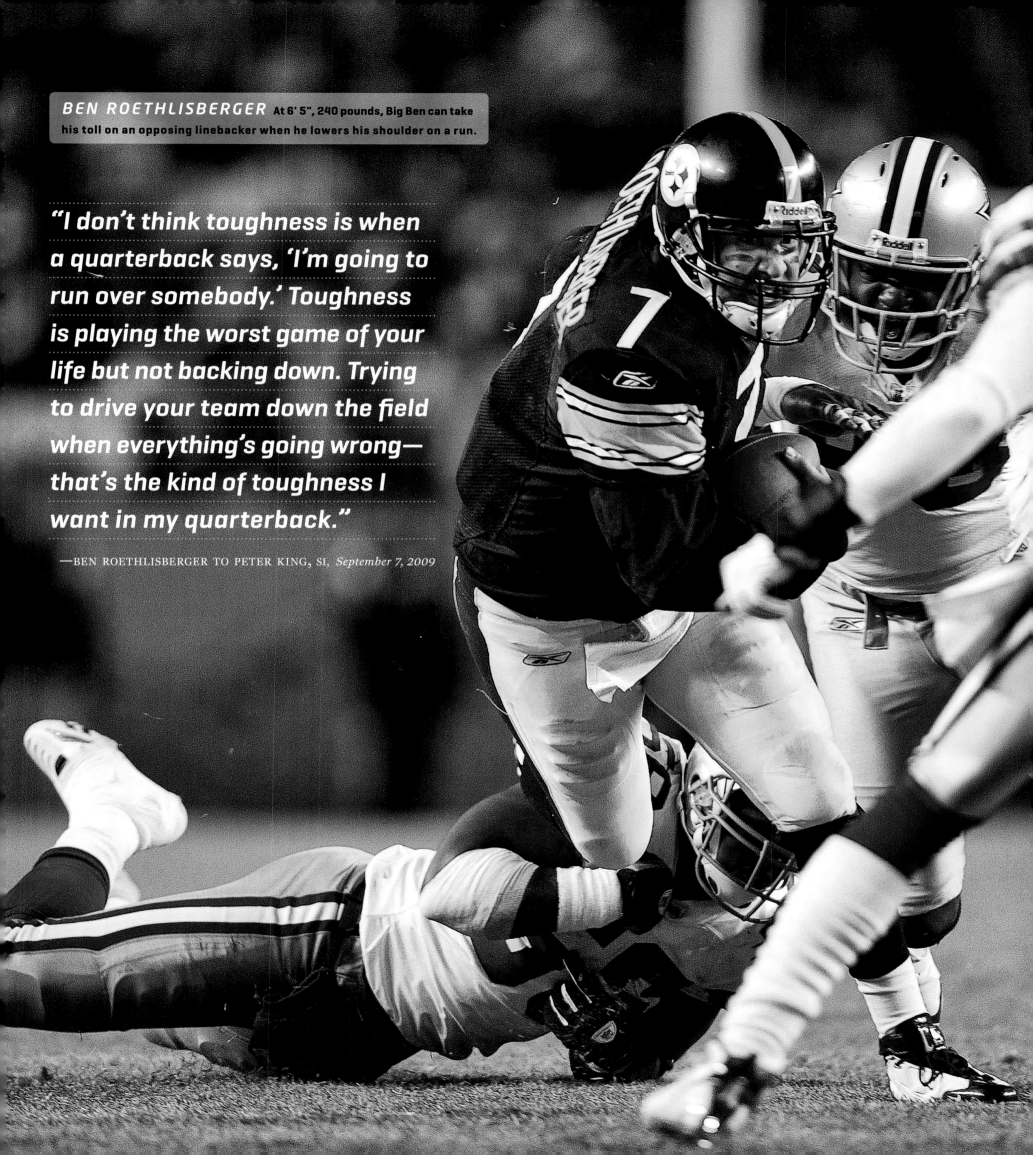

BEN ROETHLISBERGER At 6' 5", 240 pounds, Big Ben can take his toll on an opposing linebacker when he lowers his shoulder on a run.

"I don't think toughness is when a quarterback says, 'I'm going to run over somebody.' Toughness is playing the worst game of your life but not backing down. Trying to drive your team down the field when everything's going wrong— that's the kind of toughness I want in my quarterback."

—BEN ROETHLISBERGER TO PETER KING, SI, *September 7, 2009*

Game Changer

BOBBY LAYNE

IN A LONG-NEGLECTED clip file in the SPORTS ILLUSTRATED library, there's a dusty 1957 report that details an athlete's drunk-driving arrest. It describes a car, moving erratically on the wrong side of the center line with its headlights off at 2 a.m., followed by a police cruiser. The suspicious car finally pulled over, but it was still moving slowly away as the driver emerged and admitted that, no, he didn't have his license with him. That was Bobby Layne, who broke all the rules and lived his life hard, but when it came time for football, played even harder.

[It should also be noted that he somehow managed to get acquitted in that case. His lawyer successfully argued that what the officer mistook for slurred speech was really just his raspy Texas twang. Soon after, a sign appeared in the Lions locker room that read: AH AIN'T DRUNK. AH'M FROM TEXAS.]

Layne (number 22) was a star at Texas before becoming the third overall pick of the Bears in the 1948 draft. Two inauspicious years later he joined the Lions, and under his fiery leadership, Detroit won championships in 1952 and '53 and was runner-up to the Browns in '54.

He asked no quarter, and gave none either, even to teammates. "I've seen him chase guys out of the huddle, send 'em to the sideline if they missed a block," said LaVern Torgeson, a former teammate.

How tough was Layne? Long after face masks had been introduced, he was among the very last quarterbacks to keep playing without one. "I tried a new face mask every day they brought one out," he said. "But they bothered my vision, even the one-bar types they had. Sure, I had my nose broken some, but it was nothing serious."

Layne would play 15 seasons in the NFL (the last five with the Steelers). When he retired after the 1962 season he held the records for most pass completions (1,814), yards (26,768) and TDs (196), and he was a first-ballot inductee into the Pro Football Hall of Fame in 1967.

Beyond statistics, though, he's also credited as the first master of the two-minute drill, after he and coach Buddy Parker fashioned a series of plays designed to move the ball quickly upfield while preserving as much time as possible. That led to a famous quote from his old friend and teammate Doak Walker, which might also serve as Layne's epitaph after his premature death at age 59: "Bobby never lost a game in his life. Time just ran out on him." —G.K.

Photograph by Evan Peskin

DONOVAN MCNABB He famously broke his right ankle on the third play of a game in 2002 and still threw four touchdown passes in the victory.

Photographs by Robert Beck (left) and James Drake

JOHNNY UNITAS He was admired for his guts against the pass rush, but he was revered for his mental toughness and indomitable leadership.

"I often thought that sometimes Unitas would hold the ball one count longer than he had to," Rams defensive tackle Merlin Olsen once said, "just so he could take the hit and laugh in your face."

—PAUL ZIMMERMAN, SI, *August 17, 1998*

THE KING OF PAIN

PERHAPS NO QUARTERBACK EVER ENDURED GREATER SUFFERING AND MORE HORRIFIC INJURIES THAN THE PACKERS' LYNN DICKEY, WHO TOOK TOUGHNESS TO A WHOLE NEW LEVEL WITH HARDLY A WHIMPER

Excerpted from SPORTS ILLUSTRATED, *September 26, 1983* | BY RICK TELANDER

HE DEFENSE MUST MAKE VINCE Lombardi turn over in his grave, and the Packers' sweep doesn't bowl anyone over anymore, but in Green Bay they're getting ready to break out THE PACK IS BACK bumper stickers again. The reason? Simple. In this Age of Airball the Packers have the jazziest passing game in the NFC. Green Bay finished the strike-shortened '82 season with the best record (5-3-1) among NFC Central teams, and after Sunday's 27–24 win over the Los Angeles Rams, the Packers are flying high again.

In James Lofton, John Jefferson and Paul Coffman, Green Bay has the best trio of receivers in the NFC. But the unlikely hero of the Pack's air attack is Lynn Dickey, a 33-year-old, immobile, oft-injured but strong-armed quarterback. Dickey didn't play a full season as a starter until 1980, his 10th year in the NFL, but now he's leading the league in passing. Through three games he had completed 63 of 87 passes—72.4%—for 911 yards and nine touchdowns. Dickey is also the career leader among quarterbacks in the category of gruesome injuries and ailments, and despite his brilliant start this season, '83 has proved no exception in that regard.

Dickey's ills this year began when he got a headache on the Thursday before Green Bay's opener against Houston. No problem. Pain is Dickey's constant companion, the lapdog given to him at the start of his pro career. Without doubt, Dickey has been spindled, torn, battered, injected, cut, sutured, rehabbed, written off and resurrected more times than any other man still playing the game. His injuries have left him with a reputation as one tough hombre, a genuine stoic, a man who would battle Godzilla—and win—to stay at the job he loves.

The headache kept getting worse. On Friday, Dickey had to leave practice and go home because of the pain. Nobody doubted that this was real pain. Dickey, after all, had played part of the 1979 season with an 18-inch steel rod holding his lower left leg together and never complained. Nor did anyone assume that the cause of this headache, which couldn't be traced to fever or trauma, would be simple to pin down. "Lynn never has anything you can handle real easily," says Domenic Gentile, a Packers trainer for 22 years. "In the training room, if a player comes in and has an injury we can't do anything about, we call it an L.D., a Lynn Dickey." There was talk that Dickey might have to sit out the Houston game, which also would have been no surprise. In his NFL career he has missed 53 games because of injury.

It wasn't always like this. Indeed, Dickey's early years back in Osawatomie, Kans. (pop. 4,500) were relatively pain-free. He didn't miss a game in high school, and at Kansas State he was unavailable just once, because of bruised ribs. His notions of physical hardship and

limitation came from observing his older brother Larry, who was crippled by polio at age six.

Things began to change for Dickey when he arrived at the 1971 Senior Bowl. Fired up by all the gawking pro scouts, Dickey threw too hard too fast in the game after not warming up sufficiently, and his arm got sore. "I could almost hear the scouts mumbling," says Dickey, a slow-talking, self-effacing type. "I'd been told I'd be a first-round pick, but I figured I was dropping a few notches."

He figured right. He wasn't drafted until the third round, by Houston, which had already taken quarterback Dan Pastorini in the first round. Dickey rode the bench behind Pastorini that first year, but in 1972 he figured he had a shot to start. Then came a preseason game against St. Louis at the Astrodome.

With his receivers covered, Dickey tried to scramble but was grabbed from behind by a Cardinals defender, who rode him to the artificial turf piggyback style. Dickey's left knee struck the ground with such force that it jammed his left hipbone out of its socket, breaking off a piece of the socket bone and tearing ligaments in the process.

The Oilers' doctor snapped Dickey's hip back into its socket, and Dickey felt so relieved he tried to stand up so he could go back to the huddle. The doctor kept him down. Indeed, the injury was so severe that it didn't even resemble a sports injury; it was like the kind of joint damage associated with a high-speed, head-on auto collision, a "dashboard injury," as it's called in emergency rooms.

The next day Dickey was flown to Boston to undergo surgery by a hip specialist. The broken piece of socket bone was reattached with two screws. "I think it was the worst nerve injury I've ever seen," says Dr. Robert Fain, the Houston team physician who became associated with the Oilers at the time of Dickey's rehabilitation. Dickey had to get injections in his back for several weeks to give him nerve blocks for the unremitting pain. He remembers getting a shot of morphine one night and passing out, then waking up and crying himself back to sleep. One morning he had no feeling in his left leg. A doctor came in his room with a pin and an ink marker and began jabbing Dickey in the leg, making marks where he had no feeling. The doctor said that he would return in an hour and that, if the numbness hadn't subsided, he would be forced to reopen the 13-inch incision on Dickey's hip.

Dickey asked if he could get his leg out of traction for a while. When the doctor left, Dickey started beating fiercely on his leg. Eventually some feeling came back, and Dickey was able to avoid another session with the knife. The pain was still severe a month later when Dickey left the Boston hospital to begin learning to walk again.

Dickey is 6' 4" and normally weighs between 200 and 210 pounds. But when he returned to Houston, he weighed just 170. "It was scary," Pastorini recalls. "He was skin and bones. Plus he was on pain drugs and was sort of out of it. You wondered if he'd hurt his hip or his brain."

Dickey fought through the fog and, with the help of Oilers quarterback coach King Hill, began his comeback. He went from a wheelchair to crutches to a cane, and then around New Year's 1973 he walked unassisted. When he finally shuffled around a football field a short while later, he called home immediately. "Guess what?" he said to his parents. "I just jogged." Dickey made the Oilers' roster again the next fall, astonishing everyone. But he could never supplant Pastorini, and after the '75 season he was traded to Green Bay. He started for the Packers in '76, but in the 10th game he separated his right—throwing—shoulder and underwent surgery in which a screw was implanted in the joint. The operation itself was routine, but the incision became infected.

Dickey recovered during the off-season and was doing well the next year until Rams defensive tackle Larry Brooks crashed into him on the last play of a game on Nov. 13. Brooks's hit shattered the tibia and fibula in Dickey's left leg, and as Dickey lay on the sod, his left ankle pointed in at a 90-degree angle. Doctors operated, screwing a metal plate to the broken bones to secure them while they knitted. After several months the

plate was removed, and Dickey tried to run again. He worked up to a mile a day, but the pain in his leg never slackened. There was nonunion of the bones. In effect, the leg was still broken.

Dickey had to undergo yet another operation, one in which a metal rod was hammered like a railroad spike down through an opening just below his knee and into his tibia. The rod strengthened the bone, but it left Dickey with such acute tendinitis in his knee that he could barely jog. After missing all but a few plays of 33 consecutive games, he hobbled back into the starting lineup in November of 1979.

In 1980 the rod was removed from Dickey's leg—it was his seventh operation—and the tendinitis in his knee cleared up. Since then Dickey's injuries have been less severe, if not less painful. In 1980 he had tendinitis in his right shoulder; in 1981 he missed three games after getting speared in the back; this summer his back acted up, and then came that headache the week of the Houston game.

Dickey doesn't talk about his pains much. A couple of years ago he told a reporter, "If no one ever talked to me, it wouldn't bother me a bit." He likes to spend his free time with his family—wife Sherry and three daughters, ages nine, seven and three. When he goes out with the boys, he'll sit back and swap tales, referring to himself occasionally as "this pitiful specimen."

"I don't know how important it is to like the people you work with," says Lofton. "But we all like Lynn." And not just for his courage and calm. "He's got this intensity on the field," says Packers tackle Greg Koch. "I remember a game against the 49ers when he got sacked and he was screaming at the offensive line all the way to the sideline. All of a sudden I heard a helmet go whizzing over my head. Lynn had thrown it at all of us. Most quarterbacks couldn't get away with that, but Lynn can. We live and die with him."

By kickoff time of the opener against the Oilers, Dickey felt like he was going to die of his headache. He told his roommate, kicker Jan Stenerud, that it felt like "ball-peen hammers are pounding behind my temples." Stenerud was worried. "Lynn is the toughest guy I know," he says. "But he looked like death." During pregame warmups Dickey just jogged, grimacing with every step. Though his head was killing him, he decided to play. Before the game got under way, however, he told his receivers and backs to listen closely to him on the field, particularly on audibles, because he would not be able to yell. Doing so hurt too much.

At the end of the first quarter, despite continually grabbing his head in pain, Dickey was 10 for 10 for 90 yards and a touchdown. By late in the second quarter he had completed 18 passes in a row, tying him with Denver's Steve DeBerg for the second-most consecutive pass completions in NFL history. (The record is 20, by Cincinnati's Ken Anderson.) Dickey's 19th pass attempt fell incomplete, however, as did his 20th.

Dickey finished the day with 27 completions in 31 attempts for 333 yards and five touchdowns, the last figure tying a Packers record. The Packers edged Houston 41–38 in overtime, but Dickey wasn't around at the finish. After his last pass, a 74-yard TD throw to Lofton late in the fourth quarter, he staggered to the sideline, told backup quarterback David Whitehurst, "I don't feel good," and lay down. An ambulance cart took him to the Astrodome dressing room.

Dickey spent that Monday in a Green Bay hospital taking tests to find out what was wrong with him. The headache turned out to be the result of a spinal injection he had been given the week before for his bad back. Spinal fluid had been leaking from the puncture. What Dickey had done was play a brilliant football game while suffering from a post-spinal puncture headache, which can be horribly painful.

The headache is gone now. On Sunday against the Rams, Dickey had a hot hand early, completing 13 of his 19 first-half passes for 161 yards as Green Bay took a 17–3 lead. Although L.A. got rolling against the Packers' patchwork defense, eventually Stenerud drilled a 36-yard field goal to win it for Green Bay in the closing seconds.

For Dickey, the question of pain remains, as it always will. Packers coach Bart Starr says Dickey is a throwback to the old days, when players lived by a tougher code. "We don't want anybody to play injured," says Starr. "But play hurt, yes, you have to."

Dickey says he has kept playing for several reasons. Part of it, of course, is for his brother. "Larry loves sports, and I was always his arms and legs," says Dickey. And part of it is for the glory and the cash. But most of it is just because it feels right.

And the pain? "You've just got to roll with it," he says. "After a while, who cares?" ∎

STEVE MCNAIR He had surgery for a ruptured disc in 1999 and missed only five games; said a teammate, "We don't worry about Steve unless he's in a cast."

BERNIE KOSAR Was tough enough that he played without a mouthguard so he could audible and once played three quarters against Miami on a broken ankle.

Kilmer makes up in gung-ho leadership for his aesthetic failings as a passer. A Kilmer pass, in its wobbling flight, conjures up memories of Bobby Layne and Joe Kapp, while Billy's fiery inducements to his teammates are reminiscent of the take-charge attitudes of, right, Joe Kapp and Bobby Layne.

—TEX MAULE, SI, *January 8, 1973*

BILLY KILMER He was mostly a halfback for the 49ers until he shattered his leg in a car accident; he then played 12 years at QB with the Saints and Redskins.

Photograph by Long Photography Inc.

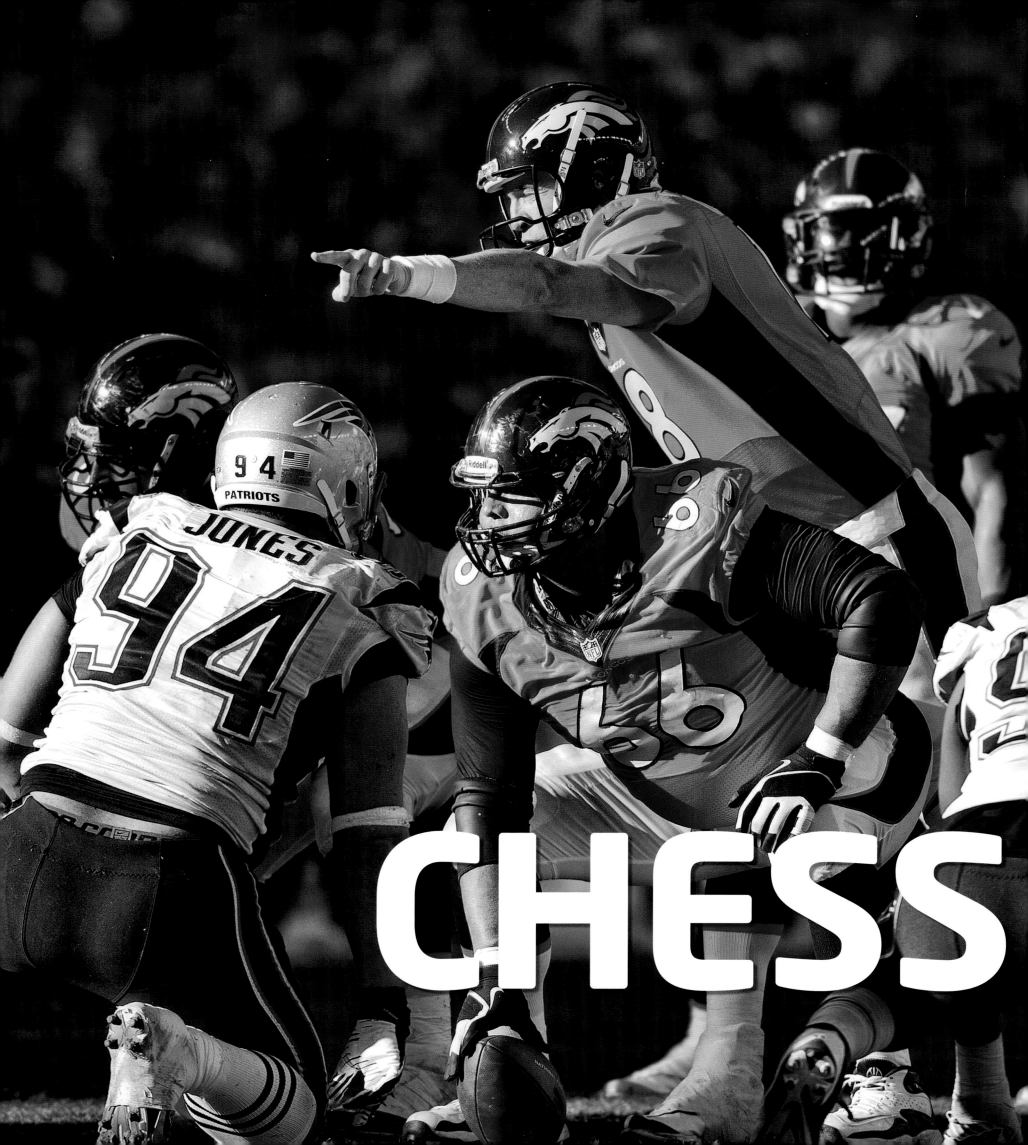

CHESS

THEY MAY NOT have the most powerful arms or the quickest feet, some are even labeled with the epithet "game manager," but that has never stopped them from having an outsized influence on the sport. They are part of a select circle of pros who have dominated the NFL with their brains, accuracy and total command of the offense

PEYTON MANNING At age 37 and two years after major neck surgery, he had a historic 2013, setting NFL records for passing yards (5,477) and TDs (55).

MASTERS

Photograph by David E. Klutho

The Thinking Man's Quarterbacks

BY CHRIS BALLARD

There is beauty IN THE DEEP BALL, ESPECIALLY WHEN LAUNCHED BY those who can really air it out. Such men are invariably described with military terminology, They possess "cannons" or "howitzers" where most mortals have only an arm. They throw "rockets" and "bombs." They are, inevitably, "gunslingers." And they are indeed a sight to behold. But they are useless without smarts and accuracy and poise, the three most valuable traits for any quarterback.

So let us now praise men of mostly modest arms, those QBs who may not be able to puncture a receiver's chest at 40 yards but will get you 10 yards when you absolutely need it and, more important, win you the game in the process. These are the Chess Masters, those ball-through-a-tire-swing deadeyes who possess the gift of touch, but more important than that, a preternatural grasp of both their team's capabilities and their opponent's. Cerebral players like Peyton Manning, relying on fluttering half-armed passes at age 37; Joe Montana, lofting the ball into the corner of the end zone to Dwight Clark; Tom Brady, completing a surreal 26 out of 28 passes in a playoff game; Bob Griese, a.k.a. "The Thinking Man's Quarterback," calling every play for the entirety of his career; and Ken Anderson, a man with a law degree who played the game with a rare precision, dinking and dunking his way to a bevy of NFL records for completion percentage.

At first blush they are not intimidating figures, and few had an easy road to the NFL. Bart Starr was drafted in the 17th round of the 1956 draft. Johnny Unitas was released by the team that drafted him, the Steelers—amazingly, head coach Walt Kiesling believed him not smart enough to quarterback an NFL team. Unitas worked construction outside of Pittsburgh to support his family, playing QB on a local semipro team for as little as $6 a game on the weekends before making

the Colts in a tryout. Len Dawson completed all of 21 passes in his first five NFL seasons and was released by the Browns before catching on with the Dallas Texans, who would go on to become the Kansas City Chiefs. During scouting workouts, Montana graded out as a 6 on a 1-to-9 scale for arm strength—and 6½ overall—before the 49ers took a chance on him with the 82nd overall pick. Tom Brady? He bears the dubious distinction of running the slowest QB time in NFL combine history in the 40-yard dash, at 5.28 seconds (for comparison, the not-exactly-fleet-footed Aaron Rodgers clocked 4.71). The result: 198 players were selected before Brady in the 2000 draft. Even Drew Brees, a college star who left Purdue as the Big 10's alltime leader in passing yards and TDs, slipped to the second round of the 2001 draft based on his six-foot stature and perceived lack of arm strength.

Each of these men made some coach, or general manager, look like a genius. (Brady is considered by some the best draft choice in NFL history.) Some, like Manning, succeed through obsessive preparation and an uncanny talent for reading defenses at the line of scrimmage. Others, like Brady and Montana, possessed an ability to maintain their poise under even the most intense pressure. Starr, born into a military family, understood the value of discipline and, above all, teamwork, making him the perfect complement to coach Vince Lombardi. Len

Dawson found his coaching muse in Hank Stram, who played to Dawson's strengths with his "moving pocket" offense. Likewise, Boomer Esiason brilliantly orchestrated Sam Wyche's then-innovative no-huddle offense. And both Anderson and Montana played in the earliest editions of Bill Walsh's West Coast offense, throwing darts on screen passes to running backs and leading receivers perfectly on slant patterns. When the two squared off in 1982, it was a showdown between perhaps the two most accurate passers in NFL history. Sure, Montana came out on top, but few remember that Anderson completed 25 of 34 passes in the game, setting Super Bowl records at the time for both completions and completion percentage.

What truly unites these men, though, is the most important marker in the game: victories. Forget passing yards and other fantasy football stats. These QBs won, in whatever fashion was required. Starr won five NFL championships, including three titles in a row, a feat unmatched before or since. Griese was the starting quarterback for the Dolphins during the 1970s when the franchise had the highest winning percentage in all of pro sports. Montana retired with a remarkable 133–54 record as a starter. Brady won a Super Bowl when he was but 24. Not only that, he was the quintessential game manager that day, despite his youth: 145 yards and one touchdown in defeating a Rams team favored by 14 points. What's more, Brady did so by leading the team on an epic drive with 1:21

remaining and no timeouts as, on the TV, John Madden recommended that the Patriots run out the clock and take their chances in overtime. As for Brees, when he finally reached the Super Bowl, he beat the Colts by completing 32 passes, a total matched only by Brady (in 2004) and bettered only by Peyton Manning (in 2014).

To see two Chess Masters square off is to see the game at its cerebral best. It has happened surprisingly often. Montana defeated Anderson in the 1982 Super Bowl, then, seven years later, did the same to Boomer Esiason, famously driving 92 yards in the game's waning moments and hitting John Taylor in the end zone with 34 seconds left. Brees not only beat Manning in his only Super Bowl win, but two months earlier he beat Brady by throwing five touchdown passes, the only time that's ever been done against a Bill Belichick team. And of course, Brady and Manning have combined to produce the rivalry of a generation, playing 15 times during their careers. (Manning is 5–10, but he's 2–1 in AFC title games.)

These men are, if you will, the craft beers of the gridiron, appealing to those of discerning taste. Underestimated, underappreciated at first, they changed the game and, collectively, collected an awful lot of jewelry. Their legacy is in their approach to the game. As Bart Starr's high school coach, Bill Moseley, once put it, "He was not a big bull of a guy, but he'd use every ounce of ability he had to polish his game the way it was best to win." ∎

Griese (12), with coach Don Shula and backup George Mira, had an accountant's mien and a killer instinct. | *Photograph by Rod Hanna/USA TODAY Sports*

"We may never know how great Bob Griese is because he plays behind the greatest offensive line ever," says Vikings quarterback Fran Tarkenton, "and he only has to throw 10 passes a game."

—DAN JENKINS, SI, *November 10, 1975*

BOB GRIESE He didn't dazzle with his statistics—for instance, he never led the league in passing yards—but he used his weapons well enough to go to eight Pro Bowls.

JOHNNY UNITAS His two-minute drill in the 1958 NFL title game became ever after the model for the take-charge, in-command quarterback.

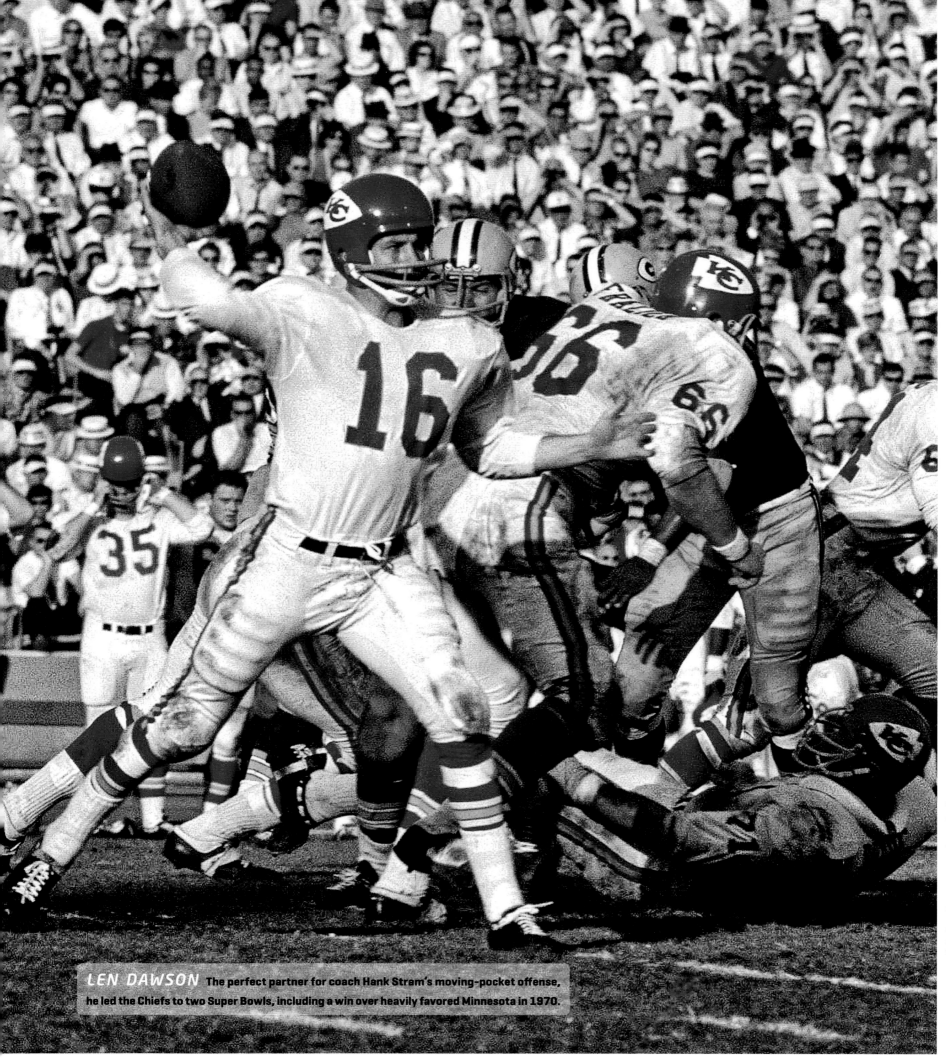

LEN DAWSON The perfect partner for coach Hank Stram's moving-pocket offense, he led the Chiefs to two Super Bowls, including a win over heavily favored Minnesota in 1970.

KEN ANDERSON He spent five seasons pioneering the West Coast offense with Bill Walsh as his QB coach and later won league MVP honors, in 1981.

NO ORDINARY JOE

COUPLED WITH THE PERFECT COACH AND THE IDEAL SYSTEM FOR HIS TALENTS, THE 49ERS' JOE MONTANA WENT FROM A THIRD-ROUND DRAFT PICK WITH QUESTION MARKS TO THE GAME'S ULTIMATE WINNER

Excerpted from SPORTS ILLUSTRATED, *August 13, 1990* | BY PAUL ZIMMERMAN

ERE'S THE THING ABOUT SCOUTING college football players for the NFL draft. It's based on fear. Scouts hedge their bets. Their evaluations all read, "Yes . . . , but . . . ." *Yes*, he can move the team down the field, *but* he doesn't have an NFL arm. If the player makes it, the scout will say, "Well, I told you he had potential," or if he's a bust, the scout will shake his head and say, "See, the arm didn't hold up, just like I said."

What terrorizes the scouts is the fear of being wrong, the big error, the No. 1 pick that was a total bust. And on draft day 1979, a lot of scouts were wrong about Joe Montana.

Eighty-one choices were made before the 49ers took him near the end of the third round. Thinking back, what were the negatives on Montana coming out of college? Strength of arm? Sure, he couldn't knock down buildings. So what? The Hall of Fame is filled with quarterbacks who didn't have a cannon. But there was something else, an undercurrent. He had trouble with his coach at Notre Dame. Uh-oh, look out.

"Trouble, what trouble?" Montana says. "I mean, I was unhappy that I didn't start when I thought I should have, and I was pretty upset when I opened my junior year as third string, but I never openly challenged Dan Devine or missed practices or stuff like that."

If the scouts had talked to some of the Notre Dame players about Montana, they might have gotten a different picture. There was a belief, almost mystical, among Montana's teammates that as long as Joe was on the field, things would turn out right, no matter what the score was. Didn't he bring them back from 20 points down in the fourth quarter at Air Force, and from 22 down against Houston with 7:37 to play in the Cotton Bowl? Cool, unshakable, treats a bowl game the same as a practice. "The guys on the team knew who wouldn't overheat," was the way teammate Dave Waymer put it.

Look at the little decisions that might have changed the course of history. "What if a Tampa Bay or a New Orleans would have taken him?" says Chuck Abramski, who was Montana's coach at Ringgold High in Monongahela, Pa. "What if, instead of having Bill Walsh to work with all those years in San Francisco, he had been in a system where he had to drop back seven steps and throw 50 yards downfield?"

Montana has reflected on that many times himself. "There's no coach I could have played for who would have been better for my career," he says. "Absolutely none."

Walsh had developed quarterbacks Ken Anderson at Cincinnati and Dan Fouts at San Diego, and he says of Montana, "When we looked at films of him in college, I said I also wanted to see his worst game. At his worst he played desperate. He'd throw late and beyond the receiver;

never early, always late. It's as if he was waiting until the last moment to make something happen. At his best, and that's true today, when he was in sync, he had an intuitive, instinctive nature rarely equaled by any athlete in any sport. Magic Johnson has it. Even watching Joe warm up, there was something hypnotic about him. That look when he was dropping back; he was poetic in his movements, almost sensuous, everything so fluid, so much under control."

By 1980 the 49ers offense was coming into focus. The running game was nowhere; it wouldn't get healthy until Wendell Tyler arrived in '83. The short, controlled pass became much of the running game. Dwight Clark, who began to emerge as a serious midrange threat, had his own thing going with Montana. "Joe once said in an interview, 'I can look all around the field; I can look away and still come back and find Dwight, that big, slow, loping receiver,'" Clark says. "He could see me moving across the field. I didn't run out of his sight line. Joe's got a knack of being able to figure out your body English, of knowing by your position on the defensive guy what you're going to do at the end of your route. He had that with me, and he has that now with Jerry Rice."

When Walsh talks about offense, he eventually mentions the "quick, slashing strokes" of attack. He'll use analogies with tennis and boxing, even warfare, which was why he was so taken with Montana's nimble feet. A quick, slashing attack needs a quick-footed quarterback. The statuesque quarterback who can throw the ball 60 yards downfield has never been Walsh's type. And when he got Montana, Walsh introduced the x-factor, which was the great escape talent of his quarterback.

"A lot of our offense was play-action," Walsh says, "and I learned through my experience that on a play-pass you have to expect an unblocked man just when you're trying to throw the ball. Your linemen have blocked aggressively. You can't expect them to hold their guys. Joe had to understand that. You're going to fool somebody downfield, but also you're going to have someone unblocked bearing right down on you. Here he comes. If you can throw and take the hit—TD. If you can avoid him, so much the better. We were on the cutting edge of Joe's ability. He was gifted at avoiding and throwing.

"We practiced the scrambling, off-balance throw. It wasn't accidental when he did it. I'd tell him, 'Timed pattern to the first receiver. If he's covered, move and look for the second. Then scramble and throw off-balance, and jerk it to the third. By the time you're reading the third receiver, someone's got hold of you.' And that's what we'd practice."

It all came into focus in the '81 postseason, in one momentous play, the last-minute touchdown pass to Clark that buried Dallas in the NFC championship. The play will always be known as the Catch—Montana scrambling to his right, with three Cowboys clutching at him; the off-balance throw; and finally Clark, on a breakoff route, ducking inside, then cutting back—just the way he and Joe had practiced it so many times. ∎

Walsh and Montana plotted strategy in a 1985 playoff win over the Bears. | *Photograph by Michael Zagaris*

TOM BRADY Questions about his arm strength and speed made him a sixth-round pick in 2000, but he's won more postseason games (18) than any QB ever.

Photographs by David Bergman [left] and V.J. Lovero

Boomer had such presence on the field, such command and camaraderie in his voice, you felt as easy in the huddle as you did in his house. Hell, the Bengals decided, who even needs a huddle? Let Boomer organize everything—last second, seat of his pants, hut, hut, hut.

—GARY SMITH, SI, *October 4, 1993*

BOOMER ESIASON As the play-caller of coach Sam Wyche's no-huddle offense, he was the NFL MVP in 1988 and led the Bengals to one of the team's two Super Bowls, in '89.

SID LUCKMAN

IT WAS A pretty simple idea in 1939 that forever changed the NFL. Put a man in motion. Until then, offensive backs were bunched behind the line, and so were their counterparts on defense, and when the ball was snapped, smashmouth football ensued. But George Halas, the owner and coach of the Chicago Bears, put his backs in a T formation, sent one of them on the move, and let Sid Luckman lead a revolution.

"The whole idea was to spread the field and give the defense more area to cover," Luckman told SI in 1998. That is the whole basis of the modern game that's still being played today, and it made Luckman *(second from left)* the progenitor of today's Chess Master QBs. He would come to camp a month early to study the Bears' voluminous playbook, and he'd watch movies of the previous season's games with Halas *(third from left)* to look for areas of improvement. He was the Peyton Manning of the '40s, only more successful, winning four NFL championships in his 12-year career.

He joined the Bears as a first-round pick out of Columbia in 1939, handpicked by Halas for his new offense. "I'd been a single-wing halfback [in college]," Luckman said. "You're set deep, the ball comes to you, and you either pass, run or spin. When I came to the Bears we worked for hours on my spinning, on hiding the ball."

By the end of his second season, his mastery of the position was obvious. He led the Bears to an 8–3 record and a spot in the NFL title game against Washington, which had quarterback Sammy Baugh and home-field advantage. The shocking final score was 73–0, Bears—still the most lopsided win in NFL history. And the rush was on for other teams to adopt the T.

If anything, Luckman only got better after that. He led the Bears to the title again in '41, and another in '43, when he was the NFL MVP and had perhaps the greatest quarterbacking season ever. Better than 1 in 4 of his 110 pass completions went for a touchdown as he threw for a record 28 TDs. (To put that in perspective, Manning's record 55 TDS in 2013 came on 450 completions, a rate of 1 in 8.)

After the season, Luckman joined the Merchant Marines, though he continued to play on Sundays; Halas had enlisted in the Navy the year before. But when the war ended they reunited for one more title in 1946. Luckman would call it quits in '50, and it was Papa Bear who paid perhaps the greatest tribute to the savviness of his old quarterback when he said, "He never called the wrong play in his life."　　　—G.K

Photograph by Bettmann/Corbis

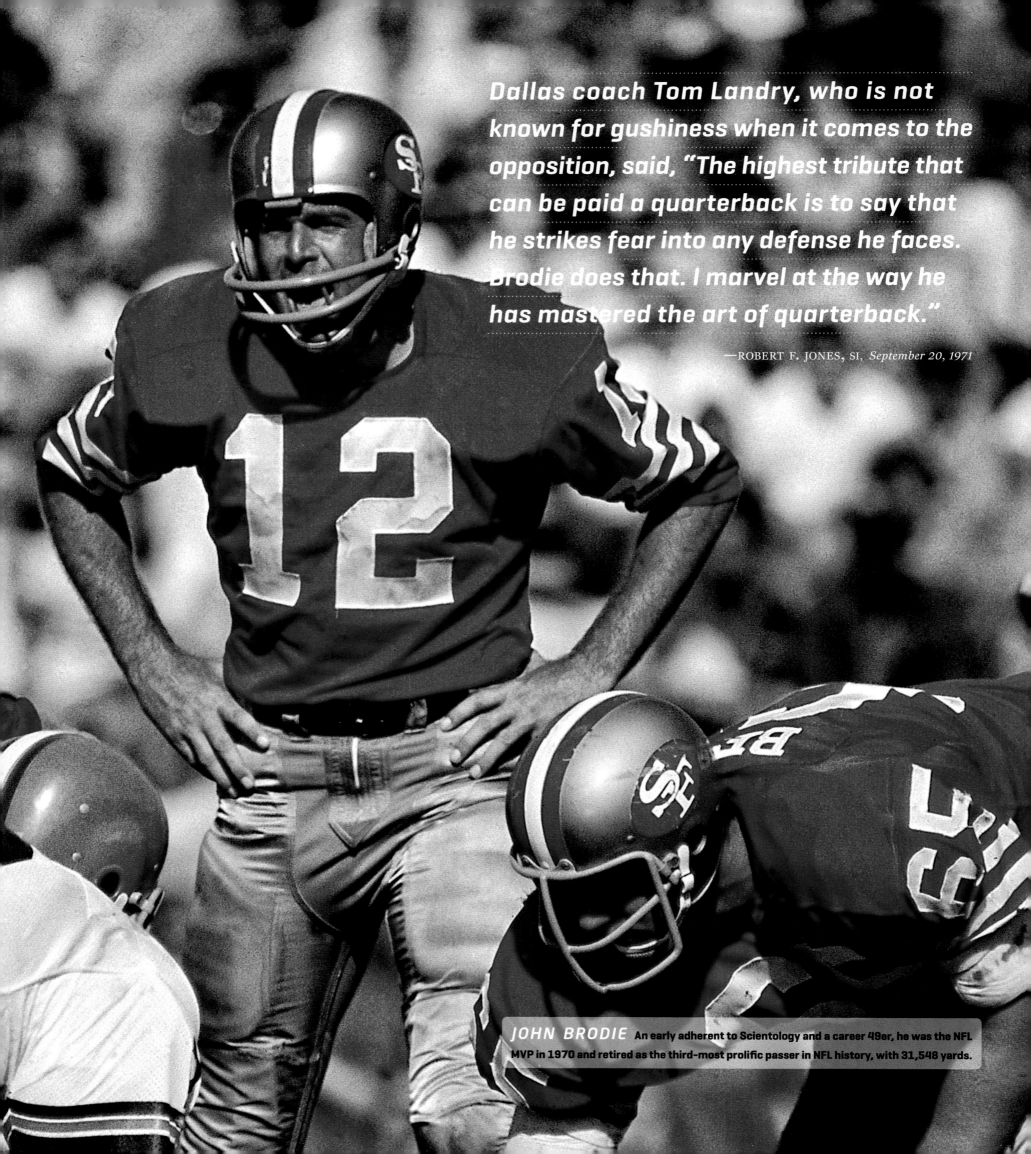

Dallas coach Tom Landry, who is not known for gushiness when it comes to the opposition, said, "The highest tribute that can be paid a quarterback is to say that he strikes fear into any defense he faces. Brodie does that. I marvel at the way he has mastered the art of quarterback."

—ROBERT F. JONES, SI, *September 20, 1971*

JOHN BRODIE An early adherent to Scientology and a career 49er, he was the NFL MVP in 1970 and retired as the third-most prolific passer in NFL history, with 31,548 yards.

BART STARR His last name was a perfect fit for his stellar career, which began as a 17th-round draft pick and ended with five NFL titles (and two Super Bowl wins).

MANNING AT HIS BEST

A NEW COACH, NEW TARGETS AND NO RUNNING GAME? NO PROBLEM. HERE'S HOW PEYTON MANNING, THE LEAGUE'S HARDEST-WORKING, MOST CEREBRAL QUARTERBACK, GOT IT DONE IN A SEASON OF CHANGE

Excerpted from SPORTS ILLUSTRATED, *November 16, 2009* | BY PETER KING

AYBE, BRIGHAM YOUNG RECEIVER AUSTIN Collie thought when he finagled an invitation to the prestigious Manning Passing Academy in 2008, this will be my breakthrough moment. Collie knew he could play in the NFL, but the world is full of 6-foot possession receivers who run 4.6-second 40-yard dashes. As a counselor at the Manning family's summer football camp in Louisiana, perhaps Collie would get to run routes for Peyton and Eli. Or he'd get pulled aside by one of the Mannings and be told, "Kid, you've got a future in the NFL."

Well, Collie never caught a ball from either Manning at the camp.

They threw to higher-profile college and pro receivers. He never had a one-on-one conversation with Peyton or Eli either. He did get to work as a counselor for some of the budding young wideouts. "Basically," Collie said last week at the Colts' facility in Indianapolis, "it was a weekend to myself. I never thought I'd see either of those guys again."

Austin Collie has seen Peyton Manning again, all right. After several clandestine Colts' scouting missions to Utah last fall to watch Collie (who led the nation in receiving yards) and a lengthy debriefing by a team psychologist, Indianapolis general manager Bill Polian chose Collie in the fourth round of the 2009 draft. In the past three months Collie and Manning, strangers at the Manning Passing Academy, have seen more of each other than they have of their wives. The football marriage is a big reason why the Colts head into their annual November showdown with the Patriots on Sunday a very surprising 8–0.

This is a story about the great season Manning is having, one in which he has been more accurate (a 70.6% completion rate) and more productive (318.1 yards per game) than in any of his previous 11 pro seasons. Which is saying something, considering that Manning has more passing yards and more touchdowns than any other quarterback in the NFL's 90-year history has had by age 33.

In September the only thing Manning seemed sure to lead the league in this year was obstacles. Wideout Marvin Harrison was allowed to leave after 11 seasons with Manning, and into his starting spot had stepped a 2008 sixth-round pick from tiny Mount Union College (Ohio), Pierre Garçon, the only player in the NFL with a cedilla in his name. Starting wideout Anthony Gonzalez went down with a knee injury in the first game, forcing Collie to play much more than planned. Rock-solid coach Tony Dungy had retired, ceding the job to an unknown, Jim Caldwell, whose only head-coaching experience was an eight-year stint at Wake Forest, during which the Demon Deacons were 37 games below .500.

Compounding the problems over the first half of the season has been a feeble running game—the Colts rank 29th in the league in rushing as they work in rookie Donald Brown—that has put Manning in constant passing situations. Defenses know he's going to throw, and yet they've been powerless to stop him. "If this year's not an indication of Peyton Manning's greatness," says Chiefs general manager Scott Pioli, "I don't know what ever would be."

MANNING, SIMPLY, HAS MADE INDIANAPOLIS SLUMP-PROOF. THE Colts have gone 112 games—seven full seasons—without losing three straight. It's not an accident that Indy is the winningest regular-season team this decade (109 victories, one more than New England). Anytime Manning steps behind center and starts gyrating and pointing, history tells us, good things are about to occur. "To understand why he hasn't struggled," Dungy says, "you have to understand the way his mind works. It drives him every day that the offense will be better, not just as good as it was. The new guys will fit in. He'll make them fit in."

Qadry Ismail learned as much in 2002, his lone year as a Colts wide receiver. On the charter to Jacksonville for the season opener, Ismail was settling in for a restful flight when Manning approached. "Hay's in the barn, game plan's done, we're all set," Ismail says. "But Peyton comes up with a serious look and his notebook, and he tells me we're going to use some different hand signals at the line. He's like, 'As opposed to giving you the fingers for that comeback route, I'm going to give you the fist' or 'If you see me do this, don't even worry about it because that's just trying to get the [defense] to think I'm going to change the play, but I'm not.' He's the ultimate micromanager. He controls everything."

Ismail shares what he calls a "CIA, burn-after-reading secret" out of the Indianapolis playbook from that Jaguars game. When Manning gave Ismail a shoveling motion or said the words "Crane! Crane!" Ismail would run a dig route—a curl or buttonhook in which the receiver goes downfield a certain distance, plants his foot suddenly and turns to face the quarterback. Having seen the signal a couple of times early in the game, Jacksonville corner Jason Craft then taunted Ismail. "I know what y'all are doing!" Craft hollered. "Every time he gives that [shoveling] signal, you run that little in route!"

Now, Ismail could have said, "Are you seriously challenging Peyton Manning?" Instead he told the cornerback he didn't know what he was talking about, then told Manning and offensive coordinator Tom Moore on the sideline, "He's bragging like he knows what we're doing. He's going to jump that route!" Manning filed the information and talked with Moore about using it later in the game. Sure enough, with the ball at the Jaguars' 12 in the third quarter, Manning told Ismail that "Crane!" would be a dummy call, and instead of the dig he should run a hitch-and-go (basically a dig, stop and sprint back upfield into the end zone).

"I made a living off double moves," says Ismail, "and that was the easiest one I ever ran. Peyton gave me the crane sign at the line. I pushed upfield five yards and stuck my foot in the ground as hard as I could. The DB made a beeline to that five-yard spot and looked for the ball, but I just ran into the end zone, all alone. What a simple TD."

Against Arizona this season, Garçon told Manning in the first half that he thought the cornerback covering him was cheating, trying to guess and jump the route. Late in the half Manning pump-faked to Garçon's side, drew the corner in and led Garçon perfectly for a 53-yard touchdown. "He always asks for information, and he puts it in his brain," Garçon says. "Sometimes he goes to it, sometimes he doesn't."

Says Ismail, "When I was there, he told me, 'Hey, I'm just a gym rat. This is what I'm about. I love the game.' He wants to squeeze out every ounce of talent he has and pour it into the art of quarterbacking, being the absolute best quarterback who has ever played."

IN OUR SYSTEM," POLIAN SAYS, "A RECEIVER HAS TO HAVE SPEED but doesn't need to be a burner. Has to have good hands. An instinctive feel to get open—very important. Size we'd like, but it's not critical. Work ethic, because he has to fit with Peyton's demands. Maturity."

And intelligence, which should go without saying because there are no simple routes in the Colts' system. Everything depends on what the receiver sees from coverage. Take a simple 12-yard out, a staple of every passing game in football. Against a Cover Two look, with a safety over the top of the receiver and the immediate cover man on the inside shoul-

der, the 12-yard out might be just what it says—12 yards, then a straight cut to the sideline. With a linebacker in coverage the 12-yard out might be a 12-yard corner route, diagonally away from the slower 'backer. A 12-yard out against tight man coverage might mean the receiver cuts and comes back at a 45-degree angle. "It's overwhelming to learn," says Brandon Stokley, a slot receiver for Indianapolis from 2003 to '06.

SI asked former Broncos coach Mike Shanahan, a longtime quarterback teacher, to evaluate some Indianapolis video and analyze how Manning has adjusted to his new receivers. He watched about 65 snaps, and one, against Tennessee on Oct. 11, he found particularly noteworthy. First down, Colts on the Titans' 39-yard line. Veteran Reggie Wayne wide left, Collie in the left slot, Garçon wide right. Corners over the top of Wayne and Garçon, linebacker Keith Bulluck shading toward Collie. At the snap Manning turned and faked a handoff to Joseph Addai, freezing Bulluck for a split second. By then Collie was three steps off the line.

"I don't care if Collie's a rookie," says Shanahan, eyes fixed on the video screen. "He's spent the whole off-season and training camp running this play. No doubt in my mind he's run that play a couple hundred times. Watch. Peyton knows from his presnap read he's probably going to get Bulluck on Collie. From playing Tennessee so many times he knows Bulluck peeks in the backfield. The linebacker's got to respect the run, and so the moment Bulluck peeks he's sucked in. It's over. Now he opens his hips to run with Collie, but it's too late. Now watch Collie. He knows he's not breaking to the post until he gets by Bulluck. Look at the ball. Beautiful. Such a catchable ball. Bulluck doesn't have a chance."

In fact, what the play shows is how, in the fifth game of his NFL career, Collie gets what it took Wayne, Gonzalez and tight end Dallas Clark a year or longer to feel comfortable with. Collie was supposed to cut to the post at about 18 yards, but as is the case on all the Colts' routes, it's more important that he cut when he knows his man is beaten. So on this route he broke to the post about 12 yards downfield. And because Bulluck was momentarily frozen, Manning knew he could throw just as Collie was jabbing his left foot into the ground to make his 45-degree cut. From a clean pocket, Manning let fly with a perfect spiral traveling 29 yards in the air, right over Bulluck's head and into Collie's hands. Collie broke a tackle at the 12, another at the four, and dived over the goal line. Touchdown.

"No hesitation by Peyton," Shanahan says. "Here's why: Collie's got a natural feel out there. What are we seeing in this entire game? Peyton might have some new guys out there with him. But if possible he might be more confident than I've ever seen him. On no throw has he hesitated. That tells me he's confident these new guys know what they're doing."

The numbers tell a good story about the young receivers' adjustment. In the Tennessee game 16 of Manning's 44 throws went to his on-the-job-training guys: Collie, Garçon and Brown. Two of his three touchdown passes that night were to the newbie Collie. Particularly, the numbers say good things about Collie's adjustment. In the rookie seasons of Wayne, Clark and Gonzalez, Manning averaged 47 pass attempts to each of them, completing an average of 31. Over the first half of 2009 Manning has thrown 46 passes to Collie and completed 32. Wayne, Clark and Gonzalez combined for four touchdowns as rookies. Collie has four in eight games.

"I've heard players say they have to adjust to the speed of the pro game," Collie says. "The difference between here and college is not the speed. It's the knowledge you have to have, what you need to know about how your route is going to change and how Peyton expects you to change. When we played San Francisco [an 18–14 win in Week 8], I had a seam route, and it looked like Peyton made the mistake and overthrew me, but in reality it was man coverage and I was supposed to do something just to get separation. I did it too late, and it was my fault. When I got back [to the huddle], he said to me, 'You gotta make up your mind. You gotta do one thing or the other.'"

"It takes years to get true timing down," Manning says. In 2009 the Colts didn't have years. They had months. That's what makes this season perhaps the best yet for this alltime great. ∎

DREW BREES He broke his own single-season NFL accuracy record in 2011, with a 71.2% mark, and of the eight 5,000-yard passing seasons in NFL history, he's had four.

In 2009, his Super Bowl season, Brees completed 70.6% of his throws, the most accurate season ever by an NFL quarterback. "He's always had unbelievable instincts, the whole skill set," says his former quarterbacks coach Brian Schottenheimer. "Now, with experience and age, he's just mastered his craft."

—TIM LAYDEN, SI, *December 6, 2010*

Photograph by Mike Ehrmann/Getty Images

THERE IS ONE unspoken objective in the game plan of every team in the NFL: Get to the opposing quarterback and, if possible, knock him out of the game. No bounties were ever really needed for that. That's why the hits are often big and the injuries frequent at the one position that matters the most in determining defeat or victory

JAY SCHROEDER The Raiders' QB probably thought a face mask penalty was not a great enough punishment for what the Bills did to him in a '91 game.

OCCUPATIONAL

HAZARDS

And the Hits Just Keep on Coming

BY GREG A. BEDARD

The myth-making machinery OF OUR CULTURE TENDS TO emphasize the positive, and that's evident when it comes to the quarterback position. The quarterback gets the glory and the glamour and in the end he gets the girl, but NFL defenses are less interested in all that than they are in grinding him into the ground. They know that there's no better antidote to a great offense than unleashing holy hell upon the quarterback. "The way to kill the snake is

to take off his head," says Giants' defensive end Justin Tuck.

He should know. He had a big hand in the beheading of Tom Brady in the 2008 Super Bowl, ending the hopes of the Patriots for an unbeaten season. The Giants continually attacked the Pats' QB and sacked him five times, including once for a fumble that ended a late-first-half drive in New York's 17–14 victory. "That was pretty much the reason why we were in the game, because we kept him off rhythm," Tuck says of Brady, whom the Giants beat in Super Bowls XLII and XLVI. "Obviously he is the main reason why [they] are successful. The way to kill an offense as potent as that one is making sure you take care of Brady."

The sack is the primary way to do that. Sacks end drives, title hopes and, sometimes, careers.

On November 18, 1985, at Washington's RFK Stadium and in front of a national *Monday Night Football* television audience, Washington quarterback Joe Theismann took a flea flicker from running back John Riggins, eluded linebacker Harry Carson and then was sacked by Lawrence Taylor. A replay showed Theismann's lower right leg buckling in half under the weight of Taylor and Gary Reasons, an injury so gruesome it had even Taylor visibly upset. It was a compound fracture of Theismann's fibula, and those watching at home still can tell him where they were at the time of the injury. Theismann

never played again. And the lesson of what can happen to an overmatched, exposed quarterback was ingrained on every signal-caller that has played the position since.

Beyond the physical pounding, sacks often have a profound psychological impact as well. David Carr was viewed as a can't-miss kid after being the first overall pick of the expansion Houston Texans in 2002. But after being sacked 249 times in five seasons, including an NFL-record 76 as a rookie, Carr was never the same. When he joined the Giants in 2008, Carr admitted he had to be completely retrained as a quarterback because of the mental and spiritual damage the sacks had done. By that time it was too late. He didn't start a game his final five seasons. Carr's career sack percentage of 10.5% is 10th-most alltime.

That might be the most telling statistic when it comes to the efficacy of the sack. Some of the game's greatest QBs were sacked a lot, none more than Brett Favre, who was taken down 525 times in his 20-year career. That's a measure of longevity, not competence. (Favre's sack percentage was a stellar 4.91.) But look at Carr and the nine players with sack percentages worse than his—including Rob Johnson, the alltime worst at 14.8%. None of them had a winning record as a starter. A couple, like Bobby Douglass of the Bears and Greg Landry of the Lions, were sacked a lot because they ran with the ball often, but the rest are a forgettable list that includes Hugh Millen, Bob Berry and Joe Pisarcik. Clearly, teams must protect their quarterback if they expect to win.

Archie Manning was one of the most exciting college players ever at Ole Miss. He was drafted second overall by the dreadful Saints in 1971, but his professional career never matched his collegiate exploits because of the physical beating Manning took behind a porous offensive line. He was sacked on 9.8% of his snaps, 17th-most alltime.

"I think the toll of sacks was more physical [than psychological]," says Ron Jaworski, who was dropped 363 times in his 15-year career, good for 17th on the alltime sacked list. "You don't want to get hit. With sacks you're unprotected. The quarterback can't roll up in the fetal position, can't lower his shoulder. You have to hang in there and expose your body to a defender that wants to bend your face mask. You just have to take the shot."

Sacks are impactful, but so are their close cousin: pressure. Sacks are the goal, but short of that, defenses want to at least let the quarterback know that they are close. They want to move a quarterback off his preferred throwing spot, to disrupt the timing and rhythm of the passing game.

"The sack is the glory stat, but there's a lot of other things," says Steve Spagnuolo, who orchestrated the upset of the Patriots in Super Bowl XLII as defensive coordinator of the Giants. "We look at affecting the quarterback. If we make him move his feet, or force a bad throw, or flush him out of the pocket, force him into a mistake, then we have affected the quarterback. And I didn't say sack."

The Broncos' Peyton Manning, who had one of the greatest seasons ever for a quarterback in 2013, wasn't sacked by the Seahawks in Super Bowl XLVIII until the score was 43–8 with 3:52 remaining in the fourth quarter. But he was under duress the entire game. In the first half, he was hurried or hit by the Seahawks on nearly 60% of his drop-backs that weren't screen passes. Before the Super Bowl, Manning felt pressure on less than a quarter of his snaps.

"There were a number of plays, Peyton never got sacked—he never gets sacked a lot—but they made him move and forced him to get off his spot," says Jaworski. "All those things, yeah, they weren't sacks but they got the job done. Seattle's pass rush was the biggest factor in the game. Even when the sacks weren't there, it was the pressure on Peyton and forcing him to move and play erratic and fast. Every quarterback is susceptible when the bodies are flying around you." ∎

Lawrence Taylor ended Joe Theismann's career with one shot in 1985. | *Photograph by Nate Fine*

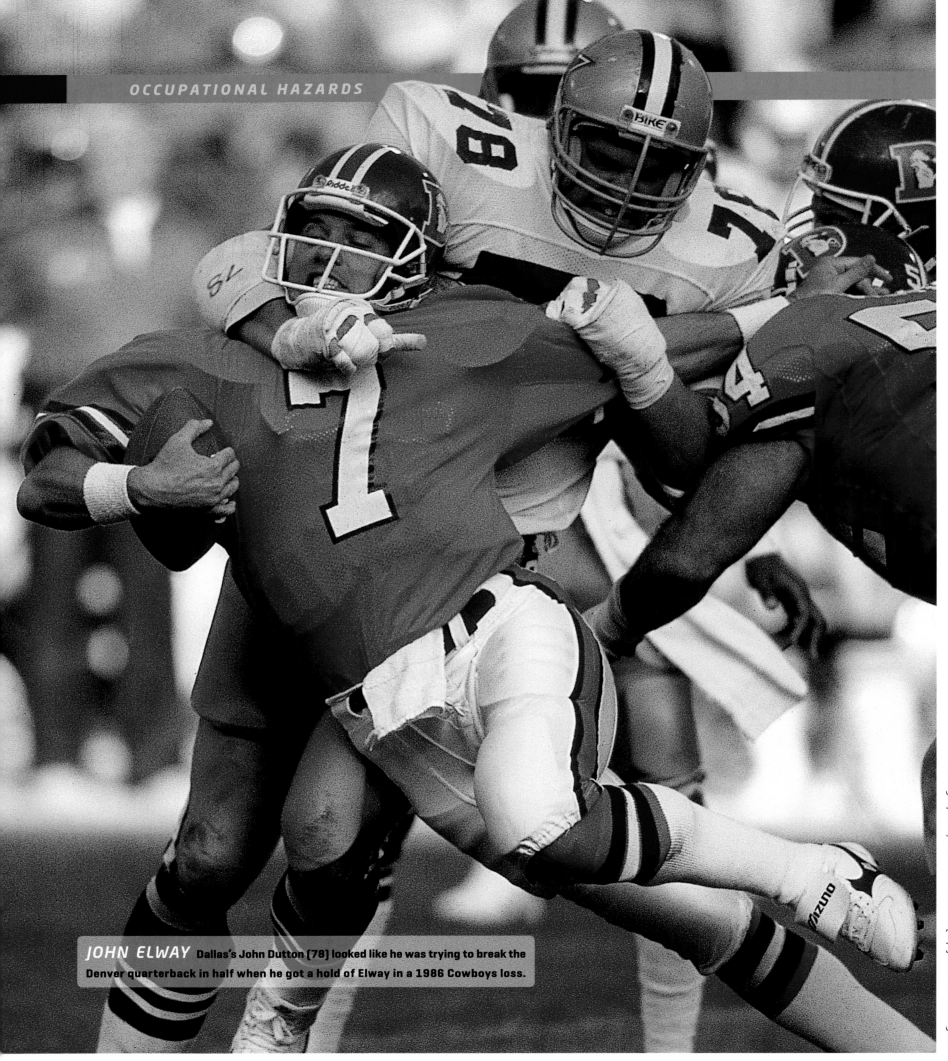

JOHN ELWAY Dallas's John Dutton (78) looked like he was trying to break the Denver quarterback in half when he got a hold of Elway in a 1986 Cowboys loss.

Photographs by Richard Mackson (left) and David Bergman

TOM BRADY The normally unruffled Pats' quarterback gave up the ball and a bit of his dignity as Calvin Pace sacked him in a 2011 Jets playoff victory.

"Do you realize that when you're lying on the ground with 600 pounds of pass rushers on top of you, it's kind of peaceful down there? It's a good time to be planning your next play (or your retirement)."

—FRAN TARKENTON, SI, *August 7, 1967*

FRAN TARKENTON There was nothing coy about what the Rams' Coy Bacon (79) did to Tarkenton (whose scrambling could annoy pass rushers) in a 1970 Rams win.

BOB GRIESE The rules have been changed significantly to protect the QB since pass rushers like Ben Davidson (83) of the Raiders laid this headlock on Griese in 1969.

GOODBYE TO ALL THAT

IN A FIRST-PERSON STORY, A VETERAN OF SIX NFL SEASONS SAID FAREWELL TO THE BEATINGS HE TOOK FROM OPPOSING PASS RUSHERS WITH A SIMPLE MESSAGE: YOU WON'T HAVE PAT HADEN TO SACK ANYMORE

Excerpted from SPORTS ILLUSTRATED, *September 1, 1982* | BY PAT HADEN *with* E.M. SWIFT

I F I SHOULD EVER GET THE URGE TO renounce my retirement and come back as quarterback for the Los Angeles Rams, or any other team, I'm going to remind myself of one play. It happened against the New Orleans Saints in 1980, in the third quarter of a game we were leading 38–14. Vince Ferragamo was doing most of our quarterbacking that year. He was the darling of Los Angeles, as I had once been, and he had already thrown five touchdown passes in the game. For some reason he came out for a couple of plays, and I came in. It was third-and-eight, so I called a pass. I dropped back and was looking around when one of New Orleans' linemen hit me from the blind side—never saw him—and the ball popped into the air. Don Reese, a defensive end for New Orleans, caught it in stride and took it 34 yards for a touchdown. I was lying on the ground, a big body on top of me, watching a 260-pound man run off with my one pass of the day. You can't imagine the frustration. Had the play not been ruled a fumble, it would have been my longest completion of the year. The boos started, and you've never heard so many, in such perfect unison, in your life.

Think of that, Pat.

Sacks and boos are two very good reasons that I will be working for a law firm in Los Angeles and doing TV commentary of college games for CBS this season. The sacks you can do something about. The boos go with the territory. I've tried to think of a position in another sport more difficult to play than quarterback, but nothing comes to mind. The simple act of throwing a ball to a receiver moving at full speed, say, 25 yards away—leading him perfectly—is difficult enough. Not many people can even do that well. Then add the other team. Start with blitzing linebackers and add a secondary with different coverages necessitating different pass routes, all of which have to be "read" in the first moments the quarterback has the ball. Add to that four guys who are faster than you, each 6' 6", 260 pounds, who will be in your face in 3.7 seconds, and you can begin to imagine the complexities of the position. That's why the quarterback is the focus of the game; why his job is more difficult than the others'; why he is compensated more and abused more.

I have heard fans boo Fran Tarkenton, Terry Bradshaw and the man I consider to be the best quarterback I've ever seen, Roger Staubach. In 1976, my rookie year, I heard Rams fans boo the hell out of James Harris and Ron Jaworski. I was the darling then, enjoying the honeymoon grace period that all new quarterbacks get. I thought: "That's not going to happen to me." It did. Many, many times.

I don't have a lot of patience with guys who complain that the new blocking rules have ruined the art of sacking the quarterback, because last season I didn't find myself getting hit any less or sacked any less than in previous years. If anything, I was hit more. Fred Dean of the San Francisco 49ers sacked me five times in one game. You could try to block Dean with a pickup truck and it wouldn't work. He's too good, too fast, and no rules committee is ever going to stop him.

You've probably heard of a "lookout" block. It's a standard joke in football, but it actually happened to me once. We were playing the Lions, and defensive end Dave Pureifory put such a strong move on Jackie Slater, one of our tackles, that Slater literally turned and yelled, "Look out!" It was too late. Pureifory's helmet was already in my face. Next thing I knew, I was sprawled out; my face mask was like a birdcage— it was broken and flapping up and down, and the birdies were going tweet-tweet. I was barely moving, there was dust all over the place, and Slater leaned over and said with great concern, "I *told* you to look out."

I've found that defensive linemen react to a sack in three basic ways. The first is to jump up and down like a lunatic, brandishing a fist in the air and slapping high fives with anyone in reach. The hot dog. The second, a particular favorite of mine, is to lie on top of the quarterback for as long as possible, until everyone else is up and you're the last guy off the bottom of the pile. The public address announcer then assumes you've made the sack, even though you may simply have been piling on. The third is to rise—not too slowly, not too quickly—then stand over your prey, the quarterback, like a lion, staring down at him. That not only gives the TV cameras a chance to focus on you, but it also lets the quarterback know that you're there and intend to be back in the near future.

No quarterback likes this sort of treatment, but we understand it. The sack is a defensive lineman's vengeance, his dance in the end zone, his toss of the ball into the stands.

Most of the great players who sacked me didn't indulge in histrionics; they let their ability speak for itself. Randy White, Mean Joe Greene (who was inappropriately nicknamed) and Alan Page simply rose after a tackle and returned to their positions. My teammate Merlin Olsen was like that, too. Bob Brazile would ask, "You O.K.?" And Lyle Alzado would often say, "Nice pass," if I had gotten rid of the football. They were the real professionals, in my opinion, and it was always appreciated.

Dean, who played with the Chargers before going to the 49ers last season, was always a thorn in my side. He was that third type, the lion who would give you the long stare. The Eighth Amendment guarantees that we will not receive any cruel or unusual punishment, but in a Rams-Chargers game in 1979, Dean violated my Eighth Amendment rights so flagrantly that I should have sued. We lost 40–16 and I had to be carried off the field twice. It was by far the worst beating I ever took, and I don't imagine too many quarterbacks in the history of football have ever had a heavier toll taken on their bodies than I did that day. I say that seriously.

The best defensive lineman I ever faced was Randy White of Dallas. In fact, all the Cowboys front four played like gods—Too Tall Jones, Harvey

Martin, John Dutton—and Dallas was the best team in the league at deflecting passes. It wasn't just a matter of me being a "small" (5' 11") quarterback, either. I watched films of the Cowboys, and every time a quarterback got set to throw, they'd put their hands up. It's amazing how many teams aren't coached to do that. I'd bet my house that the Cowboys lead the league every year in tipped passes.

White really beat me up in one preseason game, which, at that time of year, isn't supposed to happen to your starting quarterback. During the game one of our coaches must have said something to our guard who was responsible for White, because the guard came up to me and said, "I can't block him." Just like that, "I can't block him." You don't know how frightening that was. I looked at the guy and wanted to say, "What do you want me to do? Do you want to throw the ball and have me try to block him?"

My rookie year, I recall Olsen telling another of our defensive tackles, Mike Fanning, that a defensive lineman has to be part charging buffalo, part ballet dancer. That's as good a description as any. But when talking about sacks, you aren't just talking about defensive linemen. The nickel defenses have changed the game. On second-and-eight, the Rams might

send in five defensive backs and four defensive linemen, and they'd come from everywhere. Johnny Johnson, our strong safety, might lead the team in sacks one game. Or the Rams might dog a linebacker and blitz the free safety, leaving Jack Youngblood, an end, to cover Walter Payton. Youngblood cannot cover Payton, but the theory is that he won't have to do it very long.

The most difficult thing facing a quarterback these days is reading the different blitzes. If I spotted one, I could check off in the middle of the count and call something like "Blitz, 56, left!" which would change the play, the lineblocking, the routes. It was a way of saying, "Buckle your

chinstraps, here comes the cavalry." I don't believe the pocket as we know it is long for this world. Rams quarterbacks use the standard seven-step drop on most pass plays. The quarterback reads the strong safety's movements as he drops back, and that tells him what coverage to expect. He sets up nine or 10 yards behind the line of scrimmage and waits for the play to unfold. The offensive line retreats two steps to form a pocket and tries to hold its ground. If everybody does his job, the play works. If not, maybe you've got a sack and an injured quarterback or an incompletion or an interception, or some combination thereof. Pittsburgh has used the same seven-step-drop system with Terry Bradshaw with great success.

San Francisco and San Diego, on the other hand, seem to prefer a three- or five-step drop. They essentially don't care what coverage the defense is in because by flooding three or four guys into a zone, they figure somebody's going to be open. The quarterback goes One-Two-Three Boom!—it's off. The offensive linemen don't retreat, they set up at the line of scrimmage and go right for the legs of the would-be sackers. I believe that the shorter drop will be used more and more in the future. It does a number of things, including something nobody ever talks about: It enables your quarterback to take less of a beating. Joe Montana didn't miss a game last year, and Dan Fouts hasn't missed one in the past three. If you want to know how to cut down not only on sacks but also on quarterback hits, the shorter drop is the answer.

One year, Georgia Frontiere, the Rams' owner, had an interesting idea how we would cut down on sacks, which unfortunately I never pursued. She suggested I take karate, so that as I stood in the pocket with my right arm cocked, I could defend myself with my left arm. Here comes Mean Joe . . . Haiku! Katcho! Sa! . . . He's down! Haden fires the bomb! Touchdown!

Over the years the one thing I could never escape was this question: "What's it like being a small quarterback and having all those big guys coming after you?" Well, it was my belief that I had a lot of big guys in front of me keeping the other team's big guys away. The quarterback's size is a nonissue. Bob Griese played pretty well, and he was only 6' 1". Tarkenton had a little success, and he was only 6 feet. If you want a big quarterback, try Bobby Douglass—he was the biggest quarterback you'll ever see. There are good and bad of both sizes.

I think if I'd been taller, I could have carried more weight and perhaps avoided some injuries, but I'm not convinced of that. My injuries were all freakish. In the playoffs after the 1978 season I broke my thumb against Randy White's helmet while following through on a pass. I caught the little finger on my right hand in a seam of the AstroTurf in Seattle and broke it in '79. And in the opening game of '80 I broke my right hand by catching it in one of my lineman's shoulder pads on a follow-through.

I'll never forget what happened after that. I walked off the field and the doctor bandaged my hand, and a couple of minutes later, when the news flashed on the scoreboard, PAT HADEN HAS BROKEN HIS HAND, 65,000 people, a majority of them anyway, cheered. That really blew me away. I felt like a gladiator in the Colosseum, with the fans up there giving the thumbs-down gesture.

But for all the frustrations, the beatings and the booings I endured, I'd still be in football if I could be guaranteed a certain feeling just three times a game. Twice even. It's when you get into a zone or a groove—whatever nomenclature you want to use—in which everything appears to be moving in slow motion. I've heard golfers describe a similar feeling; they say they can visualize a shot going into the hole before it does. On those occasions, the 3½ seconds between the snap from center and the time you release the ball seem like a month. It's the most exhilarating feeling you could ever imagine: very pure, simple. As you stand in the pocket, even if guys are huffing and puffing and grunting and groaning and hitting and growling all around, you don't hear a thing. Complete silence. It doesn't happen every game, but when it does it's so satisfying. But it's frustrating, too, because sometimes you find yourself waiting for it to happen, and it doesn't.

I won't be waiting anymore, but I'm going to miss that blessed month in the pocket. ∎

RYAN FITZPATRICK The Bills quarterback coughed up the football (and maybe a little blood) as Vince Wilfork took him down in a 2012 Patriots win.

STEVE YOUNG He may have been one of the most elusive quarterbacks to play the game, but Young couldn't escape the clutches of the Bucs' Warren Sapp forever.

Photograph by CJ Gunther/EPA (left) and Damien Strohmeyer

GREG LANDRY A safety seems like a terrible misnomer for what happened to the Lions quarterback when he was crushed in his own end zone by Dallas's Jethro Pugh (75).

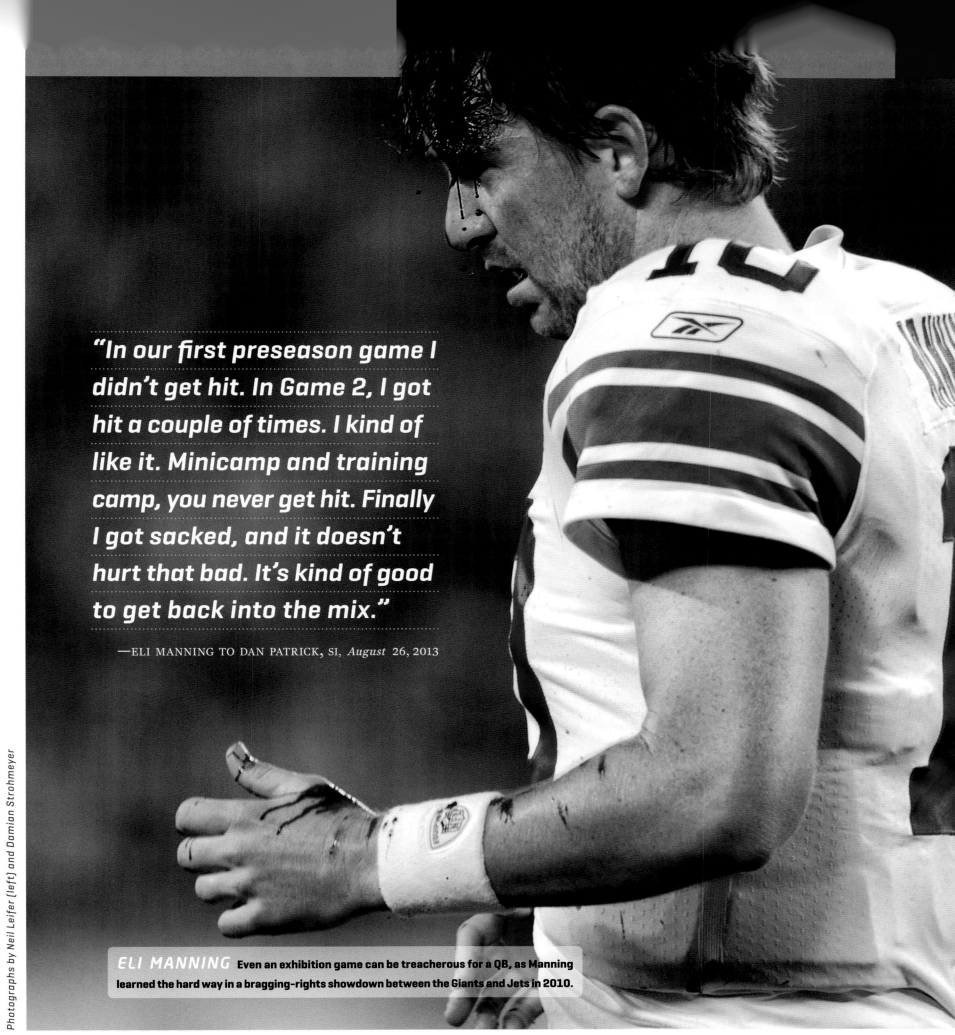

Photographs by Neil Leifer [left] and Damian Strohmeyer

"In our first preseason game I didn't get hit. In Game 2, I got hit a couple of times. I kind of like it. Minicamp and training camp, you never get hit. Finally I got sacked, and it doesn't hurt that bad. It's kind of good to get back into the mix."

—ELI MANNING TO DAN PATRICK, SI, *August* 26, 2013

ELI MANNING Even an exhibition game can be treacherous for a QB, as Manning learned the hard way in a bragging-rights showdown between the Giants and Jets in 2010.

DOUG WILLIAMS A pair of Chargers pass rushers put a jolt into the Bucs' QB, who would find better pass protection and greater success in his next job, in Washington.

BART STARR Quarterbacks occasionally have to play D, and the Packers star was knocked out of a 1965 playoff win over the Colts on the first play, trying to make a tackle after a fumble.

SAMMY BAUGH

THERE AREN'T MANY aspects of the quarterback position that the Redskins' Sammy Baugh did not revolutionize. He was the first great thrower at what was then called single-wing halfback, having perfected the forward pass as a two-time All-America at TCU before leading the NFL in pass attempts, completions and yardage as a rookie in 1937. He made the transition to T formation quarterback in the early '40s and became the paradigm of QB cool in the '41 off-season, starring in a serial for Republic Pictures called *King of the Texas Rangers*. And along with coach Ray Flaherty, he invented the play that quarterbacks have used ever since to perform jujitsu on overzealous pass rushers: the screen pass.

The QB's lot was much tougher in Baugh's day. He had no face mask to protect his head and he was fair game to be hit after he released the ball, as long as the play continued. Still, Baugh *(number 33, far right)* led Washington to the NFL title game as a rookie, facing the heavily favored Chicago Bears in frigid conditions on their home turf at Wrigley Field.

Knowing that his passing was the key to Washington's attack, the Monsters of the Midway came with everything they had at the quarterback. "They were breaking their necks trying to rack up Baugh," Flaherty later recalled. "That's what made the screen pass go. [The pass] had been nullified downfield, but we put it in behind the line of scrimmage and the Bears didn't know how to stop it."

With Chicago's defense suddenly finding itself off balance, Slingin' Sammy connected on scoring passes of 55, 78 and 35 yards in Washington's 28–21 upset. For the day he completed 18 of 33 passes for an astonishing 335 yards. (Consider that he led the league that year averaging 102.5 per game.)

Baugh would go on to lead the league in passing yards per game five more times, an NFL record only Dan Fouts of the Chargers has matched. Baugh's star value helped to bring about a change in the rules in 1938 to stop defenders from roughing the passer. In '43 he achieved a unique triple crown that will never be equaled. He led the NFL in passing completions (133), punting (with an average of 45.9 yards) and interceptions as a defensive back (an extraordinary 11 in just 10 games). It's no wonder then that when the Pro Football Hall of Fame was opened in '63 and the inaugural class of 17 was elected, it was Sammy Baugh who was installed as the Hall's first pure quarterback. —G.K.

Photograph by AP

BILLY KILMER The Dolphins' Vern Den Herder (83) and Bill Stanfill enjoyed a crunched quarterback sandwich in Miami's Super Bowl VII win, which was keyed by a Kilmer interception.

"The sacks you know are coming are worse than the ones you don't. You just try to relax and not land on your shoulder."

DREW BREES The Saints' signal-caller fell head over heels after an encounter with the 49ers' Aldon Smith (99) in San Francisco's 2012 playoff victory.

—DREW BREES, SI, *January 9, 2006*

THE SACKERS

**CHANGE WAS IN THE AIR—AND SOON A LOT OF PASSES WOULD BE TOO—
AS NFL RULES BEGAN TO MAKE IT HARDER TO GET TO THE QUARTERBACK,
AND PUT A PREMIUM ON PASS RUSHERS LIKE THE JETS' FRONT FOUR**

Excerpted from SPORTS ILLUSTRATED, *September 1, 1982* | BY PAUL ZIMMERMAN

ACKS. QUARTERBACK SACKS. "THE essence of the game," says Detroit defensive tackle Doug English. "A product of uncontrolled rage," says defensive end Lyle Alzado. "Absolutely the single greatest thing in the world," says Tom Keating, the right tackle on Oakland's record-setting sack crew of 1967.

Sacks? The greatest thing in the world? "Oh, sacks? I thought you said sex," Keating says. "Sacks are the second-best thing."

Sack. The term didn't catch on until the late 1960s. Some people think it originated in L.A., with the Rams' famous Deacon Jones–Merlin Olsen–Rosey Grier–Lamar Lundy Fearsome Foursome team. The NFL still doesn't officially recognize the term. "Opponents Tackled Attempting Passes," is the rather stuffy way the league describes sacks in its record book. But at least they're recognized now. Until '67 there was no official record for team sacks, and for a time before that the play itself didn't show up anywhere in the stats. It was a nonevent.

Some coaches feel that no other play in the game serves as such an exact barometer of success or failure. One doesn't have to look any further than the sack stats to understand how the New York Jets rejoined the ranks of the living last year. They had been notoriously weak pass rushers for almost a decade—their 16 sacks in 1976, when they finished 3–11, was one away from the alltime worst—but last year they erupted with a sacking frenzy, getting 66 of them. As a result, the Jets picked up their first playoff check in 12 years, and the front four of defensive ends Joe Klecko and Mark Gastineau and tackles Marty Lyons and Abdul Salaam picked up a catchy nickname, the New York Sack Exchange.

The Pittsburgh Steelers' fall from greatness came when their sack total decreased from 49 in 1979 to 18 in '80. When the Atlanta Falcons lost their sacking linebacker, Joel Williams, with an injury to his right knee last year, their sacks dropped from the 46 they had in '80 to 29, and their preseason Super Bowl hopes ended at 7–9. Last season each of the nine double-digit winners in the NFL finished in the top half of the league in team sacks. Of the top eight sacking teams in history, six made it into the playoffs, and another, the 1976 San Francisco 49ers, third on the alltime list with 61, had their only winning season in an eight-year stretch.

Pro football statistical analyst Bud Goode says the sack is worth three points. Klecko says a sack isn't "exactly like a touchdown, but it's a big play, both materially and emotionally." The 49ers' coach Bill Walsh says, "A pass rush late in the game is the key to NFL football."

To the league office, sacks are very unpleasant things. Bad for the game, for the quarterbacks and for the passing stats. Bad for scoring,

attendance and America. So the rulemakers have unchained the hands of the offensive linemen. And it's about time they got a break. No one ever gave offensive lines catchy nicknames, such as Gold Rush or Silver Rush or Sack Pack or Purple Gang or Doomsday Defense or Steel Curtain. All those belonged to the sack artists, but now it's time to take those defensive monsters in hand.

In 1976, as pass rushers became leaner and quicker, NFL sacks reached a high of 9.98 per 100 passes thrown. Defense was taking over. And attendance was declining. So in '77 the head slap was taken away from the defensive linemen. The next year the offensive linemen were allowed to shove off and generally use their hands more freely, and the one-bump rule was put in to limit the defensive backs. The year after that, '79, the five-yard bump zone was installed. The passing lanes opened up; quarterbacks began taking a shorter drop and throwing quicker, timed patterns; and sacks decreased every season, down to a low of 7.20 per 100 passes thrown in '81, a 28% decrease in five years. And attendance has shown a steady rise since '77, attaining a regular-season record of 60,745 per game last year.

"The league has given the offense all the weapons now," 49ers linebacker Jack Reynolds says. "It's like Great Britain against Argentina."

"I'd have a lot of trouble playing the game under today's rules," Olsen says. "My whole thrust was to try to make some initial contact with the offensive lineman, but now he'll grab you and you'll never get away. Nowadays you need stunts and tricks and designated pass rushers like San Francisco's Fred Dean. The whole idea is to avoid contact. The new rules have destroyed one of the finest parts of the game, the integrity of one-on-one battles on the line. You don't get that anymore. It's a wrestling match now, a joke. If you went back to the rules of five or six years ago, very few offensive linemen today could play the game. You can get any big strong guy off the street and teach him to pass-block. I'm sad. They've taken an art form and destroyed it. Some people are very Machiavellian. They look at the scoreboard, they look at the dollar sign. Does that mean happiness?"

Still, according to Walsh, pass rushing and quarterback sacks will determine the winners and losers this season. The hunt is on for defensive linemen, not two or three but half a dozen of them per team, all ready to come in at any time. Fresh troops. Superior athletes.

"Sometimes you see a boxing match where for seven or eight rounds the underdog holds on or even gets ahead," says Walsh. "You think an upset is in the making, but then at the end the champion gets him; the champ has worn him down. The pass rush can be like that. Constant pressure by a whole group of superior athletes will wear a blocker down. He gets a little tired, and he isn't able to deal with it anymore. The odds have run out on him."

And then it will be time for some more new rules. ∎

The Patriots' Tony Eason [11] was downgraded by the New York Sack Exchange. | *Photograph by John Iacono*

BEN ROETHLISBERGER The Steelers QB assumed the fetal position (and threw a shoe) under 550 pounds of pressure from the Bengals' Manny Lawson (99) and Domata Peko.

DAN PASTORINI Dwight White of the Steelers added insult to ignominy as he made himself comfortable on the flattened Oilers quarterback at Three Rivers Stadium.

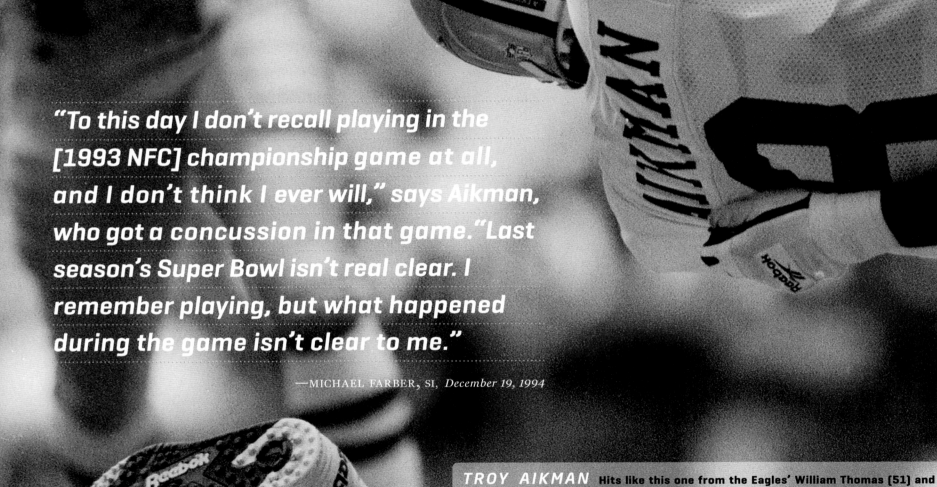

"To this day I don't recall playing in the [1993 NFC] championship game at all, and I don't think I ever will," says Aikman, who got a concussion in that game. "Last season's Super Bowl isn't real clear. I remember playing, but what happened during the game isn't clear to me."

—MICHAEL FARBER, SI, *December 19, 1994*

TROY AIKMAN Hits like this one from the Eagles' William Thomas (51) and Greg Townsend (93) helped usher Aikman out of the game at the fairly young age of 34.

Photograph by Peter Read Miller

KINGS

THE QUARTERBACK IS always the most watched player on the field, but the interest doesn't end when the game's final whistle blows. That has made the position one of the most glamorous jobs in our culture, with loads of opportunities in movies, advertising and broadcasting. Come along on a tour of the red-carpet life of the QB

JOE NAMATH Broadway Joe was a big deal as a rookie in 1965, posing on the Great White Way, but his fame would rocket with his win in Super Bowl III.

OF COOL

Photograph by James Drake

Glamour, Glory and Getting the Girl

BY STEVE RUSHIN

In this country FOR MUCH OF THE AMERICAN CENTURY, THE MOST glamorous job was not President or movie star or astronaut but centerfielder. When Woody Allen had to compile a list of things that made life worth living in *Manhattan*, he put Willie Mays second only to Groucho Marx. "I don't ask for much," Tom Hanks said in *Splash*. "I don't ask to be rich, and I don't ask to be famous, and I don't ask to play centerfield for the New York Yankees." Big league centerfielder was an unattainable

dream position, and a centerfielder in New York—especially for the New York Yankees—was the most glamorous position of all, the embodiment of style and grace. As Santiago said in Hemingway's *The Old Man and the Sea*: "I must be worthy of the great DiMaggio who does all things perfectly. . . . "

But as Mays and DiMaggio were owning the middle of the ballpark in the middle of the last century, an even more glamorous position was on the sidelines, clipboard in hand, waiting for its turn: the football quarterback.

Before long, quarterbacks were larger than the larger-than-life stars of the movies, Joe Montana eclipsing Tony Montana. And somewhere along the way, it became tough to tell who was emulating whom anymore: Were quarterbacks movie stars or movie stars quarterbacks? "The Super Bowl is like a movie," the agent Leigh Steinberg said, "and the quarterback is the leading man." We should have seen it coming, of course. The Green Bay Packers employed a quarterback named Bart Starr, who was helping position the position as the next centerfield, in the '60s.

Today, of course, they're all stars, routinely dating models and actresses and pop starlets. As the college All-America, the quarterback was always the Big Man on Campus—or even the Big Man off Campus, in the case of Johnny Manziel, who became so famous so abruptly that he couldn't attend classes in

person at Texas A&M. His first name remains the quintessential quarterback's name, appearing prominently in every era of professional football in one form or another, from Johnny Unitas to John Elway to Johnny Freaking Football.

Or maybe it's Joe: Joe Namath, Joe Montana, Joe Theismann, Joe Flacco. Either way, these All-America Joes and Johnnys (and Sonnys and Sammys and Boomers and Bretts) are at the pinnacle of American cool. After Jack Kemp played quarterback professionally for a decade, the only thing left for him to try for was President.

In many ways—salary, just for starters—President is a step down from QB. When President Reagan appeared at Baylor University in 1988, at the peak of his powers, *The New York Times* reported with some surprise on the raucous applause he received there: "Such collegiate adoration [is] usually reserved for football quarterbacks."

And why shouldn't it be? Our Bradys and Bradshaws, with their Giseles and Jo Jos, flogging their Flutie Flakes and Discount Double Checks, are perfection incarnate. In the national imagination their lives are untroubled by failure or heartache or flyaway hair, even when—as with Tittle or Bradshaw or Hasselbeck—their hair has flown away.

Bald or be-Afroed, it doesn't matter. Quarterback cool is elusive, indefinable. It embraces the self-described "punky QB"

Namath: "His wild, untamed facial hair revealed a new world of rebellion, of change." To which Grampa Simpson replied: "Look at them sideburns! He looks like a girl. Now, Johnny Unitas . . . there's a haircut you could set your watch to."

In this Faustian battle for the soul of quarterback glamour—Hip vs. Square—one had to take sides, at least until the two styles were finally and blessedly reconciled in Tom Brady, who has the air of Unitas and the hair of Namath, and as such became the sine qua non of quarterback glamour. Or indeed, of American glamour, period. Brady spent $20 million on a home in Brentwood among Hollywood stars, who receive more reflected glory by the proximity than he does.

The two worlds came together in the 1978 film *Heaven Can Wait,* in which the beau ideal of Hollywood glamour, Warren Beatty, plays a Los Angeles Rams quarterback. But as one man already knew, there was no reason you couldn't be both movie star and QB.

Bob Waterfield was the original QB glamour boy, starring for, naturally, the Los Angeles Rams. Waterfield married actress Jane Russell in Las Vegas in 1943, when Russell, a beloved World War II pinup, was under contract to Howard Hughes. Waterfield would go on to make movies himself—opposite Johnny Weissmuller in *Jungle Manhunt* in '51 and as himself in *Crazylegs*, the story of Elroy Hirsch, in '53. That same year, Russell appeared opposite Marilyn Monroe in the somewhat more enduring *Gentlemen Prefer Blondes*. Not to be eclipsed, Waterfield frequently stayed out until 3 a.m. and came home only to sleep. Or so Russell claimed at their divorce proceedings in 1968, the year Mickey Mantle retired, when NFL quarterback and Yankee center-

Jim McMahon and the straitlaced Roger Staubach, the U.S. Navy ensign who commanded more than 100 enlisted men in Chu Lai in Vietnam, coined the phrase "Hail Mary" for a last-second touchdown heave and made quarterback of the Dallas Cowboys equal to centerfield for the New York Yankees, even if the doomed romance of Joe DiMaggio and Marilyn Monroe slightly outshone that of Tony Romo and Jessica Simpson.

These two kinds of cool—countercultural and cultural—literally came to a head when Joe Namath faced Johnny Unitas in Super Bowl III, a stylistic tête-à-tête that was perfectly encapsulated on *The Simpsons*, when Mother Simpson said of

fielder were still neck-and-neck as the most glamorous positions in American sports, and perhaps in American life.

As one who knew, Russell had warned Monroe about marrying a quarterback or a Yankee centerfielder, though Monroe would go ahead and marry DiMaggio anyway. These privileged positions, with their manifold trappings of fame, could make marriage a minefield, reminding us that glamour was then (and remains now) squarely in the eye of the beholder.

"They're birds of a feather and you'll get to know lots of other athletes," Russell told Monroe of marrying a sports star. "Otherwise, it's great." ∎

AUDIBILIZING *A career of making plays seems to segue easily into calling plays, as scores of QBs have become broadcasters.*

Don Meredith (left) was a *Monday Night Football* phenom with Howard Cosell and Frank Gifford.

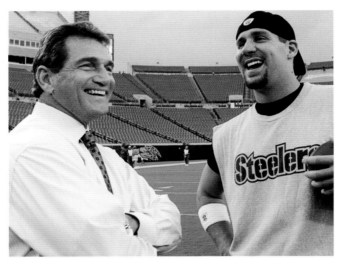

The ever-voluble Joe Theismann (left) interviews Ben Roethlisberger.

Ron Jaworski (interviewing Michael Vick) is an ESPN fixture.

Dan Fouts: on air since 1988.

Terry Bradshaw is a mainstay on *Fox NFL Sunday*.

John Brodie (with O.J. Simpson) was a longtime NBC analyst.

Boomer Esiason (with Shannon Sharpe) is a talk-radio host and CBS studio analyst.

Steve Young (left) and Trent Dilfer (center) on ESPN's *Monday Night Countdown*.

Phil Simms is a top NFL analyst for CBS and for Showtime's *Inside the NFL*.

Troy Aikman (right, with Joe Buck) has been the lead Fox analyst since 2002.

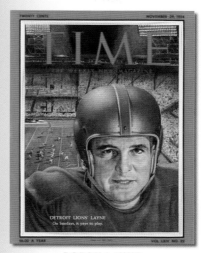

BOBBY LAYNE
November 1954

JOE NAMATH
September 1978

WELL-COVERED *Whether as playmakers, newsmakers or tastemakers, quarterbacks command more attention than any other players in the NFL.*

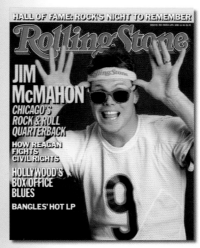

JIM McMAHON
March 1986

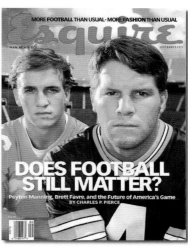

PEYTON MANNING/BRETT FAVRE
September 1997

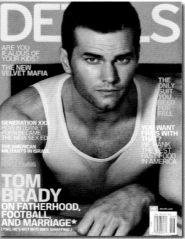

TOM BRADY
September 2009

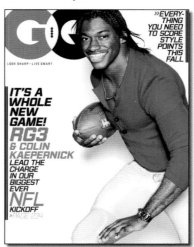

ROBERT GRIFFIN III
September 2013

Superstar Tom Brady married supermodel Gisele Bündchen in 2009.

After he wed Jane Russell, Rams QB Bob Waterfield dabbled in film too.

Tony Romo courted Jessica Simpson and controversy from 2007 to '09.

Terry Bradshaw wed Olympian JoJo Starbuck in 1976; they split in '83.

Joe Montana met wife Jennifer, an actress, on an ad shoot. They posed for SI's Swimsuit Issue in '99.

Rodney Peete married actress Holly Robinson.

Jay Cutler wed TV personality Kristin Cavallari.

COOL CUSTOMER

FRESH OFF A STORYBOOK SEASON IN WHICH HE QUARTERBACKED THE PATRIOTS TO A SUPER BOWL WIN AT AGE 24, TOM BRADY LEARNED A FAST LESSON IN NEWFOUND FAME AND THE SPOILS OF VICTORY

Excerpted from SPORTS ILLUSTRATED, *April 15, 2002* | BY MICHAEL SILVER

**C**OME FLY WITH ME, THE BRASSY billionaire said to America's newest football star, and soon the two were traversing the friendly skies in a customized Boeing 727, swapping stories, chowing down on sandwiches and preparing to mingle with 51 of the hottest women in the land. This was the usual plane of existence for the aircraft's owner, a real-estate magnate, but the wide-eyed quarterback was having the ride of his life. He sank into the Italian leather couch, stared dumbstruck at paintings that looked as if they might be on loan from the Louvre and thought, My God, how did I get here?

So it was that Tom Brady, the 24-year-old quarterback of the New England Patriots, found himself sitting in Donald Trump's private jet last month as it flew from New York City to Gary, Ind., site of Miss USA 2002. There Brady donned a tux by Calvin Klein; traded giggles with *The Price Is Right* bombshell Nikki Ziering, a fellow judge; and was besieged with requests from contestants' mothers imploring him to consider dating their lovely daughters. Amid all the obvious talent—and the requisite assemblage of former players (including host Deion Sanders) and *playas* (judge Jermaine Jackson)—it was the tall guy with the cleft chin and the amiable grin who shone brightest.

As insane as it would have seemed a year ago, when he couldn't even convince skeptics at a health club near San Francisco that he played in the NFL, Brady created Gary's biggest buzz since Professor Harold Hill and his 76 trombones. "The kid has great self-confidence and an unbelievable personality, and he's got the maturity of a much older man," Trump said later. "Let me tell you, if one thing stands out about Tom Brady, it's that he loves those women. And, guess what? They love him too."

Right now it seems that everybody—men, women, children, corporations, living legends—wants a piece of Touchdown Tommy. Two months after propelling himself to stardom by leading his team to a stunning 20–17 victory over the St. Louis Rams in Super Bowl XXXVI, Brady, that game's Most Valuable Player, is still livin' it up like Ja Rule.

In the aftermath of his triumphant performance in New Orleans, Brady jetted off to Disney World, returned to Boston for the team's victory parade (during which some women felt compelled to flash him, 25° weather be damned) and hightailed it to Hawaii to play in the Pro Bowl. Before he knew what had hit him, Brady was playing an impromptu round of golf in Kauai with John Elway; hangin' with Barry Bonds and Willie Mays at the San Francisco Giants' spring training complex in Scottsdale, Ariz.; trading mock punches with Muhammad Ali at a charity event in Phoenix; and blowing off *Vanity Fair*'s exclusive Academy Awards party because he felt he would be so hopelessly out of his element.

"One thing I've realized is that for every thing you turn down, there's something else right around the corner that's really cool," Brady said recently over breakfast in his hometown of San Mateo, Calif., about 15 miles south of San Francisco. "These last few weeks have been a whirlwind, and I'm trying to learn as I go along. I think I'm a pretty good quarterback, but there's all this other stuff that goes along with being a very recognizable person, and I suck at it. This is my new reality, I guess, and it's knocking me down."

It appears that fame is doing what neither the Rams nor the AFC's best teams nor the looming presence of longtime New England quarterback Drew Bledsoe could do last season: rattle Brady, a former fourth-stringer who in just his second year in the NFL stirred a tired team with his brash enthusiasm and preternatural poise. It's the latter quality that scored him his backstage pass into Trumpville. Americans have a thing for quarterbacks, especially the ones (Unitas, Staubach, Montana, Elway) who stare down long odds with time ticking down and rally their teams to victory.

Brady is a long, long way from being mentioned with those alltime greats, but already we have seen glimpses of his ability to respond in the clutch. In the Patriots' epic OT playoff victory over the Raiders in January, a game played during a field-blanketing nor'easter, Brady proved to be the coolest guy in the snow since Franz Klammer at the 1976 Olympics. In New Orleans two weeks later, after a St. Louis rally had hundreds of millions of viewers preparing for the first overtime in Super Bowl history, Brady needed little more than a minute to move his team 53 yards for Adam Vinatieri's 48-yard field goal on the last play of the game.

"The great thing about Tom is that no matter what he went through, it didn't seem like he allowed the pressure to bother him," says Rams quarterback Kurt Warner, Brady's immediate predecessor as the NFL's out-of-nowhere sensation. "A lot of guys might have reacted to the big stage of the Super Bowl by trying to force plays, but he just relaxed. Right now he seems like a kid in a candy store." Warner, a former supermarket stock boy and Arena League mainstay, has sustained his excellence after achieving sudden stardom in 1999, and Brady is obsessed with doing the same. "Why do some guys have one great year and then play so badly the next?" Brady asks. "Well, now I think I know why—because there are so many things that can take you away from what you need to do to focus on your job."

As Warner once did, Brady bristles at the notion that his ascent was a fluke. But while both rose to the top overnight, Brady faces different challenges in his quest to stay there. Whereas Warner, a husband and a father of four, has resolutely distilled his off-field interests to faith and family, Brady has no such constraints. If he continues his rise on the field, Brady will have a chance to become the 21st century's answer to Joe Namath. ∎

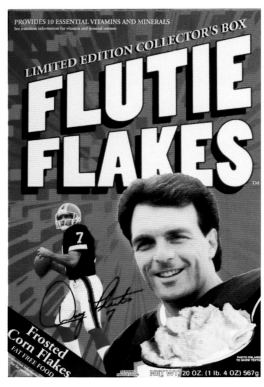

Doug Flutie flacked a line of flakes for charity in 1998.

Ubiquitous salesmen Peyton (left) and Eli Manning hawked Oreos in 2008.

BRAND NAMES *The ad world has long known that a pitch from a high-profile quarterback can score big.*

Aaron Rodgers (with Da Bears' fans) took up selling insurance for State Farm in 2012.

got milk?

Kurt Warner milked his Super Bowl victory in 2000.

UNRIVALED With movies roles, ads, his own TV show, Joe Namath set the bar for quarterback cool.

Backstage with Barbra Streisand.

Shaving his Fu Manchu for dollars.

Interviewing actor Elliott Gould on TV.

With legendary soccer star Pelé.

Styling, even when injured.

In *C.C. & Company* with Ann-Margret.

With Raquel Welch at the Oscars.

Recuperating at home, atop llama rug.

Touch football with *Playboy* bunnies.

At an ad shoot with Farrah Fawcett.

JOE WILLIE, AFTER HOURS

WITH HIS HIGH SALARY AND EVEN HIGHER PROFILE, THE JETS' JOE NAMATH BECAME A MAJOR HAPPENING IN NEW YORK CITY, THROWING PASSES BY DAY AND MAKING PASSES BY NIGHT

Excerpted from SPORTS ILLUSTRATED, *October 17, 1966* | BY DAN JENKINS

STOOP-SHOULDERED AND SINISTERLY handsome, he slouches against the wall of the saloon, a filter cigarette in his teeth, collar open, perfectly happy and self-assured, gazing through the uneven darkness to sort out the winners from the losers. As the girls come by wearing their miniskirts, net stockings, big false eyelashes, long pressed hair and soulless expressions, he grins approvingly and says, "Hey, hold it, man—foxes." It is Joe Willie Namath at play. Relaxing, Night-timing.

The boss mover studying the defensive tendencies of New York's off-duty secretaries, stewardesses, dancers, nurses, bunnies, actresses, shopgirls—all of the people who make life stimulating for a bachelor who can throw one of the best passes in pro football. He poses a question for us all: Would you rather be young, single, rich, famous, talented, energetic and happy—or President? Joe Willie Namath is not to be fully understood by most of us, of course. We are ancient, being over 23, and perhaps a bit arthritic, seeing as how we can't do the Duck. We aren't comfortably tuned in to the Mamas and the Uncles—or whatever their names are. We have cuffs on our trousers and, freakiest of all, we have pockets we can get our hands into. But Joe is not pleading to be understood.

He is youth, success, the clothes, the car, the penthouse, the big town, the girls and the games on Sundays. He simply is, man. The best we can do is catch a slight glimpse of him as he speeds by us in this life.

Right now, this moment, whatever Joe means to himself behind his wisecracks, his dark, rugged good looks and his flashy tailoring, he is mostly one thing; a big celebrity in a celebrity-conscious town. This adds up to a lot of things, some desirable, some not. It means a stack of autographs everywhere he goes ("Hey, Joe, for a friend of mine who's a priest, a little somethin' on the napkin, huh?"), a lot of photography stills for ads and news and continual interviews with the press. Such things he handles with beautiful nonchalance, friendliness—and lip.

Then comes the good part. It means he gets to sit at one of those key tables in Toots Shor's—1 and 1A, the joke goes—the ones just beyond the partition from the big circular bar where everyone from Des Moines can watch him eat his prime rib. It means that when he hits P. J. Clarke's the maitre d' in the crowded back room, Frankie Ribando, will always find a place for him, while, out front, waiter Tommy Joyce, one of New York's best celebrity-spotters, will tell everyone, "Joe's inside." It means he can crawl into the Pussy Cat during the late hours when the Copa girls and the bunnies are there having their afterwork snacks, even though the line at the door may stretch from Second Avenue to the Triborough Bridge. It means he can get in just as easily at two of his other predawn haunts, Mister Laffs and Dudes 'n Dolls, places long ago ruled impenetrable by earth people, or nonmembers of the Youth Cult.

Easing into the clubs and restaurants that he frequents, Joe Willie handles his role well. "Don't overdo it, man," he says. "I can hang around till 3 or 4 and still grab my seven or eight." He sits, he eats, he sips, he smokes, he talks, he looks, and maybe he scares up a female companion and maybe he doesn't. "I don't like to date so much as I just like to kind of, you know, run into somethin', man," he says.

Namath is unlike all of the super sports celebrities who came before him in New York—Babe Ruth, Joe DiMaggio and Sugar Ray Robinson, to name three of the more obvious. They were grown men when they achieved the status he now enjoys. They were less hip to their times and more or less aloof from the crowd. Joe thrusts himself into the middle of it. Their fame came more slowly, with the years of earning it. Joe Willie Namath was a happening.

He happened first when he was a sophomore passing whiz who made Alabama coach Bear Bryant change his offense. He happened again as a junior when he proved to be such an away-from-the-field mover that Bryant had to kick him off the team for drinking and carousing before the last two games of the season. He happened again when he returned to take Alabama to the 1964 national championship on a gimpy leg. Then Sonny Werblin, the owner of the New York Jets, made him really happen when he gave him that $400,000 contract on the second day of '65. No football player in history had ever been worth half that much. But this wasn't all. He quickly had to undergo an operation on his knee to have a torn cartilage removed and a loose ligament tied. He was already a celebrity then, but his image grew throughout '65 when a certain amount of suspense built as to whether his knee would allow him to play any football at all for Werblin's $400,000. During it all, the wisecracks flowed like cocktails.

"I'd rather go to Vietnam than get married," he said as the draft board in his home town of Beaver Falls, Pa. requested that he appear for his physical. Then after he flunked it and a lot of superpatriots bristled, as they did at Cassius Clay's attitude, Joe said with brutal honesty, "How can I win, man? If I say I'm glad, I'm a traitor, and if I say I'm sorry, I'm a fool." Once when he was asked to point out the difference between Bryant and Jets coach Weeb Ewbank, Joe grinned and unwisely said, "Coach Bryant was always thinking about winning. Weeb is mainly concerned over what kind of publicity you get." When a writer tried to tease him about his classes at Alabama, asking if he majored in basket weaving, Joe Willie said, "Naw, man, journalism—it was easier."

But all that was a year ago. Now in this season as he goes about proving that he is worth every cent of his contract (he has thrown nine touchdown passes and put the Jets in first place in the AFL's Eastern Division through five games), he is becoming the quarterback that Werblin gambled he would be—a throwing artist who may eventually rank with the best—and he is still a swinger. Namath may be Johnny Unitas and Paul Hornung rolled into one; he may, in fact, be pro football's very own Beatle.

He lives in a penthouse on New York's Upper East Side, one that features a huge white llama-skin rug, a marble bar, an elaborate stereo hookup, an oval bed that seems to increase in size with each glance, a terrace and a couple of roommates—Joe Hirsch, a writer for *The Morning Telegraph*, and Jets defensive back Ray Abruzzese, whom he knew at Alabama.

Of Hirsch, Joe Willie says, "I got my own handicapper." Of Abruzzese, he says, "I got my own bartender," referring to Abruzzese's onetime summer job tending bar at Dudes 'n Dolls. And of his apartment, he says proudly, "I had the same decorator that Sinatra had for his pad." He whirls around the city in his gray Lincoln Continental convertible, the radio blaring, parking by fireplugs whenever possible, wearing tailor-made suits with tight pants and loud print linings, grabbing checks, laughing, enjoying life, spending maybe $25,000 a year ("On nuthin', man") and wondering why anyone should be offended.

"I believe in letting a guy live the way he wants to if he doesn't hurt anyone. I feel that everything I do is O.K. for me and doesn't affect anybody else, including the girls I go out with," he says. "Look man, I live and let live. I like everybody. I don't care what a man is as long as he treats me right. He can be a gambler, a hustler, someone everybody else thinks is obnoxious, I don't care so long as he's straight with me and our dealings are fair. I like Cassius Clay, Bill Hartack, Doug Sanders and Hornung, all the controversial guys. They're too much. They're colorful, man. But I like everybody." Joe's eyes sparkle, as if he is getting ready to make a joke, and he says, "Why, I even like Howard Cosell."

Joe Willie's philosophy is more easily grasped when one realizes what he lifted himself up from in Beaver Falls. It is a picturesque but poor town in the hills about 30 miles outside of Pittsburgh. He was the youngest of five children, and his parents were divorced when he was in the sixth grade. His father was a millworker. He lived with his mother, and there was little money, so Joe hustled. He shot pool, he shined shoes, he ran messages for bookies, he hustled; he got by. "Where I come from," he says today, "ain't nobody gonna hustle me, man." As he prepared for his senior year of high school the idea of going to college was remote. An older brother, John, was a career man in the Army, a warrant officer now in Vietnam. Joe was set on joining the Air Force and making it a career. What stopped him was a lot of touchdown passes.

Contrary to popular notion, Joe did give the St. Louis Cardinals, who drafted him in the NFL, some serious consideration. "And they weren't that far off in money," he says. "But they had it laid out wrong, like I had to do a radio show for part of my salary. I couldn't believe that. I said, man, I'm just a football player, and what I make will be for football only." He did guess that the Cardinals, who had an established passer in Charley Johnson, might be dealing for him on behalf of the New York Giants, who had nothing, and, one way or another, he wanted to "get to this town." Bryant's only comment was that Ewbank had won a couple of championships at Baltimore and, if Joe was still interested in winning, he might give that some consideration.

He wasn't a winner right off, of course. The Jets' 5-8-1 record last season made New York the worst team Joe had ever played on. Admittedly, he didn't know the first thing about quarterbacking a pro team. He had the quickest delivery anyone had ever seen, and he got back into the Jets' exceedingly secure passing pocket, formed by Sherman Plunkett, Dave Herman, Sam DeLuca, and Winston Hill—his "bodyguards"—so fast that Kansas City's All-AFL lineman, Jerry Mays, said, "He makes the rush obsolete." But there was so much he had to learn.

At Alabama he had raced back only five yards and released the ball in approximately 1.3 seconds. Ewbank demanded that he get eight yards deep and go 3.2 seconds before throwing. His firmly braced knee prevented him from using the threat of the run, which he had done so well for two and a half seasons in Tuscaloosa. He had to learn how to read defenses, how to look for tips among the defensive backs, how to hit his receivers on the break, how to set up when he threw, how to call audibles and how to convince his Jets teammates that he could lead them.

"Last year," says defensive end Gerry Philbin, "there was an undercurrent of resentment—nothing you could pinpoint, but it was there—about Joe's money and his publicity. That was at first. It disappeared when everybody found out what a great guy he is." Curley Johnson, the punter, says, "Mainly we wanted to see how good he was. He really didn't throw the ball that damn well for a long time. Now, we know how good he is—the best." Says the ace receiver, Don Maynard, "At first he'd knock us over on short patterns. Now his timing is great, and he adjusts to situations like a veteran." To this, George Sauer Jr., another top Jets receiver, adds, "He never knew how to throw on the break last season. The ball was always early or late. Now it's there."

If he stays healthy, Joe Willie may achieve his deepest ambition, which is "to become known as a good quarterback, not a rich one." He may even become what Boston owner Billy Sullivan says he is now: "The biggest thing in New York since Babe Ruth." Slowly, because trying to fathom youth is always a slow process, you get the impression that Joe is quite serious about it and, despite his hip ways, is working hard to make it. Beneath the gaudy surface there somehow beams through a genuine, considerate, sincere, wonderfully friendly and likable young man. But he's going to be himself. He's going to do it his way, and nobody else's. ∎

Namath routinely charmed the press, in this case a fashion reporter at a New York restaurant. | *Photograph by Barton Silverman*

DISCOMFORT ZONE
A quarterback's poise under pressure is always being tested, and five of them have faced the ultimate trial: hosting Saturday Night Live.

Peyton Manning menaced Fred Armisen in 2007.

Tom Brady, with Amy Poehler, was a genial genie in 2005.

Fran Tarkenton looked up to Coach Belushi in 1977.

Joe Montana met the Church Lady in 1987.

Eli Manning in drag in 2012.

TAKE A KNEE A Hail Mary from QB Tim Tebow became a big deal when suddenly everyone started Tebowing.

Lindsey Vonn

Paul Pierce

Broncos mascot, Thunder, Tebowing in 2011

Alec Baldwin

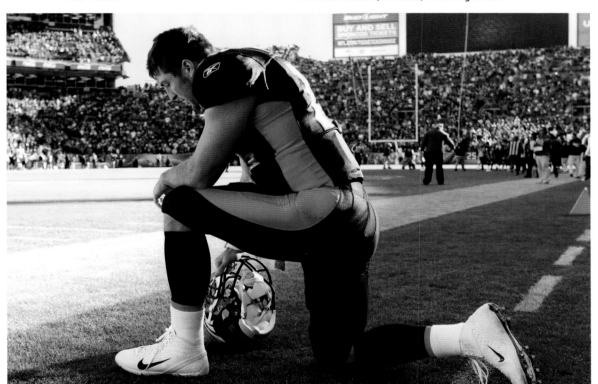

The original, with the Broncos in 2011

Nuggets mascot, Rocky

The Broncos' marching band

Marine Sgt. John Martinez

Virginia state delegate Rob Bell

Charlton Heston was a Saint in 1969's *Number One*.

Alan Alda played George Plimpton in 1968's *Paper Lion*.

SCREEN PASSERS The movies may not have won Oscars, but there have been some memorable football films in the annals of sports cinema, and just like in real life, the star can most often be found at the quarterback position.

Keanu Reeves QB'd *The Replacements* (2000).

Adam Sandler in *The Longest Yard* remake (2005).

Warren Beatty was a deceased Ram in 1978's *Heaven Can Wait*.

Mac Davis (16) in 1979's *North Dallas Forty*.

Dennis Quaid in *Any Given Sunday* (1999).

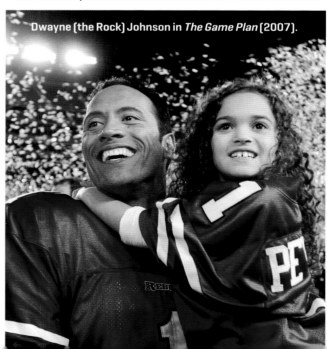

Dwayne (the Rock) Johnson in *The Game Plan* (2007).

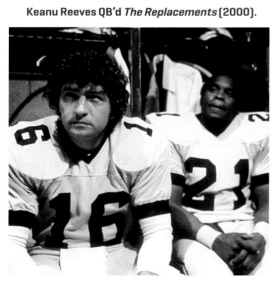

Burt Reynolds was a former NFL QB in prison in *The Longest Yard* (1974).

THE HARDEST JOB in pro football might be finding a great quarterback, and to get one almost always requires a high draft pick. That's what makes the mistakes so embarrassingly memorable. Meet the members of a fraternity that no one wants to join, the high-profile busts whose names—fairly or unfairly—will forever live in infamy

RYAN LEAF The second overall choice in '98, Leaf was a toxic mix of arrogance, inability and injury until the Chargers released him three years later.

BORN UNDER A

BAD SIGN

A List That Will Live in Infamy

BY AUSTIN MURPHY

Pity the poor BUST, HIS NAME A SYNONYM FOR FUTILITY AND UNDER-achievement, doomed to roam cyberspace for eternity, handcuffed to his briefcase of ignominy. In that briefcase is the damning list, the Biggest Busts of All Time, from which his name will never be expunged. Also in that satchel of sadness: the names of the Pro Bowlers and Hall of Famers selected in the same draft class, but after him. *Oh my God—look who we could've had!*

On second thought, go ahead and pile on the Bust, who shouldn't be poor at all. Among the prerequisites to be a full-fledged, genuine Bust, he had to have been drafted in the first round—usually the first half of the first round. Which means that before he imploded, he got paid.

Things end up working out just fine for him. Usually. Tim Couch, whom Cleveland (in)famously chose with the first over-all pick in 1999, was beaten out by journeyman Kelly Holcomb in the final year of his disappointing, five-year stay with the Browns. But Couch did end up marrying former *Playboy* Play-mate of the Year Heather Kozar. He wins. After flaming out spectacularly with Washington, Heath Shuler served three terms in the U.S. House of Representatives and is now a lob-byist in D.C. Former Bengals bust David Klingler is at peace with his disappointing NFL career: He teaches Bible studies to seminarians in Houston.

"I kind of got out of the spotlight, and life's never been this good," Ryan Leaf told ESPN.com in April of '08. This period of tranquillity was short-lived. A year later, he pled guilty in Texas to burglary and controlled-substance charges and was placed on probation for 10 years. He'd go on to serve time in a federal prison in Montana for violating his probation and for a burglary conviction. So life hasn't been so good.

(In his case, pity the poor sportswriter. With the '98 NFL draft coming up, I was assigned to write the Leaf half of a story asking which quarterback you'd take first, Peyton Manning or Leaf. "It's only 100 words," the editor said. "Have fun with it!"

It was a tiny portent of the calamity awaiting San Diego that I could muster only 82 words on behalf of Leaf, who several years ago passed the mantle of the Biggest Bust in NFL History to JaMarcus Russell. *Give me the linebacker-sized Leaf,* I wrote, *who at 6'5", 238 pounds is more rugged, less susceptible to injury than the 6'5", 222-pound Manning.* Great point! Because, at 6'5", 222, Manning was a sylph, a stripling—how would he survive his first scrimmage? *Leaf is a better athlete, stronger of arm and more fiery than Manning.* Too bad he harnessed that fire not to lead comebacks, but to rage late at the bars—which may be why he napped during meetings. *To those who point out that he's also rawer, I say: So what? No quarterback does squat until he's been in the league at least three years.* (Manning won 13 games and led the Colts to a division title in his second season.)

The cold truth is, there's a small part of us that takes pleasure in rubbernecking at the wreckage of a Bust's career, unless he is torpedoing *our* team. His failure imparts a frisson of moral su-periority. Surely his struggles are the result of some defect in his character. Surely if we had hit the genetic jackpot, we would have lasted 10-plus years. Just as we love the pluck of undrafted free agents who succeed despite limited skills, we reserve our scorn

for those who are blessed with vast talent and then squander it.

It may feel good. But is it fair? If the immature, narcoleptic Leaf had passed an actual torch to the overall No. 1 pick in the 2007 draft, the blubbery, apathetic Russell, it would've been made of paper—sheaths of rolled-up evaluations put together by scouts and GMs who got it completely wrong. Behind every Bust lurks a legion of gurus who are paid well to know better.

When a club thinks it's drafting a franchise quarterback but ends up with a clipboard caddy, it pays the price for years. The team is out more than the Bust's salary and the opportunity cost. Often, general managers part with a king's ransom in picks to move up in the draft, for the privilege of selecting the player who will eventually get them fired. The Chargers coughed up three high picks—plus Pro Bowl returner Eric Metcalf—to move up a single spot in '98, for the right to select . . . Leaf.

When a high pick at quarterback fails to pan out, the club's misery often seems to be compounded. Few teams have spent more seasons trapped in this "bust-and-bust" cycle than the Bengals, who took Klingler with the No. 6 overall pick in 1992. Cincinnati gave up on him in '95, after it became evident that his gaudy college stats were due to Houston's high-octane offense. Chastened little by the experience, it would seem, Cincinnati used the No. 3 overall pick in '99 to select . . . Akili Smith. He threw for five touchdowns and 13 interceptions in his four seasons with the club.

On rare occasions, the miscalculations of one franchise migrate to and pollute another team, like a chemical spill moving downstream. Consider the 1987 Cardinals, who squandered that year's No. 6 overall pick on Kelly Stouffer, who instead of expressing his gratitude to the club for its (grotesquely misplaced) faith in him, held out for an entire season. Cutting their losses, the Cardinals unloaded him on the Seahawks, whose decision to Adopt-A-Bust—Stouffer won five games as a starter over five seasons for Seattle—seemed to have a pernicious and cascading effect. When it became clear that Stouffer was not the answer, the Seahawks used their first-round pick in '91 on 6'8" Dan McGwire. With two touchdowns and six picks in just 12 games over four seasons, McGwire was the franchise's most disappointing pick ever . . . *until* '93, when Seattle used the No. 2 overall pick to select its third Quarterback of the Future in six years, a prospect Bill Walsh himself had described as "the next Joe Montana."

Alas, Rick Mirer turned out to be more like the next Dan McGwire. And Seattle didn't make the playoffs until 1999.

Just as Dante divided his Inferno into nine circles, there are varying levels of Bust. In the deeper rings are Leaf and Russell, for whom it's tough to muster sympathy. Given the opportunity of a lifetime, they responded with apathy and sloth. Greater forgiveness is afforded those who were rushed into action before they were ready, playing behind lines that couldn't protect them. As the shrink played by Robin Williams repeatedly shouts at Matt Damon in *Good Will Hunting*, "It's not your fault!"

That may be true for some Busts. But it's not going to get them off The List. ∎

KELLY STOUFFER He refused to sign with the Cardinals, who took him sixth overall in '87, and instead was slipshod in Seattle for four seasons.

JAMARCUS RUSSELL The Raiders loved his big arm and made him the No. 1 overall pick in '07, but he went 7–18 as a starter in three seasons.

SAD SACK

THE CHARGERS PAID A KING'S RANSOM TO ACQUIRE RYAN LEAF WITH THE SECOND OVERALL SELECTION IN THE 1998 DRAFT, AND THEY WERE REWARDED WITH A ROOKIE SEASON FROM HELL

Excerpted from SPORTS ILLUSTRATED, *December 28, 1998* | BY AUSTIN MURPHY

RYAN LEAF, THE SAN DIEGO CHARGERS quarterback, was seated in a chair on the stage of the Matthew Sherman Elementary School auditorium, playing Santa Claus. The beneficiaries of his largesse on Dec. 14 were not Chargers' opponents, for a change, but rather the students at the San Diego primary school, who received from Leaf goody bags and stockings stuffed with toys. These items, unlike the 19 turnovers that Leaf has committed this season, weren't gift-wrapped.

In another switch, Leaf wasn't booed by the hometown audience. "All the kids knew was that there was a Charger in their school," says Sylvia Soria, an instructional aide at Sherman Elementary who had arranged Leaf's visit. A loyal San Diego fan, Soria isn't inclined to give up on Leaf just yet.

"He's still a young man," she says. "We have a lot of underprivileged kids here, and we tell them, 'Just because you've had a hard start doesn't mean you can't have a beautiful finish.' " Steve Young had a hard start. Troy Aikman had a hard start. Leaf had a catastrophe, the result of having not only the worst quarterback rating (39.0) in the league in the '90s but also the worst public relations instincts. He has thrown two touchdown passes and 15 interceptions, completed 45.3% of his throws and been sacked 22 times. His rookie year has been a study in bad reads, bad passes and bad behavior. His off-field misdeeds include a profanity-laced tirade at a reporter that aired on nationwide TV and an infamous weekend of barhopping and hell-raising near the campus of his alma mater, Washington State.

Is there a beautiful finish on Leaf's horizon? "It's in his hands," says June Jones, San Diego's interim coach, who will become the University of Hawaii's head man after the Chargers' season finale at Arizona on Sunday. "His commitment in the off-season will dictate how he does."

Few NFL insiders doubt Leaf's physical attributes, but privately, those who have worked most closely with him say he won't reach his potential until he adopts a more professional attitude. Leaf, on the other hand, has no doubts about his future. "Everybody tells me, 'You're going to be fine,' " he says. "Well, I know I'm going to be fine." San Diego general manager Bobby Beathard traded a king's ransom—two first-round draft picks and a second-rounder, plus wideout-return man Eric Metcalf and linebacker Patrick Sapp—to move up one spot in last year's draft for the opportunity to take Leaf, a junior coming out early, with the second pick. "Ladies and gentlemen, we have the player who's going to lead us to the Super Bowl," Chargers owner Alex Spanos said after San Diego had selected Leaf. Three days into training camp Leaf agreed to a five-year, $31.25 million contract that included an $11.25 million signing bonus, and shortly thereafter he was named as the Chargers' starter.

However, by mid-November, when Leaf was benched, Beathard would say, "A career could be crumbling if he doesn't wise up and understand he isn't handling things the right way." Beathard now says, "There's a maturity factor with Ryan," which means that Leaf is immature. When might Leaf start acting his age? "I don't know the timing on that," Beathard says.

It needs to have happened yesterday—or so it seems if you listen to the talk in the San Diego locker room. In a game against the Seattle Seahawks on Dec. 13, Leaf relieved Craig Whelihan, who'd thrown five interceptions. Leaf, who was seeing his first action in five games, didn't exactly take the Kingdome crowd out of the game: He tossed two more interceptions and lost a fumble that was returned for a touchdown.

The day after that 38–17 defeat, Chargers strong safety Rodney Harrison and linebacker Kurt Gouveia criticized unnamed teammates for not preparing sufficiently and for taking losses too lightly. Gouveia left little doubt that one of the players he was talking about was Leaf when he said, "College is over. This is the NFL. You are expected to play well, and you are getting good money to play." Gouveia, who returned this season after cracking a vertebra in his neck in 1997, is one of the most respected San Diego players. Three days after the loss to Seattle, he elaborated on his remarks. "I'm in the league 13 years, and I still have a sense that I'm going to lose my job if I don't play well," he said. "I approach every day with a sense of urgency. Every guy on this team needs to ask himself if he has that urgency.

"Ryan lost this team this year, and it was a tremendous loss because of the wasted effort by the defense. [The Chargers lead the NFL in total defense but have only a 5–10 record.] If we were just average on offense, who knows where we'd be? You're in the pros now. Stand up and be accountable. Futures are at stake. Livelihoods are at stake. This is not a place for kids who've got a lot of money to joke around."

Upon learning that a reporter was working on a Leaf story, another Chargers veteran said with disdain, "Rip his ass off. Kid's got the world by the balls, and he doesn't even know it."

In the five weeks he spent on the bench after the Chargers' Nov. 8 loss to the Denver Broncos, Leaf had plenty of time to reflect. He knows he has lost his teammates' confidence and is itching to win it back. Admitting that he was ceded the starting job "based on where I was drafted," he says, "now I want to earn it. I want my teammates to want me in there. I want to deserve to be in there."

Or does he? Citing unnamed players, the *San Diego Union-Tribune* recently reported that Leaf has fallen asleep in meetings and, since being pulled, has been going through the motions in practice. "I don't think he's learned a thing since he was benched," said one Charger. ∎

Leaf threw for just two TDs in his first season, with 15 interceptions and eight fumbles. | *Photograph by Patrick Murphy-Racey*

190

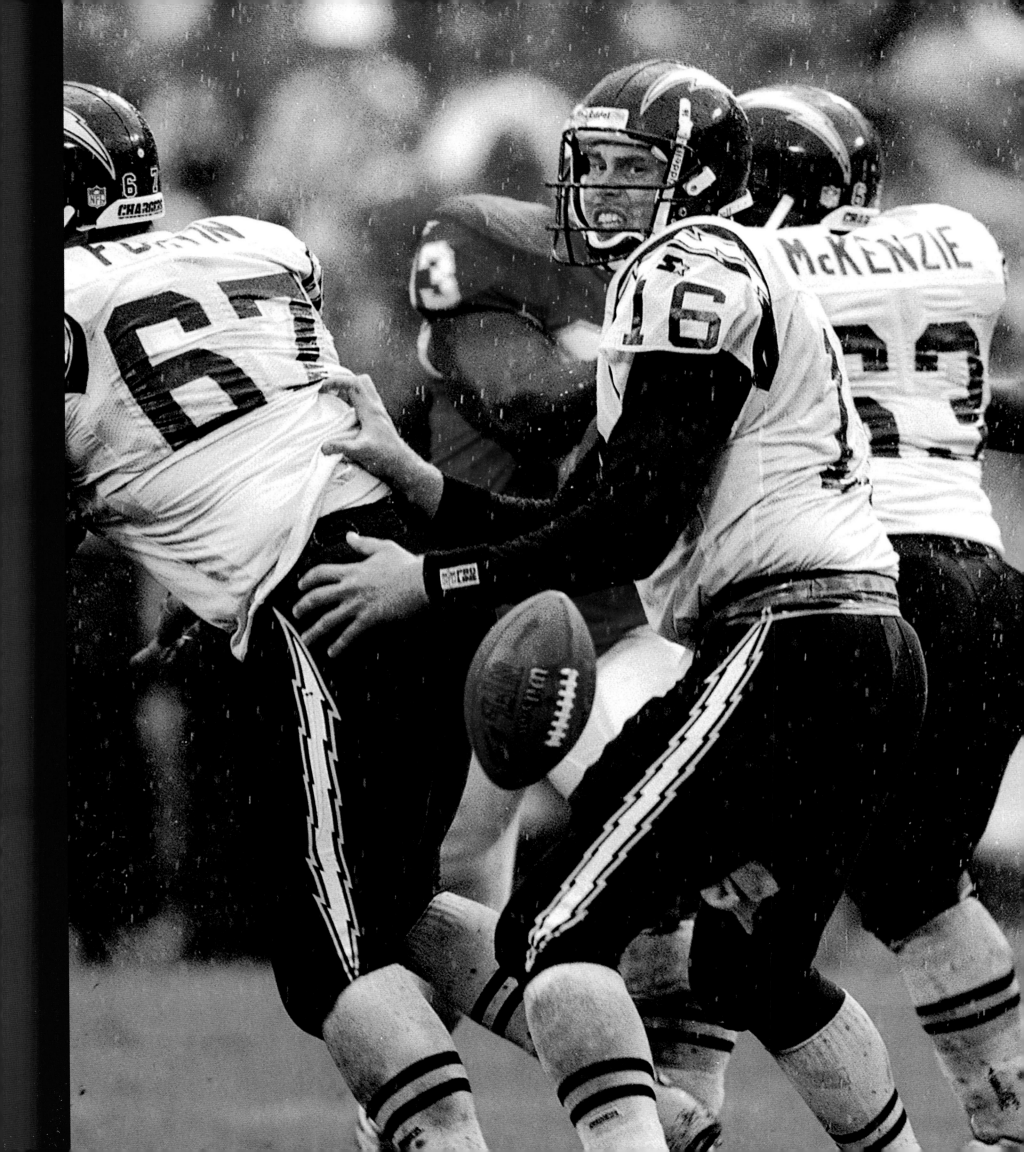

DAVID CARR Playing behind a ragged line as the top pick of the expansion Texans in '02, a totaled Carr was sacked 76 times, which is still a single-season record.

AKILI SMITH **The Bengals turned down a draft-pick bonanza from the Saints to take Smith third overall in '99; he would end up 3–14 as a starter over four seasons.**

He was bred to be a quarterback—his father, Marv, stretching his son's infant hamstrings, teething him on iron-rich frozen liver— [but] his football-only upbringing left him unprepared for adult urges; and wasted, arrest-riddled years followed.

—BEN REITER, SI, *February 6, 2012*

TODD MARINOVICH Raised on a junk-food-free diet, the Raiders '91 first-round pick also had an appetite for drugs that helped end his NFL career after two seasons.

RICK MIRER The "next Joe Montana" out of Notre Dame, Seattle's top pick in '93 played eight seasons with five teams and a 24–44 mark as a starter.

ART SCHLICHTER

TO ALL APPEARANCES, Art Schlichter was a very safe choice when the Colts grabbed him with the fourth overall pick in the 1982 draft. He had been an All-America at Ohio State, where he threw 50 TD passes and ran for 35 more in his four seasons as a starter. Cowboys personnel chief Gil Brandt had said, "He looks like the kind of guy you'd want to start a new franchise with." Instead he became the poster boy for rigorous background checks.

Schlichter was a hero with a fatal flaw: an insatiable urge to gamble. Horses, poker, basketball, football, even backgammon. He bet until he lost, then he'd double his bets to try to get even. He was beaten out in Colts training camp by rookie Mike Pagel, and he comforted himself by betting more. One Friday he had a streak of good luck and won $120,000. "I called the book to collect," he told SI in 1986, "and they said they couldn't pay me until Tuesday." By Monday he had lost the $120,000, and $70,000 more.

The Colts finished 0-8-1 in the strike-shortened season, and Schlichter (number 10, left) mopped up in just three games. Three months later, news broke that the FBI had arrested four bookies who had threatened to break his arm if he didn't pay up $159,000 in losses. The NFL investigated and ultimately suspended Schlichter, causing him to miss the 1983 season.

After Schlichter, NFL background checks on top picks became far more rigorous "We thought we were being thorough," said Dick Szymanski, the Colts' GM who drafted Schlichter. "We talked to his coaches and got a lot of good info. He checked out." They did not, however, talk to law-enforcement sources, who could have told them about the quarterback's gambling in college. Digging deeper has became standard procedure since.

With Schlichter crashing and burning, the Colts still needed a quarterback, only now they had the top pick in the '83 draft. They took John Elway, even though he had already told them he wouldn't play for them, forcing the Colts to trade his rights to Denver. The cost of mishandling two No. 1 picks? The Colts would appear in one playoff game, a loss, in the next 12 years.

Schlichter would lose all six of his starts with the Colts in '84 and '85, and then his NFL career was effectively over. Rehab and imprisonments have followed since, but his compulsion has always triumphed. The latest and heaviest blow to the one-time golden child came in 2012 when he was sentenced to almost 11 years in federal prison for fraud, forgery, theft and drug use while under house arrest. —G.K.

Photograph by Bruce Dierdorff

DAVID KLINGLER He once threw 11 TDs passes in a college game at Houston, but only had 16 in six losing seasons after the Bengals took him sixth overall in '92.

ANDRE WARE Another college wunderkind at Houston, he went from Heisman to history in Detroit, starting just six games in four years from 1990 through '93.

THE MAN WHO ISN'T THERE

HE WAS THE OVERALL NO. 1 PICK IN THE 2007 DRAFT, AND THEN HE WAS
OUT OF THE NFL TWO YEARS LATER. JAMARCUS RUSSELL, THE MOST
MALIGNED FIGURE IN ALL OF FOOTBALL, TELLS HIS SIDE OF THE STORY

Excerpted from SPORTS ILLUSTRATED, *October 31, 2011* | BY L. JON WERTHEIM

 NSIDE MAYSVILLE BARBER SHOP, TIME doesn't act its age. Small but tidy, the place has been at the same spot on Dublin Street in Mobile for decades, and there's little indication that it's a day beyond 1975.

The air is thick with wintergreen, baby powder and testosterone. Above the soda machine that sells Cokes for 50 cents, a television is tuned to daytime fare you haven't seen in years. (*Family Feud* is still on the air?) The decor is mostly yellowed photos of local sports stars. There are only three hydraulic chairs inside the shop. But two benches along the walls accommodate at least a dozen people, the equivalent of church pews or ringside bleacher seats. At all hours of the day, men come to talk sports and sex and politics, swap jokes and conspiracy theories. They tell and retell stories, a disproportionate number of which turn on the phrase, *But then I come to find out. . . .*

There's another regular, originally from the neighborhood, who seldom rolls up in the same car twice in a row. On this day it's a tan SUV. He goes 6' 6", maybe 280 pounds, wearing a Phillies cap, a gold tube of a necklace, a red T-shirt reading WITHOUT VICTORY THERE IS NO SURVIVAL. With a boyish, meaty face set off by a thin mustache, he looks both older and younger than his 26 years. JaMarcus Russell comes to Maysville three or four times a week, ostensibly to get his head shaved clean but also to get his ego stroked. The shop is where he's accepted, adored even, where he hangs comfortably. As the razor hums, he can express his mix of emotions—pride and embarrassment, defiance and remorse. And if it comes in a swirl of contradictions, here, somehow, it still makes sense.

In the spring of 2007, the Raiders selected Russell, a junior at LSU, with the No. 1 pick, and the barber shop erupted. His name hasn't prompted nearly the same enthusiasm since. Russell played three seasons, and won few fans and fewer games—just seven of the 25 he started—before Oakland released him in May 2010. No other team picked him up.

Russell's fall has been spectacular: He has replaced Ryan Leaf, by an order of magnitude, as the biggest bust in NFL history. And it has been accompanied by a level of glee that verges on creepy. If Michael Vick exposed the fans' capacity for forgiveness, the depth of their compassion, their love of a comeback, Russell has inspired the opposite: To an unprecedented degree he has become a vessel for every disgruntled fan's bile. Call it regression to the mean.

It's been two autumns now since Russell last played a down of organized football. This fall, when capable quarterbacks have been in high demand and short supply, he's gotten no calls.

Trips to the barbershop notwithstanding, Russell has found security in obscurity. He has little use for media—mainstream, digital or social.

He's unsure whom he despises more, the pundits who routinely rip him on the air or the bloggers who do the same anonymously. Going nowhere in particular, Russell often drives the interstates of the Gulf Coast, past fog-shrouded bayous, magnolias and gumbo shacks. Hidden by tinted windows, he lets his texts and voicemails backlog. "He can be a mystery man," says an uncle, Albert Russell, a chemistry professor at Tuskegee University. "He doesn't really like to talk about everything he's been through. You can understand it." Every man, though, has a breaking point. Russell has stood by as his name has become a punch line.

But now it's a few days after the death of Al Davis, the Raiders' idiosyncratic owner, the man who drafted Russell and conferred on him tens of millions of dollars. Russell has decided he's in the mood to talk. It's time, he reckons, to give his side of the story.

His massive torso covered by a leopard-print cutting cape, Russell settles into the first chair at Maysville. Gray-haired proprietor Moses Packer, known to all as Black Sheep, is ready to work.

Russell orders the blinds pulled. He tells the gallery they're welcome to stay, and they all do. But no one else can enter. The vertical bars on the door are fastened, the CLOSED sign unfurled. "I'm warning y'all," says Russell, smiling, "there's gonna be some cursing." The gallery whoops. And with that, in a rumbling drawl, JaMarcus Russell begins his defense of the outstanding charges.

Russell has become the poster dude for lethargy. —*San Francisco Chronicle*
During his time in Oakland, Russell's work ethic was considerably less than exemplary. Most damning were reports that he fell asleep during team meetings. "My first year, I had to be in at 6:30 before practice and be on the treadmill for an hour," he says. "Then meetings come, I sit down, eat my fruit. We watch film, and maybe I got tired. Coach Flip [quarterback coach John DeFilippo] pulled me aside and said, 'What are you doing for night life?' I said, 'Coach, I'm just chilling.' He said, 'I need to get you checked out.' I did the sleep test, and they said I had apnea."

JaMarcus Russell is so fat he eats out of a satellite dish. He sweats gravy.
—comment at *National Football Post*
During Russell's time with the Raiders his weight fluctuated, not least when he returned to the Gulf Coast in the off-season and indulged in various deep-fried specialties. "I put weight on easy, and I can take it off easy. Do I look fat now?" If Russell were a steak, you might say he's heavily marbled. But fat? No. He's not in NFL shape, but he doesn't look far off.

JaMarcus Russell: Purple Drank Connoisseur. —*Moviemike.blogspot.com*
Over the Fourth of July weekend in 2010, Mobile police, acting on a tip, raided Russell's mansion near Mobile Bay. Next to his bed they found a cup containing a codeine-laced liquid. Though Russell admits he failed

a drug test for codeine while in the NFL, he says he was taking cough syrup at the time to combat his sleep apnea. As for the arrest, a friend of Russell's who was in the house claimed the drink was his. The charge against Russell was dropped. "I don't have a drug problem," he says. "What I do have is police trailing every car I got like I'm a dope dealer."

JaMarcus Russell is broke. —*Yardbarker*
Claims that Russell is in dire straits circulated over the summer when TMZ reported that his Oakland Hills mansion had fallen into foreclosure after he failed to make mortgage payments amounting to close to $200,000. Not so, Russell says. He just sold the house. "Football isn't paying me now," he says. "You make $1 million a game and you can do whatever. It's not like that anymore; I need to put myself in a place where those zeroes in the bank last for a long time. But I'm not broke. Far from it."

SO HOW DID THE TOP PICK IN THE NFL DRAFT, WITH NO PHYSical injury, find himself out of the league at 24? How did a player so coveted become so unwanted so quickly? Analyze Russell's downfall and you get an algorithm for bad luck, bad advice and bad decisions.

Start with the Raiders. Drafting Russell was a classic case of overvaluing a player based on intuition and misleading data. While few doubted his abilities in the run-up to the draft, some voiced concern over less quantifiable aspects of Russell's game, in particular his maturity. Was his laid-back nature a reflection of poise or apathy? "The only thing that's going to keep [Russell] from being great is him," NFL Network draft expert Mike Mayock said at the time.

"Basically, Al Davis fell in love with [Russell], and if anyone had doubts, he didn't want to hear it," says a former Raiders executive. "You could justify JaMarcus, but it was based mostly on his arm strength. Great, but how many times a game does a guy throw 60 yards on the run?" A congenitally dysfunctional organization, the Raiders could scarcely have been a worse fit. They surrounded Russell with mediocre talent: Justin Fargas was no Marcus Allen, Ronald Curry no Tim Brown, Lane Kiffin no John Madden. The front office and coaching staff were crippled by infighting.

And during his time in Oakland, Russell says 11 of his family members or friends died, including his uncle Ray Ray Russell, a father figure. "I went through so much no one knew about," he says. "Go to a funeral on Saturday, fly into the game on Sunday. Then I hear, 'He doesn't lead by example.' Really?" The wounds still clearly raw, Russell can recall, word for word, entire passages of dialogue with Raiders teammates and staff. The coaches who complimented Russell (or blamed his linemen) to his face, and then ripped him behind his back. The teammates who complained of his leadership but didn't accept his offer to come to Mobile, all expenses paid, and work out with him in the off-season.

"Things weren't going right, and it felt sometimes like everything fell back on me," he says. "I take some responsibility, but I was one guy. . . . I may have missed a throw, but I didn't give up 42 points, I didn't miss a block."

Russell, of course, bears plenty of responsibility himself. As a rookie he held out through training camp before signing a six-year, $61 million deal on Sept. 12, 2007, with $32 million guaranteed. That contract would become Exhibit A when the NFL owners argued for a rookie wage scale this past off-season, one of the key elements in the new collective bargaining agreement. The outsized contract created outsized expectations. "With that kind of money," says Albert Russell, "there were negative judgments before he threw his first pass."

When JaMarcus did throw one, too often it fell to the ground. He completed just 52.1% of his passes, threw more interceptions (23) than touchdowns (18) and lost 15 fumbles. Russell's 65.2 career passer rating is anorexic, but it was in keeping with his approval rating among fans. A few wayward passes or sacks and the Black Hole would break out in spontaneous chants: *JaMarcus sucks! JaMarcus sucks!*

Russell grew up on Marine Street in the Oakdale section of Mobile, raised by a single mom, Zina, who held a variety of minimum-wage jobs. Unlike some friends and neighbors, Russell didn't go hungry. And he always had a seersucker suit to wear to church. But the family was not rich. Says Russell, "Put it this way: I got free lunch."

When Russell signed his NFL contract, he became unfathomably wealthy overnight. "And you know what?" says Terry Green, his aunt. "He spent it like any other 21-year-old kid would." Yes and no. True, he bought items that had once seemed abstractions: jewelry, a fleet of cars and a gated waterfront estate that looks like something out of *Gone with the Wind*. For this Russell is unapologetic. "What am I supposed to do?" he says. "Not get nicer clothes to wear and nicer cars to drive?"

But Russell also spread considerable wealth around Mobile. If you live in town and have eaten Thanksgiving turkey through a food drive these past few years, there's a good chance Russell paid for it. He's bought supplies and library books for local schools and uniforms for local sports teams. When he heard about a family that had lost its home in a fire, he says he drove up, handed the mother $10,000 in cash and drove off. He underwrote the renovation of his church, Sure Word Outreach Ministries.

Russell recently noticed that an alarming number of his old Mobile neighbors were confined to wheelchairs. Sometimes it was diabetes.

Sometimes, as in the case of a boyhood friend, Ralph Wiggins, it was because of a gunshot wound. Russell bought supplies, and he and his cousin Daryl Davis built ramps at many of their homes. Last year Russell hosted a party at the park where, growing up, he spent countless hours playing sports. He fed hundreds, and if kids could show him a report card of straight A's, Russell bought them bikes, MP3 players and GoPhones.

"Like Santa Claus!" interjects one of the Maysville congregants. "If I do go broke," says Russell, who is unmarried and has no children, "it's going to be from providing for my neighborhood and my family." ∎

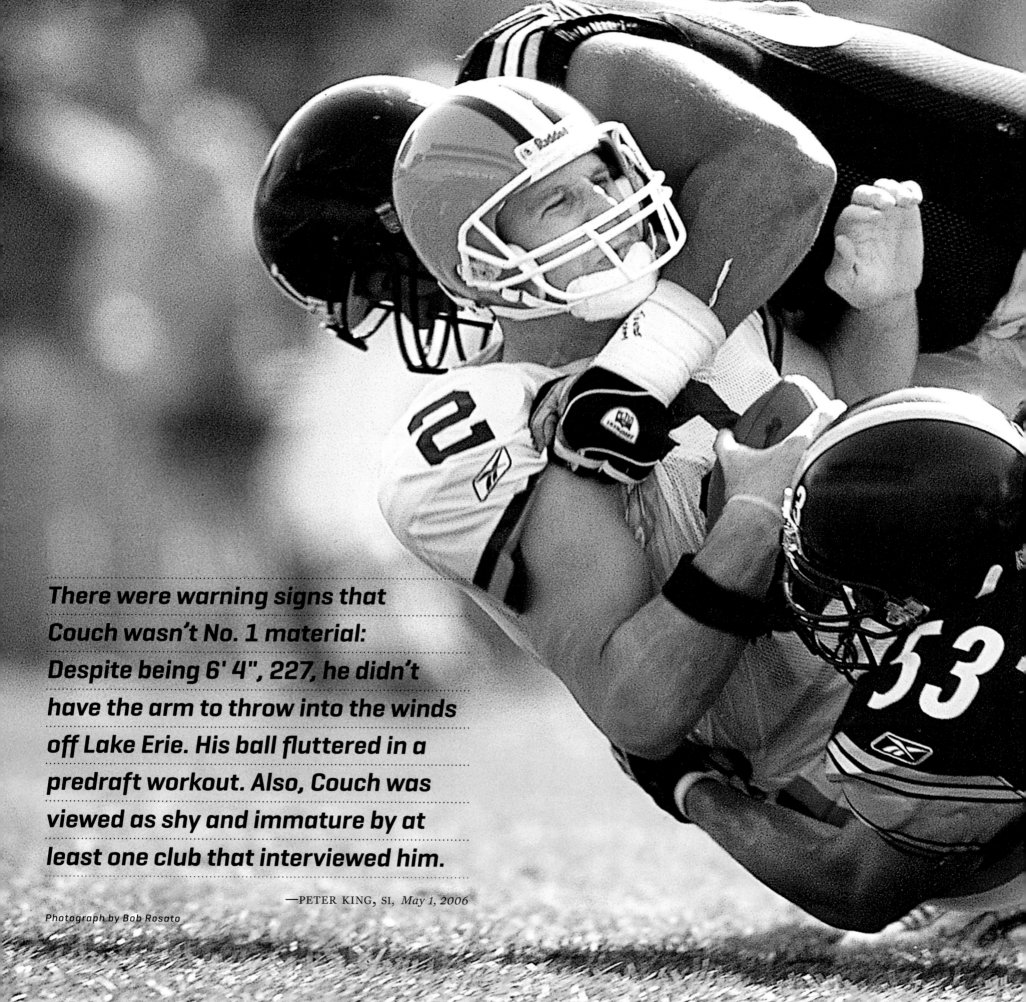

TIM COUCH The expansion Browns passed on Donovan McNabb to take Couch first overall in '99; he had one winning season, in 2002, but was out of the NFL after 2003.

There were warning signs that Couch wasn't No. 1 material: Despite being 6' 4", 227, he didn't have the arm to throw into the winds off Lake Erie. His ball fluttered in a predraft workout. Also, Couch was viewed as shy and immature by at least one club that interviewed him.

—PETER KING, SI, *May 1, 2006*

Photograph by Bob Rosato

RACIAL

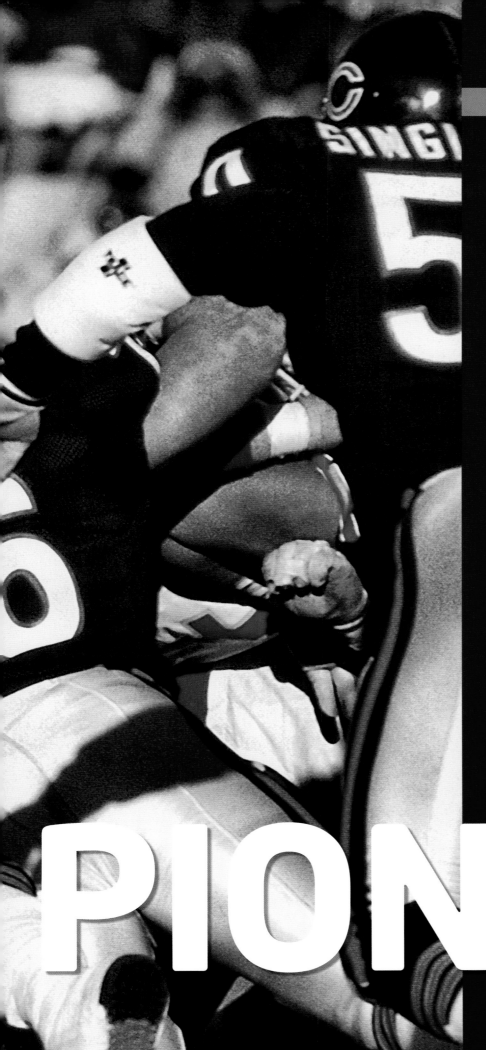

THE HISTORY OF the NFL quarterback is strikingly pale-complexioned for a reason. For many years, black players weren't allowed to play at all, and it was many more years before they were allowed to play the game's most vital position. Here are the intrepid souls who broke the color barrier and paved the way for a more equitable league

DOUG WILLIAMS He was the first black QB to be taken in the first round of the NFL draft, in 1979 by the Bucs, but he would earn lasting fame in Washington.

PIONEERS

Photograph by John Iacono

A Slow March To Equality

BY PHIL TAYLOR

On January 31, 1988, MARLIN BRISCOE WAS SITTING IN A SAN DIEGO jail, locked up on drug possession charges, watching Doug Williams become the first African-American quarterback to win a Super Bowl. After a nine-year pro career during which he became the first black quarterback in modern pro football history, for the Denver Broncos, Briscoe's life was in ruins from a crack cocaine addiction. Yet when the Super Bowl ended, the tears that ran down his face were joyful.

"I was so proud at that moment," he says. "I knew something historic had happened, and I felt that I had played a part in getting us to that day."

He was right. Briscoe, who ultimately conquered his drug problems and went on to become an administrator at Boys & Girls Clubs in Southern California, was one of the trailblazing black quarterbacks who chipped away at the racial stereotyping that for decades had made quarterback a whites-only position in the NFL. Some of these pioneers had distinguished careers, like Williams and Warren Moon. Others had just a brief chance to take snaps under center, like Briscoe and the aptly named Willie Thrower. But they were all instrumental in breaking down the league's racial barriers.

Like a lot of longtime American institutions, the NFL has a racial history that is in many ways shameful. Although one of its first stars was Fritz Pollard, the black quarterback and coach of the Akron Pros in the old American Professional Football Association, which would eventually become the NFL in the 1920s, the league eventually fell in step with the segregationist times. From 1934 through 1945 the NFL was all-white, as an unspoken agreement among its owners completely excluded black players. Highly decorated college stars were snubbed because of their skin color, including Kenny Washington, a dynamic UCLA running back who led the country in total yards in 1939 yet went unchosen in the league's 22-round draft. (It was Washington who eventually broke the color barrier when the Rams signed him in 1946, due to pressure from the Los Angeles Coliseum Commission.)

Even after the blackballing ended, opportunities for blacks to play quarterback were limited because of a prevailing belief that they lacked the intelligence and leadership ability to play the position. For years African-Americans who had played quarterback all their lives hit a wall once they reached the NFL. After starting at QB in college at Minnesota, Tony Dungy went undrafted and had to accept a switch to safety when the Steelers signed him as a free agent in 1977. The league was similarly uninterested in Moon as a quarterback, even after a stellar career at Washington that included the Rose Bowl MVP award in '78. Moon signed instead with the Canadian Football League and starred there for six seasons before attitudes changed enough for him to get his chance in the NFL, where he became a first-ballot Hall of Famer.

It's regrettable enough that dozens of would-be black quarterbacks from the 1930s to the '80s experienced similar resistance from the NFL. But there is also no telling how many other young black athletes were either steered away from the position or chose not to play it at the youth level because they saw no chance of a professional future at QB.

After the anomaly of Pollard, progress was slow. In 1949 George Taliaferro became the first black player ever to be drafted by an NFL team when he was selected in the 13th round by the Bears. He signed instead with the L.A. Dons, who took him in the first round of the All-America Football Conference's draft, and he threw for 790 yards that season. A year later, though, he joined the NFL's New York Yanks and, while he did attempt seven passes, he was listed as a halfback and never took snaps under center.

It wasn't until Oct. 18, 1953 that an African-American took a snap as a T formation quarterback in an NFL game. Thrower, a former Michigan State quarterback who had gone—not surprisingly—undrafted, replaced struggling Bears QB George Blanda against the 49ers at Soldier Field in Chicago. Thrower completed 3 of 8 passes for 27 yards before coach George Halas reinserted Blanda. Thrower didn't throw another pass that season and never played in the NFL again, finishing his career

in Canada. But his brief appearance inspired at least one future QB, namely Moon, who thanked him in his Hall of Fame acceptance speech.

Every time a black quarterback took the field, however briefly, it pushed the door open wider for the next one, even if only a sliver. After Thrower, it was 15 years before Briscoe became the next black QB to appear in a pro game. The Broncos turned to him in 1968 after their starter was injured and his backups were ineffective, and although he threw for 14 touchdowns in 11 games, he was released before the next season. He signed with the Bills, who converted him to wide receiver. Briscoe never played quarterback again.

Such were the small advances that black QBs made when opportunities arose. There was no Jackie Robinson, no one who broke through and immediately became such a great player that it was impossible to keep him on the bench. Instead it was the cumulative effect of all of the black QBs, over the course of decades, that slowly made the difference. It was because of them that the idea of an African-American under center became a slightly less foreign concept, which helped lead to James Harris becoming the first black full-time starter at the position for the Los Angeles Rams in 1974.

Then came Williams, whose Super Bowl performance was impossible for the football world to ignore. After a week of pre-Super Bowl questioning from the media about the historical significance of being the first black quarterback to reach the title game, Williams responded to the pressure by throwing for 340 yards and four touchdowns while winning the MVP award in the Redskins' 42–10 rout of the Broncos.

After that, it was no coincidence that the influx of black quarterbacks became, if not a flood, then at least more than a trickle. Until then, there had rarely been more than one black starter in the league at any time, but in the 10 years after Williams's MVP performance, multiple QBs, including Moon, Randall Cunningham, Rodney Peete, Jeff Blake, Steve McNair and Kordell Stewart all became starters.

The QBs that would follow them in the decades to come—Donovan McNabb, Cam Newton, Robert Griffin III and Russell Wilson among them—stand on the shoulder pads of these pioneers. With their talent and even more than that, their persistence, they made the NFL a racially more enlightened league in which the sight of a black quarterback is no longer uncommon. The NFL cannot be proud of the discriminatory parts of its history, but at least it's just that—history. ∎

Thrower won a title at Michigan State before becoming the first African-American to take snaps at QB in the modern NFL. | *Photograph by AP*

VINCE EVANS It was rare to see a black man lead the huddle when he joined the Bears in 1977 but far less so when he finished his career as a Raider in '95.

GEORGE TALIAFERRO He completed almost 500 passes for over 2,200 yards as a pro, but he was always listed as a halfback, never taking snaps under center.

ONE SUPER SHOW

UNDER THE PRESSURE OF BEING THE FIRST BLACK QUARTERBACK IN A SUPER BOWL, DOUG WILLIAMS DELIVERED A REDSKINS VICTORY AND ONE OF THE GREATEST QB PERFORMANCES IN THE GAME'S HISTORY

Excerpted from SPORTS ILLUSTRATED, *February 8, 1988* | BY PAUL ZIMMERMAN

OR TWO WEEKS LEADING UP TO THE Washington Redskins' 42–10 victory over the Denver Broncos in Super Bowl XXII, Doug Williams was asked the same question. Often it was disguised by another question, or buried in a mass of them, like a tin whistle in a Cracker Jack box. But it was always there.

At one interview session it wasn't even put as a question. A newsman merely said, "Black, Doug." Williams smiled and said what he had been saying all along: "[Coach] Joe Gibbs and [GM] Bobby Beathard didn't bring me in to be the first black quarterback in the Super Bowl. They brought me in to be the quarterback of the Washington Redskins."

The 32-year-old Williams had put up with much adversity in his nine years in professional football, but all week his press conferences in San Diego were filled with friendly faces. Indeed, how could you not like Williams, who treated every person with a microphone or a notepad, as well as every fan, with kindness and consideration?

He chose his words carefully. He said that both on and off the field he thought he was a role model for young players, white and black alike. "I'm glad if I've opened doors for young [black] quarterbacks like Rodney Peete [of Southern Cal] and Don McPherson [of Syracuse]," he said. He also said that he didn't feel he had to have a spectacular game. "I don't have to play well for us to win," said Williams. "What I have to do is not beat the Redskins by throwing interceptions or turning the ball over."

But on Sunday he did play exceptionally well. He was especially impressive in one furious quarter of football, a quarter in which records toppled so fast the statisticians could barely keep track of them, a quarter that earned Williams MVP honors and Washington its second Super Bowl win in three tries. (The Skins won in 1983 and lost in '84.) So breathtaking was his team's second-quarter outburst and the blowout it led to that even Williams was a bit stunned. "Can you express the joy you feel now?" he was asked after the game.

"Not yet," he said. "Catch me next week in Zachary, Louisiana."

First the numbers. In five possessions the Redskins established a postseason record for one quarter of 35 points on five TDs. They turned a 10–0 deficit into a 35–10 lead, thereby ending the show before the Rockettes could even get warmed up for their halftime number. Williams had nine completions in 11 attempts for 228 yards and four touchdowns. His scoring passes covered, in order, 80, 27, 50 and 8 yards. In that quarter Washington racked up a playoff-record 356 yards of offense. It may be a regular-season record as well. "We don't keep one-quarter records," said Seymour Siwoff, head of the Elias Sports Bureau, which handles NFL stats, "but geez, 356 yards. Who could have gained more than that?"

Gone were the painstaking, clock-killing drives that have become a Washington trademark under Gibbs. The most plays consumed on one drive—a 79-yarder—were seven. Another, covering 80 yards, required only one play. The other drives covered 64 yards in five plays, 74 in two and 60 in three. Total plays, including a quarterback kneel to close the half: 19. Total time of possession: 5:54.

The best thing about it, if you are a Washington fan, was that it was far from a one-man show. It was simply a team reaching perfection on all levels: Williams's passing; the running game, featuring a little-known rookie named Timmy Smith, who added slash and dash to the Skins' old five- and six-yard standby, the Counter Gap play; a defense that clogged Broncos quarterback John Elway's passing lanes, kept the pressure on him and gave him little room to maneuver outside the pocket; a brilliant little receiver named Ricky Sanders, who had made his reputation catching Jim Kelly passes in the USFL; and a line that blocked the way you draw it on the play charts.

Smith, Sanders and Williams all set Super Bowl records. Smith, a fifth-round draft pick out of Texas Tech, got his by rushing for 204 yards (on 22 carries). Sanders, who made nine catches starting in place of the injured Art Monk, broke the mark for receiving yardage with 193, and Williams, who finished with 18 completions in 29 attempts, threw for a record 340 yards. As a team, Washington went into the books with 602 total yards and 280 on the ground. But the game was won in that wild second quarter.

The Skins' second-half score, a four-yard run by Smith, was frosting. A game that had been billed as potentially the first down-to-the-wire Super Bowl since the Baltimore Colts' 16–13 win over the Dallas Cowboys in '71 was a rout.

Williams's counterpart on the Broncos, Elway, had taken a beating. He threw for 257 yards but completed only 14 of 38 throws. Denver's whole offensive operation seemed to be overmatched by the coverages and pass-rush schemes devised by Washington defensive coordinator Richie Petitbon. "We've got to be a better football team—I don't think we're good enough to win the Super Bowl," said a disconsolate Elway.

On his way to a victory celebration and rehab on a sore left knee he'd twisted in the first quarter, Williams was asked one final question. "What was your lowest moment as a pro?"

"I'll tell you one thing I'll always remember," he said. "When I was with Tampa Bay and we lost to Dallas in the [1981] playoffs and I got sacked four times, I got this beautifully wrapped package with a nice bow on top. When I opened it, there was a rotten watermelon inside. The note said, 'If it wasn't for your black ass, Tampa Bay would have won.' You don't forget things like that."

Super Sunday will be a far better memory, for sure. ∎

Williams made history by completing 9 of 11 passes for 228 yards and four TDs—in the second quarter alone. | *Photograph by Andy Hayt*

MARLIN BRISCOE

PRO FOOTBALL CAN be about as proud of its record on integrating the quarterback position as Mississippi is on desegregating its schools. Of course, it didn't require the intervention of federal troops, as it did in Mississippi in 1962, but it did take the pros six more years, an injury to a starter and the poor play of three backups before the AFL's Denver Broncos gave Marlin Briscoe a chance in 1968.

Briscoe *[15, right]* was an NAIA All-America quarterback at Nebraska-Omaha before he was drafted in the 14th round in 1968, but, as was usual then, he was quickly moved to defensive back. To be fair to the Broncos, he was only 5' 11", 177 pounds, and they did give him a tryout at QB. No surprise, he was then assigned to the defense.

But starter Steve Tensi was injured late in camp, and in the first two games of the season, both losses, backups John McCormick, Jim LeClair and Joe DiVito were outscored 58–12. So with Denver trailing 17–10 with 9:52 left against the Patriots on Sept. 29, coach Lou Saban gave Briscoe his shot. He led Denver on a five-play, 80-yard scoring drive late in the game, and though the Broncos lost 20–17, Briscoe earned a start the following week. He was conscious the whole time of his place in history. "I think other black athletes, like Jackie Robinson, must have had the same feeling," he said.

The good feeling didn't last. Briscoe threw for 1,589 yards the rest of the way and his 14 passing TDs are still a Denver rookie record, but in the off-season he wasn't even invited to QB meetings, and he was eventually granted his release when he objected to being put back on defense.

He signed with Buffalo, which already had Jack Kemp and James Harris at QB, so he moved to wide receiver—a position he had never played before. It's a testament to his athleticism that he became a Pro Bowler as a wideout and won two Super Bowl rings there in his next stop, with Miami.

His life after football has been filled with triumph and despair. He was a successful bond trader for many years before he developed a crack cocaine addiction and lost everything, becoming homeless. He eventually got himself clean and went to work for Boys & Girls Clubs in Southern California.

But he'll always have the satisfaction that he changed the game. As he said then, when he broke the color barrier, "Maybe there are great black quarterbacks coming out of college now who won't get switched [to another position]. It's nice knowing you helped."   —G.K.

Photograph by Bill Johnson/The Denver Post/Getty Images

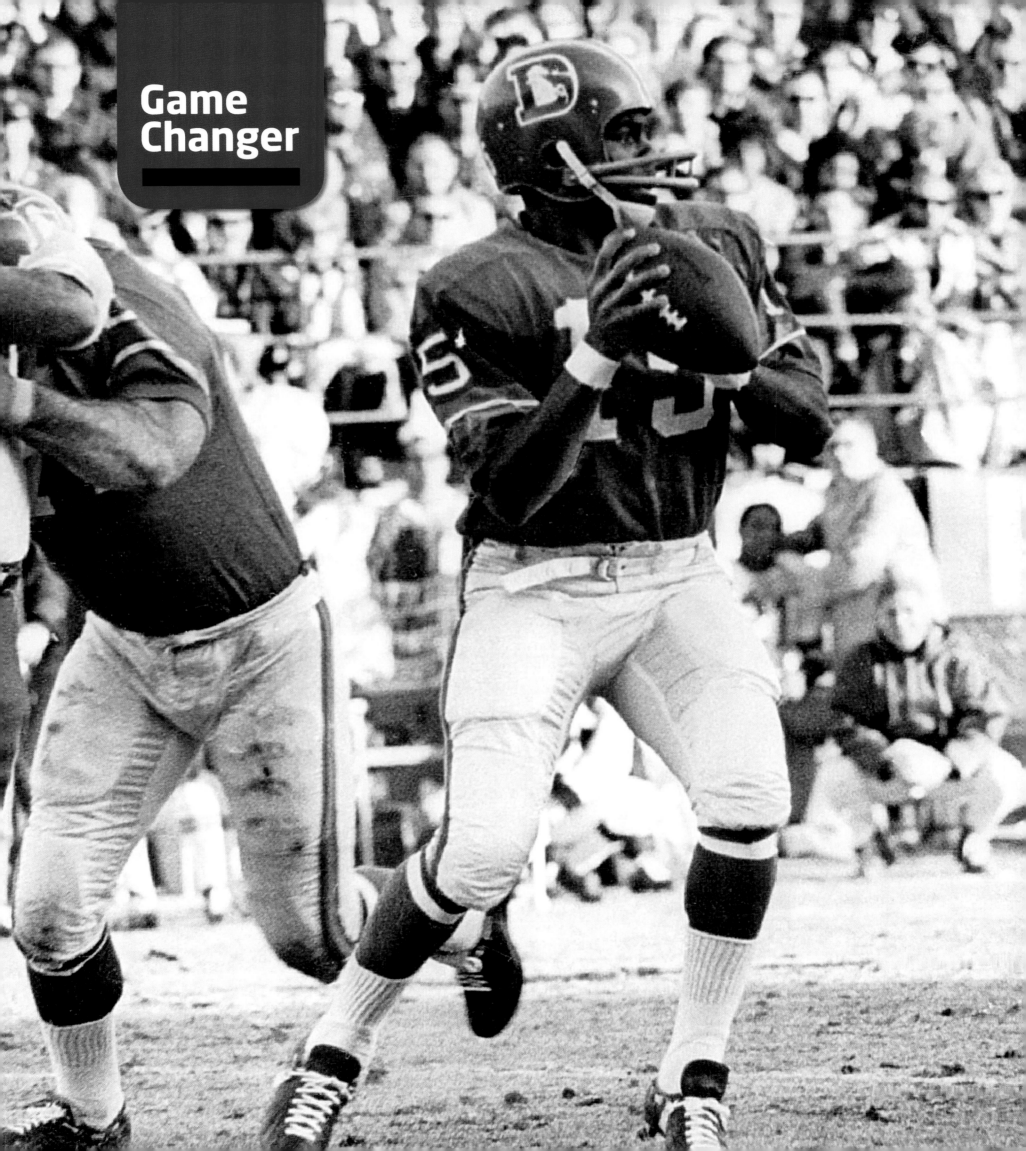

JAMES HARRIS He was the first African-American quarterback to win a postseason game, with the L.A. Rams in 1974, and the first to go to a Pro Bowl.

Gilliam led the Steelers to four wins and a tie in their first six games in 1974, but after a bad performance in the sixth game, a 20–16 win over Cleveland, he was replaced by Bradshaw. Gilliam was to stay on the bench for the next year and a half.

—ROBERT H. BOYLE, SI, *November 5, 1979*

JOE GILLIAM His 1974 opening day victory—the first by a black QB in the postwar NFL—put him on the cover of SI, but drug use and poor play drove him out of the NFL by '76.

FATHER MOON

AT EVERY STAGE OF HIS CAREFULLY PLOTTED LIFE, OILERS
QUARTERBACK WARREN MOON FACED DOUBT AND DISCRIMINATION,
AND HE RESPONDED WITH A WISDOM WELL BEYOND HIS YEARS

Excerpted from SPORTS ILLUSTRATED, *September 27, 1993* | BY LEIGH MONTVILLE

SHE KICKED OFF HER SHOES TO DANCE. Felicia Hendricks liked to dance and this was a party and kicking off your shoes seemed to be an obvious thing to do. Her boyfriend told her she was crazy. Why take off your shoes? Someone could steal them. They could be lost. This was somebody else's house.

Why take off your shoes in somebody else's house? Anything could happen. "Don't worry, Warren," Felicia Hendricks said. "No one will take my shoes."

How about this guy? He was so different from the other kids she knew. Daddy. That was his nickname. Harold Warren Moon. Everybody's daddy. The average teenage boy in Los Angeles in the early '70s seemed to be a pinball of emotions and noise, bouncing off the city walls, screaming into the adolescent night. Not this boy.

The party, that night she kicked off her shoes, was a celebration in a couple of ways. First, Hamilton High had beaten neighboring Crenshaw High in football, and second, Moon, the Hamilton quarterback, was still alive. There had been a death threat that week. A Crenshaw player had told Felicia that if Hamilton won, Moon was going to be killed. Simple as that. In other places this perhaps could be dismissed as pregame trash talk. But in Los Angeles in 1973 gangs had begun their rise—the Crips and the Bloods and all the rest—and this Crenshaw player was a known gang member. When he talked, it paid to listen. Moon, for one, had listened.

Felicia pointed out the guy on the street, and Moon went straight for him. Felicia thought there would be trouble, a fight. Moon put out his hand to shake. "Hi," he said. "I'm Warren Moon. Good luck on Friday night." So different. Following a sensible discussion with the Crenshaw player, he had nevertheless sensibly informed his mother, his coach and the appropriate authorities, and then he proceeded to play the game in which he sensibly cleaned Crenshaw's clock. Now there was the victory party. Felicia danced and Moon danced, and at some point in the festivities, some kids from Crenshaw arrived. Moon stopped dancing. Were they here for him? No. A Hamilton kid was dancing with a Crenshaw kid's girl, and as the fight began, as the kid from Crenshaw grabbed a lamp and swung it at the Hamilton kid's head, Moon grabbed Felicia's hand and pulled her out the front door. He started running down the street and she ran with him, and when the sound of pistol shots came from the house, Moon and Felicia dived to the sidewalk together. "My shoes," she said. "They're still back there."

"I told you not to take off your shoes," he said. "Maybe now you'll learn." Daddy. Daddy Warren. She never saw the shoes again and never went to another party for the rest of the season. Daddy Warren wouldn't allow it.

He is the father. Always the father. . . .

This was not a normal postgame moment in a locker room. The son was crying, and the father had fathering work to do. The newly enriched quarterback of the Houston Oilers had to conduct an extemporaneous lesson on racism. The night was Dec. 2, 1991. The Oilers had lost to the Eagles 13–6. The week before, he had thrown five interceptions against the Steelers. The quarterback was married now to Felicia, and they had four children. Joshua, 9, was the oldest. He was sitting in the stands with his mother at the Astrodome, and the crowd became ugly.

The quarterback was on the verge of signing a five-year contract extension, and the news was public. The Oilers could not cross the goal line, and the boos increased. The words became nastier. On the way out of the stands, Joshua heard a man say, "I can't believe they gave that n----- $14.3 million."

Joshua wasn't really sure what the word meant, but he knew it was bad. His father had to explain. There were cameras and reporters in the room. It was the worst possible situation in which to talk about deep and disturbing subjects, but that did not matter. "I am the type of person who confronts things when they arise," Moon says now. He explained the word to his son. He explained that there are ignorant people in the world who say ignorant things. He said that while the man was directing those things at him, he was not the only target. The man hated a race of people. He would say ignorant things about a lot of people. Most people didn't feel that way, but a few did. That was a sad fact of life. The reporters who watched—John McClain of the *Houston Chronicle* was one of them—were touched. McClain says, "It made you want to cry."

The amazing aspect of the episode was the fact that Moon already was a solid member of the Houston community. This was his eighth season since coming down from Canada; he had picked Houston over five other NFL cities in a flat-out bidding war. He was a civic pillar, living year-round in Houston, making appearances everywhere, even establishing his own charitable foundation. What more did he have to do? The team's record, even with the loss, was 9–4. Was he a quarterback when he won and a "black quarterback" when he lost? Or was he always a "black quarterback," no matter what he did?

The days that followed were ugly too. His foundation logged over 200 calls that echoed the racist words in the stands. The talk shows were brutal, and it continued until Moon responded in the middle of the week on his TV show. He apologized.

Apologized? He told the people that he was sorry that he had played lousy, that he would try not to do it again. He said the loss was his fault. He said he hoped to play better. It was an astonishing response. "It defused everything," wide receiver Haywood Jeffires, a friend, says. "How could you beat that? An apology. I think of myself, if I heard those words, I'd be saying, 'Oh, yeah, well, come down here if you want a piece of me.' What Warren did.... He could have said a lot of things. Those five interceptions weren't all his fault. I think I was responsible for two of them myself. He could have talked about passes that were dropped, routes that were run incorrectly. He did none of that. He took the load the way he always does. That is why he is such a leader. How could you not follow someone like him? He is like Cesar Chavez or Arthur Ashe or Martin Luther King Jr." The response to the apology was as amazing as the apology itself. The phones rang again. People called to apologize for what they had said. The talk-show dialogue flipped to his accomplishments instead of his failings. The Oilers beat the Steelers 31–6 in their next game.

FOOTBALL WAS HIS MAIN GAME. HE DECIDED THAT EARLY. He looked at his mother and older sisters and decided that he wouldn't grow tall enough to be a pro basketball player. Baseball seemed to be a bore. He decided that he could play only one sport in high school because he had to work the rest of the year to help the family, and the sport would be football. Quarterback would be the position. He had discovered that he could throw a football longer, harder and straighter

than anyone he knew. He would take that arm all the way to the pros. That was his goal.

By the time he was a high school senior he was successful enough to be a Division I-A prospect, recruited by Arizona State and USC and other powers. But they wanted him to be a defensive back or a wide receiver. When what he wanted to be was a quarterback. Was he not being viewed as a quarterback because he was a black quarterback? Or was it because he was a city quarterback matched against quarterbacks from those heralded football programs in the suburbs? Or was it ... what? Whatever it was, it left him with an uneasy feeling of injustice.

He ended up at West L.A. Junior College, a place where he had been allowed to move freely as a quarterback, breaking passing records almost weekly as a freshman. Then the big colleges had finally decided to take a look at him as a quarterback ... with a little help. To spread the word that he was available, he mailed out his own game tapes to four-year colleges. He had a job in the athletic department, and when no one was around, he "borrowed" the coaching staff's game tapes, sending them out with the message that "it is important this tape be returned as soon as possible." Washington was the first school to express interest, and he was assured that he would have a fair chance to win the quarterback job. This was not a lie. Before the team had finished its first weeks of practice, Moon was the starter. The problem was that he won the job over Chris Rowland—an incumbent, a senior and, worse yet, a Washington native. The Huskies were still perennially low in the Pac-8 standings, doomed to extending their run of failure before coach Don James's rebuilding program could take hold. Shouldn't the local kid at least have a chance to play? Amid the bad feelings it became easy to put Moon's face on the team's failure. An easy black face. It wasn't a total racial situation; much of it was a case of the hometown hero against the interloper. But race was in the mix. As Moon played out his sophomore and junior seasons, and as he began his senior season, he was booed and heckled. By the end, as he quarterbacked Washington to an upset win over Michigan in the Rose Bowl, strangers were coming up to him on the street, all ages, all sizes, some with tears in their eyes, apologizing for anything they might have said.

He always has known the right move to make at the right time....
Life in Canada was not bad. It was very good, in fact. For the first time, he felt that race was not an issue. He felt that way from the moment he signed with Edmonton. It was curious that he had had to go to another country, to an overwhelmingly white city, to feel that he was just a player, good or bad, color not involved. He had left the U.S. with all of the old stereotypes unresolved. The NFL basically had rejected him as a quarterback. He was the Pac-8 Player of the Year, yet there was no interest in his talents. The mumbled word was that "he didn't have an arm." Didn't have an arm? That was the one thing he did have. His height, at 6' 2", might be average, and he never was the quickest runner, but he always thought he could throw with anyone.

Not one NFL team expressed serious interest in him. The talent hunters had little desire to see the Pac-8 Player of the Year throw the ball. What was the (black) Player of the Year to think? His agent, Leigh Steinberg, after making various calls, estimated that Moon would be drafted between the "fourth and seventh" rounds. Moon thought the fourth was being generous. Doug Williams, a black quarterback from Grambling, was projected as a certain first-round pick, but Moon did not think that fact eliminated the possibility of racism in his own case.

"Williams was a can't-miss guy, about 6' 4" and coming out of a pro offense with great statistics," Moon says. "I've always said the racism doesn't come with the obvious can't-miss guys. It's the guys who have to be developed, who have to sit on the bench for a while, who are affected. The NFL teams won't wait for them, for the black quarterbacks, to develop. They say, 'Go to Canada, then come back when you're ready.' The white quarterbacks sit on the bench in the NFL and learn."

He went to Canada. He never even waited for the NFL draft, signing early enough with Edmonton to be passed over by every team in the NFL. He was quarterback on a Canadian team that won five straight Grey Cup titles. The football was free-form and fun. The camaraderie was the best, the players and their families trapped together in this cold-weather city, almost forced to become closer friends. Canada was great, but.... There was interest at last from the NFL. The USFL had been born in 1983, and the two leagues were fighting for talent. Moon was a measurable, successful talent. A free agent. He announced his availability and entertained suitors. He visited six cities, talked with officials, researched teams and environments and offenses. In the end his choice was Houston. The contract was $6 million for five years. He became the highest-paid player in the game. Just like that. ∎

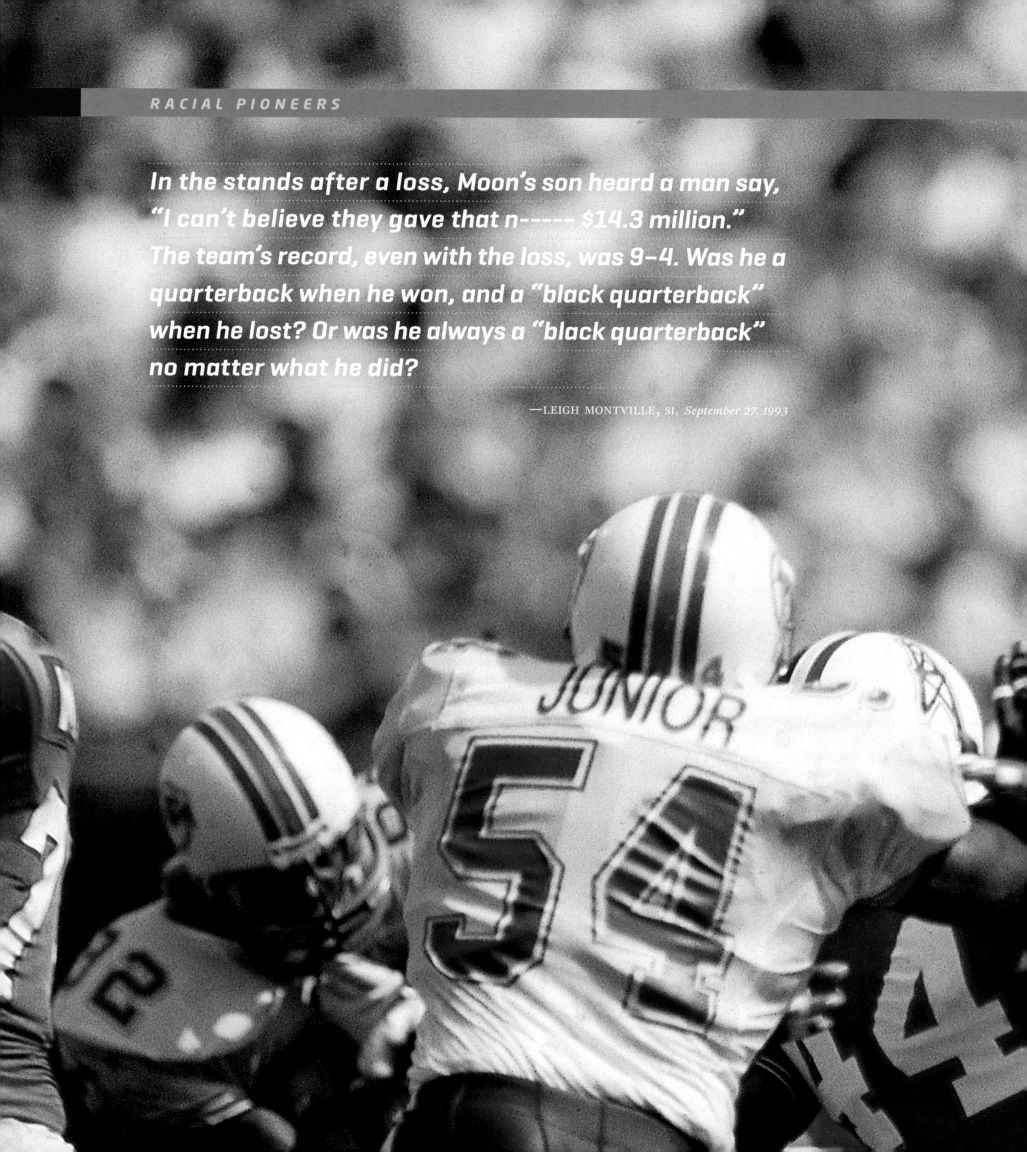

In the stands after a loss, Moon's son heard a man say,
"I can't believe they gave that n----- $14.3 million."
The team's record, even with the loss, was 9–4. Was he a
quarterback when he won, and a "black quarterback"
when he lost? Or was he always a "black quarterback"
no matter what he did?

—LEIGH MONTVILLE, SI, *September 27, 1993*

WARREN MOON Lukewarm NFL interest drove him to the CFL out of college, but he would become the NFL's highest-paid player with Houston in 1989 and go to nine Pro Bowls.

Photograph by Damian Strohmeyer

RIGHT OR WRONG, there is one thing that defines a pro football quarterback's legacy above all others: winning titles. A ring can elevate a mediocre QB, and not winning can diminish a great one. There have been 48 Super Bowls since the game's introduction in 1967, but only these 31 quarterbacks can say they have won the NFL's greatest prize

BART STARR In the minutes before the start of the first Super Bowl, Starr (15) could not have known how momentous this new event would become.

ULTIMATE

Photograph by Vernon Biever

In a League of Their Own

BY AUSTIN MURPHY

Contrary to news REPORTS, THE COAT WAS NEITHER MINK NOR chinchilla. Striding on rickety knees across the field to flip the coin before Super Bowl XLVIII, the 70-year-old Joe Namath was largely obscured inside a bulky, hooded coyote fur coat with white trim harvested from Norwegian foxes. As one wiseacre tweeted, "I'm not a big PETA guy but I don't agree with what #JoeNamath did to Lassie." Others exhibited more outrage. But sports fans of a certain age

had to chuckle. They got it. Namath, they realized, was evoking his glory days as Broadway Joe, his star turn as a New York Jets quarterback and unapologetic Lothario who rocked fur coats, modeled pantyhose and got a kick out of shocking bourgeois sensibilities.

If there was something vaguely surreal about his choice of outerwear on this 50° night at MetLife Stadium, Joe Willie got a pass. He was making use of privileges granted him as a member of a very exclusive fraternity.

But what if he hadn't led the Jets to a 16–7 victory over the Baltimore Colts in Super Bowl III, some 45 years earlier? Three days before that game, Namath famously guaranteed a Jets win over the heavily favored Colts. What if he'd failed to deliver that victory? Namath would just be some grinning, eccentric; a deluded septuagenarian satyr.

Broadway Joe doesn't have to worry about any of that. He won the big game. You win a Super Bowl, you earn a lifelong membership in a club that slightly warps and distorts logic. According to the bylaws of this establishment, journeymen Trent Dilfer and Brad Johnson are more accomplished than Hall of Famers Dan Marino and Jim Kelly, their careers more complete. Yes, Dilfer and Johnson, who respectively quarterbacked the Ravens and Buccaneers to victories in Super Bowls XXXV and XXXVII, were game managers whose unspoken

instructions going in were: Just don't screw it up. In a peripatetic career spanning four teams and 15 seasons, Johnson had a career quarterback rating of 82.5, which is a dozen points higher than that of Dilfer, who threw 113 touchdowns against 129 interceptions in his career, and was unceremoniously let go by the Ravens following that Super Bowl win.

And Dilfer's career quarterback rating comes in five points higher than that of Namath, whose 65.5 is the lowest of any Super Bowl–winning quarterback, and whose touchdown-to-interception ratio, 173 to 220, makes Dilfer's look downright . . . Montana-esque. Not that any of those gentlemen give a fig about a bunch of ancient statistics. They're smoking Cuban cigars and yukking it up in the Winners' lounge.

So powerful and potent is this contest, this unofficial national holiday, that it doesn't just determine a champion. The Super Bowl plays an outsized role in shaping individual legacies, as well. Some people have a problem with that. Fran Tarkenton, for one, doesn't think it's fair. The Super Bowl, he wrote in early 2014, is just "one football game, played on one day of the year . . . Winning or losing that one game doesn't make you a better or worse team, player or quarterback than you were the other 364 days of the year.

"Joe Montana and Tom Brady aren't great because they won so many Super Bowls," Tarkenton opined. Their greatness derived from "their great play every game, every season."

Tarkenton, you may recall, lost all three of his 1970s Super Bowl starts for the Vikings, making his assertion both wrong-headed and self-serving. What truer measure of greatness is there than how an athlete performs on the biggest stage? Brady and Montana share a preternatural, icy cool under pressure that served them especially well on Super Sunday. Their wins in those games—four for Montana, three for Brady—are inextricably bound to their reputations as champions.

While Jeff Hostetler, Doug Williams, Eli Manning and Jim Plunkett wouldn't insult your intelligence by claiming to be better quarterbacks than Marino or Kelly—or Warren Moon, or Dan Fouts, or Tarkenton, for that matter—they wouldn't trade places with those guys, either. They're just fine with their place in the annals of the game. They felt the heft of the Lombardi Trophy. They will probably only ever enter the Hall of Fame as spectators, but they won a Super Bowl. (Manning and Plunkett won it twice). They'll take that trade-off.

The converse is likely true. In a transcendent 17-year career Marino threw for 61,361 yards and 420 touchdowns. How many tens of thousands of yards, how many dozens of TDs would he exchange to feel even once the deep fulfillment that Terry Bradshaw and Montana each earned four times?

When Marino made it to the Super Bowl in just his second season, but lost—Montana and the 49ers drilled the Dolphins 38–16—the Dolphins faithful could take solace in his youth. He had thrown an astounding 48 touchdown passes going into those playoffs. Not only would he return to the big game, it was safely predicted, Marino would win it multiple times.

Instead he spent 15 futile seasons trying to get back to the big game, but never could. To his credit, Marino doesn't pretend that this yawning void on his résumé doesn't rankle, doesn't sting. "That's just part of life, man," he told a radio interviewer in 2010. "I never had that feeling, and that's the feeling you want to have as a player"—the feeling of achieving the goal toward which "you've worked your whole life."

Marino, Kelly, Moon and Fouts were exceptional talents and superb leaders who could've used a little more help from their GMs. None of the teams they often had to carry were renowned for the ferocity of their defenses. A pyrotechnical passing game will keep fans slack-jawed. But the old bromide still applies: Defense wins championships.

Just ask Brad Johnson, whose Buccaneers picked off Oakland's Rich Gannon five times in Super Bowl XXXVII. Ask Seattle's Russell Wilson, who was steady and effective against the Broncos in 2014, but who was also the beneficiary of one of the greatest defensive performances in the game's history.

Just as a relentless, suffocating defense can compensate for a host of offensive woes, a Super Bowl win on a quarterback's résumé can cover up a variety of flaws and shortcomings—like a capacious fur coat, come to think of it. Or a good pair of pantyhose. ∎

Four Super Bowl victories have burnished Montana's legend for preternatural poise. | *Photograph by John Iacono*

BART STARR SUPER BOWL I
PACKERS 35, CHIEFS 10

BART STARR SUPER BOWL II
PACKERS 33, RAIDERS 14

JOE NAMATH SUPER BOWL III
JETS 16, COLTS 7

LEN DAWSON SUPER BOWL IV
CHIEFS 23, VIKINGS 7

JOHNNY UNITAS SUPER BOWL **V**

COLTS 16, COWBOYS 13

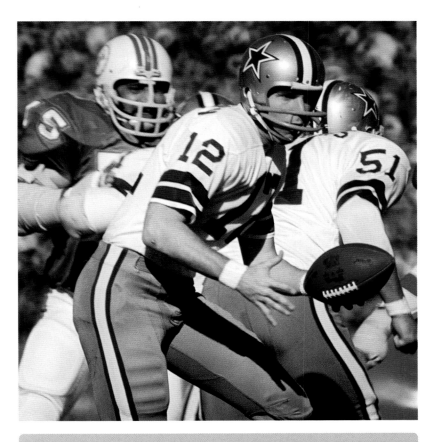

ROGER STAUBACH SUPER BOWL **VI**

COWBOYS 24, DOLPHINS 3

BOB GRIESE SUPER BOWL **VII**

DOLPHINS 14, REDSKINS 7

BOB GRIESE SUPER BOWL **VIII**

DOLPHINS 24, VIKINGS 7

TERRY BRADSHAW SUPER BOWL IX
STEELERS 16, VIKINGS 6

TERRY BRADSHAW SUPER BOWL X
STEELERS 21, COWBOYS 17

KEN STABLER SUPER BOWL XI
RAIDERS 32, VIKINGS 14

ROGER STAUBACH SUPER BOWL XII
COWBOYS 27, BRONCOS 10

TERRY BRADSHAW SUPER BOWL **XIII**
STEELERS 35, COWBOYS 31

TERRY BRADSHAW SUPER BOWL **XIV**
STEELERS 31, RAMS 19

JIM PLUNKETT SUPER BOWL **XV**
RAIDERS 27, EAGLES 10

JOE MONTANA SUPER BOWL **XVI**
49ERS 26, BENGALS 21

LI'L ABNER MAKES IT BIG

WHEN PITTSBURGH'S TERRY BRADSHAW WON HIS FIRST TWO SUPER BOWLS, HE WAS PRAISED PRIMARILY FOR HIS STRONG ARM. AS HE WON HIS NEXT TWO, THERE WAS NO DENYING HIS ARRIVAL AS A PLAY-CALLER AND LEADER

Excerpted from SPORTS ILLUSTRATED, *December 18, 1978* | BY RON FIMRITE

TERRY BRADSHAW WATCHED THE DYING rays of a December sun shimmer on the pond beyond the forest of hickory and pine. At his feet, the Doberman puppy, Jessie, was menacing the dachshund puppy, Rowdy, snatching up the tiny sausage of a dog in his powerful jaws. "That's enough, Jessie," Bradshaw admonished. "Man, sometimes I think that big dog wants a piece of the little fellow. And Rowdy is my pal. Heck, there's no dog I don't like." Buff colored cows sauntered through an open gate, nodding uncomprehendingly at their master. "They're my babies," said Bradshaw paternally as they passed. "I love 'em."

He looked out over the rolling, green, wooded hills of northern Louisiana, blue eyes squinting against the pale sunshine. He wore a fringed buckskin jacket and jeans, and a straw cowboy hat sat atop his balding pate. He was a rancher now, not a football player, and his strong resemblance to the television rancher, Chuck Connors, was more arresting than ever. "In springtime," Bradshaw said in a soft drawl, "this is the most beautiful place you've ever seen."

Time, place and circumstance collaborated to give Bradshaw this bucolic respite. The day before, he had quarterbacked the Pittsburgh Steelers to a bruising 13–3 win over the Houston Oilers. It was a game in which the final casualty figures listed eight Oilers and four Steelers with injuries, some serious. On that bloody afternoon, the Astrodome could have passed for the Alamo. But two Roy Gerela field goals and a Bradshaw touchdown pass had enabled the Steelers to clinch their sixth AFC Central Division championship in seven years and a berth in the playoffs.

As a reward, coach Chuck Noll had given his battered legions an unprecedented two days off. Because Houston is only 200 miles from his native Shreveport, La., Bradshaw capitalized on the holiday by driving with his parents, Bill and Novis, to the 400-acre cattle and horse ranch he owns south of his hometown. "The ranch is medicine to me," he says.

Bradshaw has always sought regeneration in his roots. He was born and reared in this God-fearing country. He first achieved celebrity as a star quarterback and record-setting javelin thrower at Shreveport's Woodlawn High, and he set passing records at Louisiana Tech in Ruston, 80 miles to the east. For all of his national exposure these past nine NFL seasons, the North remains a strange and hostile place to Bradshaw. Northern Louisiana is where he can kick off his boots and, within the bounds of Christian morality, "let the good times roll." This is not bayou country, with its Cajuns and its New Orleans, for that is as foreign to him as the cold, uncompromising North. This is ranching and farming and Bible-thumping country, as Southwestern in most ways as it is Southern.

When the world is too much with him, he looks homeward. After a disastrous rookie season in 1970, he pulled himself together back home, vowing to "show 'em" next time around. And when, a few years later, not only his career but also the very foundations of his life seemed to be in jeopardy, he turned once more to the fundamental beliefs of his childhood, "rededicating" himself to that old-time religion.

For a man thought by the glib and the uninformed to be simple, Terry Bradshaw has had a rather complex life. He was the first player selected in the 1970 draft, and he became, thereby, famous overnight. Nothing in his upbringing had prepared him for such recognition, and he squirmed in the limelight, a frightened and bewildered star. His country ways caused him to be too quickly characterized as an Ozark Ike type, and his Bible Belt philosophy made him appear more foolish than sincere among the supposedly sophisticated. He tried and failed to conceal his naiveté behind unnatural bravado, exposing himself to even more ridicule.

He has been married twice, to a beauty queen and an international ice-skating star. He has acted in a Hollywood movie (*Hooper*) opposite Burt Reynolds, and he enjoyed a brief, not entirely unsuccessful career as a country-and-western singer, a career he may well resume. Whatever he may become, now he is a football player who is having his best season, with a team-record 26 touchdown passes and 2,784 yards passing, and he is at long last earning his due as one of the game's finest quarterbacks.

Bradshaw has come some distance from a woeful beginning and a calamitous mid-career. The Steelers, who had not won any sort of championship in their previous 35 years in the NFL, had finished 1–13 in 1969, the season before Bradshaw's arrival. Fans and players alike had become hardened to defeat. In Bradshaw, who had passed for more than 7,000 yards in small-college football and had received top marks from all scouts, particularly because of an arm that could throw the ball on a line for what seemed like the entire length of the field, they saw a savior.

"When he arrived we were more or less desperate for anyone to turn us around," recalls Andy Russell, the retired linebacker. "Terry was portrayed as a magician who could transform perennial losers into Super Bowl champs." To acquaint the young Mandrake with his new teammates. Russell invited Bradshaw to a team party at his house. This otherwise friendly gesture had unhappy consequences. "Here he was, a rookie from the country faced with a bunch of cynical old veterans," says Russell. "You can imagine the scrutiny he was put under. I'm not sure a quarterback can ever become one of the boys—everyone, consciously or unconsciously, thinks he gets too much credit—but Terry just wasn't one to go out and match those old Steelers beer for beer and shot for shot. He wasn't into that silly macho thing. Still, we thought he could lead us out of the woods. I remember I went once to hear him give a speech before a church group. He was what they called 'witnessing.' Well, I'd never been to anything like that, but as I listened to him I sat there wondering if he could somehow convert that religious fervor into action on the field."

Bradshaw completed only 38.1% of his 218 passes his rookie season. He

and the other coaches were not as discouraged as Bradshaw believed them to be. From 1–13 to 5–9 in one year represented dramatic progress to them, and as Noll has said, "Terry was always the guy with the most talent." When Bradshaw reported to training camp in 1971, he was startled to see his name first on the depth chart. He rewarded Noll's confidence by completing 203 of 373 passes for 2,259 yards and 13 touchdowns, a superb season for a second-year man.

In 1974 his troubles began anew. He was divorced from his wife of 18 months, Melissa Babish, Miss Teen Age America of 1969, and in training camp he lost his starting job to third-year man Joe Gilliam. If an athlete's career is life in capsule—youth, middle age, old age, all in a dozen years—then Bradshaw suffered a mid-life crisis at 26.

"I'm a Baptist, a Christian," he says, "I pulled away from it in that year. I felt a lot of guilt over the divorce, and I'd lost my job. I'd failed. I didn't become an alcoholic or a whoremonger, but I was moody and depressed and I drank and hustled women in bars. I have never enjoyed those things. I'd been a devout Christian for so long, getting away from it affected me mentally. The ton of guilt brought me to my knees." It was then, he said, that he looked back to what he had been—a young man who cared more about the scriptures than the playbook. He prayed for another chance, although "I had a hard time believing God could forgive a jerk like me." Apparently He did, for within a year Jo Jo Starbuck entered his life.

Born Alicia Jo Starbuck, she was, like Bradshaw, both an athlete and a devout Christian. She had competed in two Olympics and skated professionally with the Ice Capades. Bradshaw, rededicated, saw her perform in Pittsburgh and immediately asked her out. She refused. Later, when she learned of his churchgoing ways, she sent him tickets to her next show in Pittsburgh. They had dinner that night. He proposed after two weeks. They became engaged a month later and were married on June 6, 1976. Though their jobs frequently separate them, they communicate regularly on the road and faithfully read the same passages of the Bible every day. "Jo Jo," says Terry, "is an angel."

Freed of his guilt and self-pity, Bradshaw regained his starting job midway through the 1974 season and led the Steelers to their first NFL championship with a 16–6 win over the Vikings in Super Bowl IX. The next year, with Bradshaw throwing 18 regular-season touchdown passes, the Steelers repeated, defeating the Cowboys 21–17 in Super Bowl X. The decisive TD in that game came on a 64-yard Bradshaw-to-Lynn Swann pass, a play called at the line of scrimmage when Bradshaw correctly detected Dallas in a safety blitz. He released the ball before he was hurled to the ground by a pack of Cowboys, and Swann caught it in open space. It was the sort of call one expects from intellectual quarterbacks like Tarkenton, Griese or Stabler. But Bradshaw? Yes, he is a smart quarterback, his unfortunate image to the contrary. Although he has been picking NFL defenses to pieces all year, he remains, in the eyes of the ignorant, "dumb." Noll, who is as outwardly emotional as a throw rug, bristles at any suggestion that his quarterback reads defenses remedially. "That's ridiculous," he snaps.

When the 49ers foolishly tried to blitz him in November, he deftly threw three touchdown passes. He engineered a masterly 11-play, 80-yard drive against Houston that transformed a bitter defensive struggle into a clear-cut Steeler victory. Bradshaw is nobody's fool, and he is exasperated and hurt by the slurs on his intelligence. "It is a thorn in my side, and it always will be," he says.

Griese, smallish and bespectacled, looks like a quarterback. Bradshaw looks as if he should be rushing one. And yet, says Russell, groping for the right word. "He is really . . . uh . . . well, vulnerable."

Maybe that is because he is more at home on the range. He is assured enough back at the ranch as he walks bowlegged toward his quarter horse, Flying Bolo Bars, soothing the beast with a country song and some sweet nonsense. He turns to a companion. "I love football now more than I ever did," he said, "but I don't have to have it. There are other things. No one plays forever." He mounts his steed.

"You look right at home up there," he is told.

Bradshaw smiles. "It's a good place to be," he says, galloping off, by heaven, into the sunset. ∎

threw for six touchdowns and was intercepted 24 times, hardly a magical debut. In the final game, a 30–20 loss to Philadelphia, he was sent in to punt for the injured Bobby Walden. "He was kicking from the end zone," Russell recalls, "so we suspected they'd be coming strong. They did. They just crushed that punt. For Terry it was the final humiliation." Still, the Steelers finished with a 5–9 record, their best since 1966. It was small consolation to the shattered young quarterback.

"My rookie year was a disaster," Bradshaw can say now. "I was totally unprepared for pro ball. I'd had no schooling on reading defenses. They'd blitz me, and I'd just run away. I had never studied the game, never looked at films the way a quarterback should. I'd never even played on a team that had another quarterback besides me. I had no idea how important I was to the team. We had another good quarterback in Terry Hanratty. He was an All-America from Notre Dame, and he was from Pennsylvania. He had polish. He was one of the guys. I was an outsider who didn't mingle well. The other players looked upon me as a Bible-toting Li'l Abner."

He went home to Shreveport discouraged but not defeated. "I was embarrassed. I started studying this game. I worked and worked." Noll

JOE THEISMANN SUPER BOWL **XVII**
REDSKINS 27, DOLPHINS 17

JIM PLUNKETT SUPER BOWL **XVIII**
RAIDERS 38, REDSKINS 9

JOE MONTANA SUPER BOWL **XIX**
49ERS 38, DOLPHINS 16

JIM McMAHON SUPER BOWL **XX**
BEARS 46, PATRIOTS 10

PHIL SIMMS SUPER BOWL **XXI**
GIANTS 39, BRONCOS 20

DOUG WILLIAMS SUPER BOWL **XXII**
REDSKINS 42, BRONCOS 10

JOE MONTANA SUPER BOWL **XXIII**
49ERS 20, BENGALS 16

JOE MONTANA SUPER BOWL **XXIV**
49ERS 55, BRONCOS 10

JEFF HOSTETLER **SUPER BOWL XXV**
GIANTS 20, BILLS 19

MARK RYPIEN **SUPER BOWL XXVI**
REDSKINS 37, BILLS 24

TROY AIKMAN **SUPER BOWL XXVII**
COWBOYS 52, BILLS 17

TROY AIKMAN **SUPER BOWL XXVIII**
COWBOYS 30, BILLS 13

STEVE YOUNG SUPER BOWL **XXIX**
49ERS 49, CHARGERS 26

TROY AIKMAN SUPER BOWL **XXX**
COWBOYS 27, STEELERS 17

BRETT FAVRE SUPER BOWL **XXXI**
PACKERS 35, PATRIOTS 21

JOHN ELWAY SUPER BOWL **XXXII**
BRONCOS 31, PACKERS 24

JOHN ELWAY SUPER BOWL **XXXIII**
BRONCOS 34, FALCONS 19

KURT WARNER SUPER BOWL **XXXIV**
RAMS 23, TITANS 16

TRENT DILFER SUPER BOWL **XXXV**
RAVENS 34, GIANTS 7

TOM BRADY SUPER BOWL **XXXVI**
PATRIOTS 20, RAMS 17

BRAD JOHNSON SUPER BOWL **XXXVII**

BUCCANEERS 48, RAIDERS 21

TOM BRADY SUPER BOWL **XXXVIII**

PATRIOTS 32, PANTHERS 29

TOM BRADY SUPER BOWL **XXXIX**

PATRIOTS 24, EAGLES 21

BEN ROETHLISBERGER SUPER BOWL **XL**

STEELERS 21, SEAHAWKS 10

THE BIG EASY

CALL HIM A HANGDOG HERO, A SAD-SACK SUPERMAN, BUT WOULD YOU BET AGAINST THE GIANTS' ELI MANNING, THE TWO-TIME MVP OF THE SUPER BOWL, WHEN IT'S ALL ON THE LINE IN FEBRUARY?

Excerpted from SPORTS ILLUSTRATED, *December 17, 2012* | BY S.L. PRICE

OU WANT TO WIN, RIGHT? THEN YOU'LL have to reimagine how a quarterback should be. That's obvious now. This won't be easy if you grew up with Tittle's bloodied head or Namath's nightclub grin, with Montana's ice-cool gaze or Marino's red-faced rage; if you buy the football-as-war thing and envision a QB as some glory-eyed field general, Patton in cleats, beloved and feared and renewing one of the last archetypes of American manhood with each last-second miracle.

Eli Manning stays on his feet . . . airs it out down the field. . . . It is . . . caught! By Tyree!

Because that's the essence. That's what we talk about, really, when we talk about The Quarterback. Is he clutch? How does he fare in the ultimate moment, when 100 million fans are watching and an unforgiving city demands success? Nothing else matters. Which brings us to the wondrous and puzzling boy king of New York.

Oh, my God . . . I don't know how he got out of there! I thought he was on the ground, and then he came out of the pile and just slings it!

The Giants' Eli Manning owns a middling career passer rating and is, in the words of his former center, Shaun O'Hara, "one of the most unathletic quarterbacks in the NFL." He lacks Tom Brady's glamour, Drew Brees's accuracy and big brother Peyton's near-oppressive aura of authority. Yet after last February's Super Bowl title—his second in five seasons—after a year in which he set the NFL record with 15 fourth-quarter touchdown passes and 10 road wins and tied the alltime mark with eight game-winning drives, it's clear that, at 31, Manning is the best quarterback alive if you want to win a title; the best ever to play for one of the most iconic franchises, the best, in fact, to take Manhattan, better than Charlie Conerly, Phil Simms and even sexy Broadway Joe.

Thirty-nine seconds left. . . . Manning lobs it. . . . Burress alone. Touchdown, New York!

This is, in many precincts, sacrilegious talk. The Big Apple likes its heroes (and villains and fools) larger than life. Manning is the opposite, country twang and all. His body language falls somewhere between mumble and sigh. Where his passing peers project macho cool, Eli appears to have just rolled off a couch, blinking and bed-headed, to take the snap. His hype-deflating demeanor on camera—even the cellphone that snapped him gazing at his flooded Hoboken, N.J., apartment lobby following Hurricane Sandy—can leave one doubtful that this guy knows whether he's just won, lost or been hit by a natural disaster.

Four-man rush. Eeee-Li, throwing into traffic on the sideline . . . and they rule it a catch by Manningham!

An absolutely picture-perfect throw. The window on that thing is about THIS big. That's why he was the Super Bowl MVP.

Pro football has never quite known what to make of him, and God has laughed at every try. After three years of playing alongside him, running back Tiki Barber in 2007 called Manning's leadership "comical." Five months later Eli guided the mercurial Giants 83 yards in the final 2:42 to beat the 18–0 Patriots for one of the greatest upsets in Super Bowl history. Pundits giggled when, in response to a radio host's prompting, Eli described himself last season as "elite." So in February—in Peyton's old Indianapolis stomping ground—he drove the Giants 88 yards to win his second Lombardi Trophy. And a month ago, in the midst of a three-game touchdown drought and speculation that he might have a "dead arm," Simms declared that Manning was, indeed, not an elite quarterback. Thirteen days later Eli fired three touchdown passes to beat the streaking Packers and break Simms's franchise career record of 199.

On Sunday the Giants scored 52 points to beat the Saints, yet the usual spectacular-shaky mix—Manning threw four touchdowns and two interceptions, one a pick-six—had analysts mapping the ways they could miss the playoffs entirely. Meanwhile, the Redskins and the Cowboys are surging, and oh, yes, Peyton has come back from oblivion to fashion one of his typically flawless campaigns in Denver. Eli, in other words, has 'em all right where he wants 'em.

For Eli, life just feels better when it's played like an endless two-minute drill. "I definitely don't get nervous," he says. "That's maybe the difference with other people. They may think, If we don't score here, we lose. I look at it the other way: Hey, we're about to win. It's two minutes, we're *about* to throw it every down—and as a quarterback that's what you want. When you're down, you got nothing to lose."

There have been low-key star quarterbacks before, of course. But Bart Starr and Bob Griese carried themselves like NASA engineers. Eli Manning, peering out from under a 10-year-old's haircut, is the NFL embodiment of cognitive dissonance. He inspires confidence despite stretches where, as former Jets QB Boomer Esiason says, "he can look like he has no clue." At certain harried moments Manning resembles no one so much as Dukakis in the tank. No wonder his favorite *Seinfeld* episode is "Bizarro Jerry," where everything is reversed. In Eli's world last is first, omega man trumps the alpha males and the lesser quarterback always wins.

"He doesn't fit," says Esiason, who cohosts a sports talk show on New York's WFAN. "When he's fundamentally sound, he looks good, like a Manning. When he's not, he's gangly, all over the place, and when he runs, the whole thing is awkward. To have two Super Bowl parades and be on the lead float, looking like a bobble-head doll? What is going on here? But that's the beauty of Eli. I can't tell you just how amazing his story is. If I had a vote, even if his career ended today, he'd be in the Hall of Fame." ∎

Manning has beaten the Pats—and Tom Brady—twice on the NFL's biggest stage. | *Photograph by Robert Beck*

PEYTON MANNING SUPER BOWL **XLI**

COLTS 29, BEARS 17

ELI MANNING SUPER BOWL **XLII**

GIANTS 17, PATRIOTS 14

BEN ROETHLISBERGER SUPER BOWL **XLIII**

STEELERS 27, CARDINALS 23

DREW BREES SUPER BOWL **XLIV**

SAINTS 31, COLTS 17

AARON RODGERS SUPER BOWL **XLV**

PACKERS 31, STEELERS 25

ELI MANNING SUPER BOWL **XLVI**

GIANTS 21, PATRIOTS 17

JOE FLACCO SUPER BOWL **XLVII**

RAVENS 34, 49ERS 31

RUSSELL WILSON SUPER BOWL **XLVIII**

SEAHAWKS 43, BRONCOS 8

THE
NEXT

OVER THE LAST decade and a half, the NFL has witnessed a Golden Age of quarterbacks, but a number of great ones have retired and more are inching closer to the inevitable end. So what is the state of the position? It's in good hands, and in many cases on more active feet, as a coterie of young guns and rising stars will attest

ANDREW LUCK Despite his surname, it has been all skill driving the Colts' QB's results: Two seasons, two 11–5 marks, two playoffs, two Pro Bowls.

WAVE

Photograph by David E. Klutho

The Future Is Now —And It's Mobile

BY GREG A. BEDARD

Peyton Manning, at AGE 37, ENTERED SUPER BOWL XLVIII LOOKING to put an exclamation point on one of the greatest seasons ever by a quarterback and on his own sterling career. Instead, after being pressured, hit and harassed on seemingly every play by a swarming Seahawks defense, it looked as if Manning's career was taking its final breaths in a 43–8 loss. He was an aging, statuesque target in the pocket, and every yard gained seemed like a monumental

effort as his minuscule average of 5.7 yards per pass attempt would corroborate.

Manning's counterpart, 25-year-old Russell Wilson, looked as if he was playing in a pickup game. Despite operating behind one of the worst pass-blocking lines in the league, he was in complete control. When he threw, Wilson averaged 8.2 yards per attempt. On the rare occasion when he felt pressure, Wilson tucked the ball and gained an average of 8.7 yards. He looked as if he barely broke a sweat. The new school of NFL quarterback won easily over the old school. Short, mobile and instinctive beat tall, pocket-bound and precise.

Were we all witness to a new NFL? Not exactly. We've been here before. Steve Young looked like he was changing the game with his unique blend of pocket accuracy and dangerous mobility as he led the 49ers to a victory over the Chargers in Super Bowl XXIX. But that was in 1995, and he never won another. Randall Cunningham, Steve McNair, Donovan McNabb and Michael Vick all looked like game changers too, but none of them ever hoisted the Lombardi Trophy. Packers quarterback Aaron Rodgers was the perfect blend of arm, running ability and game-plan mastery when he delivered another championship to Titletown after the 2010 season, but then Eli Manning and Joe Flacco led the Giants and Ravens to Super Bowl titles predominantly from the pocket.

What the NFL is witnessing is not a quarterback revolution, but an evolution, mostly thanks to developments in the college game. The NFL has its prototype quarterback—6'4", strong, with a cannon arm—but it can't create examples out of thin air. It has to pick its players from the pool available at the college level, and that game has changed.

Up until the mid 2000s, the NCAA had two types of quarterbacks: run-first athletes who directed rushing offenses, and classic pocket passers operating pro-style offenses. The advent of the spread and zone-read offenses, and then the combination of both schemes, has caused a profound shift. Now, nearly every NCAA offense features schemes that spread the field with multiple wideouts and try to gain a tactical advantage by using a quarterback who is a threat to run. (With a pocket passer, the reasoning goes, the 11 defensive players only have to account for 10 players because the QB doesn't move; a mobile quarterback makes it 11 on 11 and evens the odds for an offense.)

As a result, the collegiate pocket passer has become an endangered species in recent years. Instead of producing players like Peyton Manning, Tom Brady and Drew Brees—who only leave the pocket if it's on fire—the NFL has been going mobile. These are the quarterbacks taken in the top 18 picks from 2008 to '11: Matt Ryan, Joe Flacco, Matthew Stafford,

Mark Sanchez, Josh Freeman, Sam Bradford, Cam Newton, Jake Locker, Blaine Gabbert and Christian Ponder. Newton was the only player not to fit the traditional prototype for an NFL quarterback. Of the quarterbacks taken in the top 18 since (Andrew Luck, Robert Griffin III, Ryan Tannehill, E.J. Manuel) and the top three projected QB picks in the 2014 draft (Blake Bortles, Teddy Bridgewater and Johnny Manziel), only Luck and Bridgewater operated true pro systems in college. At 6' 4", 240 pounds, Luck has joined Rodgers as the *new* prototype in the NFL: tall, strong, with a big arm and the ability to run when a play breaks down.

"I think anytime you get into a situation where quarterbacks extend plays, particularly when the play shouldn't be

extended, it's a body blow to the defense," says Packers coach Mike McCarthy. "Andrew is excellent at it. He's a big, strong, physical quarterback that's able to step out of tough situations and make any throw, a lot like Aaron. I think people found out that he's a much better runner than they were aware of when he came into the league."

Every team in the NFL would take Luck if it could, but that kind of college star is becoming a rare breed. Instead, the best QBs coming out now are like Wilson, Colin Kaepernick, Newton and Griffin, players who aren't as adept at passing from the pocket but are more dynamic runners. They come with a risk, though, as the league saw with RGIII's first two seasons. His forays out of the pocket left him with a torn ACL and LCL in his right knee at the end of a brilliant rookie year, and the Redskins with a 3–13 record the following season.

"Having a mobile quarterback I think is harder to defend than a stationary pocket guy," says Jets coach Rex Ryan, one of the league's top defensive minds. "That said, I'd probably rather defend a mobile quarterback than Peyton Manning or Tom Brady."

Put another way, NFL coaches don't want to defend against mobile quarterbacks, but, ideally, they don't want them running their offense, either, because most games are ultimately decided from the pocket. After all, the Seahawks would not have been in the Super Bowl if not for a terrific 35-yard, game-winning touchdown strike by Wilson—from the pocket—to Jermaine Kearse to beat Kaepernick and the 49ers in the NFC championship game.

So the search will continue for classic pocket passers. (Penn State's Christian Hackenberg is believed to be the next great one, but he's not available until the 2016 draft at the earliest.) And as defensive coordinators take away the running game in college, the trend will no doubt swing back again.

Hall of Fame quarterback Fran Tarkenton, one of the first true dual-threat NFL quarterbacks, was predicting the extinction of the pocket passer as far back as 1967, when he said this in a first-person piece for SPORTS ILLUSTRATED.

"The quarterback of tomorrow is going to be better than we are today, and he will be able to do a zillion things, including scrambling," Tarkenton wrote. "He's going to have the ability to throw from the roll, the moving pocket, the drop-back pocket, the bootleg and the busted play. . . . The quarterbacks coming out of colleges nowadays are better athletes than ever before; they can do everything. They're just not producing any more of those stay-in-the-pocket, rocking-chair quarterbacks. The new breed will make the game of football wilder and more interesting than ever before."

Sounds a lot like the quarterback of today, so maybe he was right. Then again, the golden age of the pocket passer started some 15 years *after* his remarks. There will be no revolution. But evolution goes on and on. ∎

NICK FOLES In just his second season, in 2013, his ratio of 27 TDs to two interceptions set an NFL record, and his seven TDS in one game tied another.

Photographs by Al Tielemans [left] and Robert Beck

COLIN KAEPERNICK A starter for less than two seasons, he's nevertheless led the 49ers to a Super Bowl and an NFC championship game appearance.

A-PLUS FOR D.C.'S RG3

IN PERHAPS THE GREATEST DEBUT GAME EVER BY AN NFL QUARTERBACK, ROBERT GRIFFIN III SET THE NATION'S CAPITAL ABUZZ WITH HIS POTENT MIXTURE OF PASSING AND RUNNING

Excerpted from SPORTS ILLUSTRATED, *September 17, 2012* | BY PABLO S. TORRE

HEN HE WAS A FIRST-GRADER, ROBERT Griffin III's parents concocted a system of incentives to motivate their only son. This, everyone involved can now agree, was completely unnecessary. Griffin already "wanted to be the guy raising his hand," he says, "telling everyone what two plus two equals." Nonetheless, if Griffin's report card ever showed all A's, Robert Jr. and Jacqueline, both Army sergeants, would hand over five dollars. The rewards eventually expanded to include Ninja Turtles action figures, computer games and larger sums of money. Then one day, before young Robert graduated seventh in his class at Copperas Cove (Texas) High, the system finally collapsed. Considering the family's balance sheet, Robert Jr. conceded the obvious to his wife: "Robert is breaking us."

By the second quarter of Griffin's NFL debut, the entire city of New Orleans could relate. Never mind the deafening Superdome, a determined Drew Brees or a Saints defense intent on seeking vengeance for a seemingly interminable summer (the result of the Bountygate scandal that saw head coach Sean Payton suspended for the 2012 season, assistant head coach Joe Vitt banned for six games and defensive coordinator Gregg Williams banished from the team for good even before his indefinite suspension by the NFL). Never mind that Griffin, a 22-year-old rookie, was the eighth quarterback to start for the Redskins in the past eight years.

The new kid began with a scorching eight completions on his first eight pass attempts, rated a perfect 158.3 for the first half and finished 19 of 26 for 320 yards with two touchdowns and zero interceptions, a performance that no other first-time NFL starter has ever matched. Taking into account the Redskins' 40–32 upset, with New Orleans natives Jacqueline and Robert Jr. watching proudly from the stands, it all adds up to Griffin III's finest report card yet.

"We all knew he had the potential to do it," left guard Kory Lichtensteiger said of beating the heavily favored Saints, "but he surpassed everybody's expectations. He was the leader for the whole game. He was unbelievable."

Yes, and he made it all look so very easy. Griffin's first touchdown was a masterpiece: a first-quarter play-action bomb, thrown on the backpedal, that wideout Pierre Garçon took 88 yards for a score, leaving the quarterback to raise both hands into the air from his seat on the turf. But the more remarkable moment, the one more exemplary of his rare talent, came when he handed off to running back Alfred Morris in the third quarter. Griffin, an Olympic-caliber hurdler, got so far ahead of the play that he ended up blocking downfield for his tailback, who took the ball 18 yards.

"Coach [Mike Shanahan] took the reins off of me and allowed me to do a lot of the things I was used to doing in college," said Griffin. "We balled out."

And then, after the game was over, the victorious No. 2 overall pick in the 2012 draft skipped away into the visitors' locker room while the remaining crowd in the Superdome chanted *R-G-Three! R-G-Three!*

No matter how much that popularity spreads—and Griffin already has endorsement deals with companies ranging from Nissan to Subway to Castrol motor oil—all the Redskins really want is to fill a void that has existed for well over a decade. It is ironic, if not plainly humiliating, that the nation's capital of all NFL cities has been so starved for leadership under center that two years ago some fans resorted to calling then 33-year-old Donovan McNabb the Franchise when he arrived at Redskins training camp for what turned out to be a very short tenure.

In truth, Griffin has been trying to halt that cycle of disposability since the spring. During the off-season, before he'd ever even met any of the offensive linemen who would be blocking for him, he sent them motivational text messages. "I'm doing my part down here to get ready," the guard Lichtensteiger recalls the contents of one reading. Coming from a rookie—indeed, the first NFL starting quarterback who happened to be born in the decade of the 1990s—this kind of message raised eyebrows.

Griffin also sought out some retired signal-callers, such as former league MVPs Kurt Warner and Rich Gannon, to ask for advice, hoping to find an edge. "He wants to be great—he wants to do the work," says Gannon. "But you've got to be realistic. The Redskins are a developing team, and you have to manage the bumps in the road."

When that struggle inevitably arrives, what will be of most help to Griffin is the experience of his final (Heisman-winning) season in college. Before Griffin's arrival at Baylor, the school was known primarily as a Big 12 Conference cellar dweller. The miasma in Waco was not terribly dissimilar from what has long plagued the District. But then Griffin's Bears set to tying or breaking no fewer than 101 school offensive records as the junior led Baylor to a 10–3 record and a No. 12 final BCS ranking. Suddenly anything seemed within range.

On Sunday night, several hours after his first NFL victory, the quarterback walked across the field inside the now silent Superdome, cradling his inaugural touchdown ball, and paused to reflect on all of the things that had once been gifted to him. "I might give this [ball] to my parents," he said. "The greatest thing was coming off the field and seeing the smiles on my mom and dad's faces." That memory would be his own reward. ∎

Griffin had a stunning inaugural, but by year's end a knee injury clouded his future. | *Photograph by Simon Bruty*

JOHNNY MANZIEL There are questions about his size (6' 1") and his love for the nightlife, but no one questions the excitement that Johnny Football creates.

What happens when a quarterback beats eventual national champion Alabama on its home field, leads the SEC in rushing while throwing for 3,706 yards and 26 TDs, becomes the first freshman to win the Heisman, helps his team crush Oklahoma in the Cotton Bowl, throws out the first pitch at a Rangers' game and shoots a 79 at Pebble Beach? He makes a new bucket list, of course.

—ANDY STAPLES, SI, *August 5, 2013*

TEDDY BRIDGEWATER He shocked Florida in the Sugar Bowl as a sophomore in 2012 and came back to complete 71% of his passes for almost 4,000 yards in 2013.

WHOLE LOT OF LUCK

BUOYED BY PRECOCIOUS ROOKIE QB ANDREW LUCK, AND INSPIRED BY THE COURAGEOUS BATTLE OF COACH CHUCK PAGANO, THE COLTS TURNED INTO UNLIKELY CONTENDERS

Excerpted from SPORTS ILLUSTRATED, *December 3, 2012* | BY PETER KING

HE COLTS HAVE TRANSITIONED so quickly from the Peyton Manning era—the Indianapolis faithful going from bemoaning the loss of the greatest quarterback they'd ever seen to embracing a new one in what seemed like 10 minutes—that it's worth retracing how it came about that the Colts are 8–4 following their 20–13 victory over the Bills on Sunday.

We could start with the hiring of 40-year-old Ryan Grigson, a former beat-the-bushes scout who has churned the roster like no other GM in football. Of the 61 players on his active and practice squads, 42 weren't on the roster the day he took over in January. That's a 69% turnover. "Our depth chart is a living, breathing organism," says Grigson, whose leading tackler is Jerrell Freeman, a 26-year-old rookie from mighty Mary Hardin-Baylor (Texas) by way of the Saskatchewan Roughriders, and whose fifth cornerback, Teddy Williams, signed in Week 9, is an All-America sprinter who never played a down of college football. Then there's cornerback Darius Butler. Three hours before a game in Jacksonville, his sixth since joining the team, he walked down the aisle of the team bus, past some coaches.

"Who's that?" quarterbacks coach Clyde Christensen asked another assistant.

"That's Butler, the corner," he was told. "He's playing tonight."

Or we could start with the guy Grigson and owner Jimmy Irsay hired as their coach, the itinerant, 52-year-old Chuck Pagano. He was the Ravens' defensive coordinator in 2011, his 12th coaching position in 28 seasons, and had never interviewed for a head coach job at any level. Early in Pagano's interview, Grigson wrote on his legal pad, "[Players] will run through a brick wall for this guy." And that was it.

A diagnosis of acute promyelocytic leukemia, a cancer of the blood and bone marrow, wasn't part of the plan. Who knows why the Colts are 6–2 since Pagano got the crushing news during the Colts' bye week in late September? It's always dangerous to invoke Hollywood in a life-and-death story, but as interim coach Bruce Arians, Pagano's close friend, says, "This whole story's for Steven Spielberg. I can't explain it."

If this were a movie, it would certainly include the scene in which Pagano, in the first game he attended after the diagnosis, climbed on a chair in Grigson's stadium suite to pound on the window, trying to get the attention of the Colts' coaches about a play he wanted them to run.

Or we could start with Pagano's stand-in, the 60-year-old Arians, hired to be Luck's offensive coordinator, then finding himself thrown into something he never could have expected. The first thing Arians, formerly the Steelers' coordinator, did when he took the interim job was to flip on the light switch in Pagano's office and, energy conservation be

darned, order that it stay on until Pagano's return. Tutoring Luck would have been more than a full-time job alone, but adding his first head-coaching duties and the awkwardness of stepping aside when Pagano intercedes with a text makes the job a balancing act that no other coach has ever had to deal with.

But really, to be simple and straightforward about it, we should start with the importance of one player. Andrew Luck was drafted No. 1 overall by the Colts on April 26, but because NFL rules dictate that seniors can't report to their teams until after completing their degrees, Luck couldn't report to Indy until mid-June, six weeks before training camp By comparison, Robert Griffin III and Russell Wilson could report full time to Washington and Seattle, respectively, in mid-May.

Why this matters: Luck played in a mostly short-passing, move-the-sticks West Coast scheme at Stanford, and Arians hates the West Coast offense. He doesn't think it sufficiently empowers a QB to change his protections or his hot (safety valve) receivers at the line of scrimmage. "My quarterback has to be able to fix problems," says Arians. Learning how to do that would take time, even for a sponge like Luck. But from the time he arrived in Indianapolis, Luck showed the learning curve wasn't going to intimidate him.

In one of his first practices, Luck faced eight snaps against blitzes. It was a disaster. He completed one pass, appeared discombobulated, and as one defensive player recalls, "If that had been a heavyweight fight, it would have been a first-round knockout."

"I have no idea what just happened," Luck said to Christensen as he walked off the field. "It was like a tsunami."

Later, watching film with Arians, the quarterback realized, "God, that's easy." He just had to learn which players to move where in protection. For instance, if he had an empty backfield in shotgun and he saw a blitzer threatening the A gap (the holes on either side of the center), he could call out a code word to reposition a tight end as a sidecar in the backfield. If he saw a defensive back creeping up to blitz, he could shift every lineman one assignment in that direction.

"In the next blitz period," recalls defensive coordinator Greg Manusky, "he'd call out who we were bringing and our coverages, right at the line. You could tell he'd studied the crap out of each play. He had an answer for everything. That's something you see in a second- or third-year quarterback, maybe. Or in a Manning."

In Indy, Luck is already famous for this learning ability. After his first minicamp, Christensen sent him home with a binder of all the Colts' three- and five-step-drop passes. The next afternoon Luck called Christensen and asked, "I got it; what have you got for me now?"

"He gets the most irritated when I repeat something, like I shouldn't be wasting his time," says Christensen.

You'd think his nerdiness might rub some veteran players the wrong

who throws deep a lot isn't likely to have a starry completion percentage. Two: The Colts are 6–1 in games that have been decided by six or fewer points. In those games, Luck had eight drives that resulted in points during the final two minutes of the second or fourth quarter, or in OT. And three: Unaccounted for in his passer rating are his fleet feet, which lend Indy an added option on the goal line. He has five rushing TDs, trailing only RG3 among quarterbacks.

True, in watching video of Luck you see some impetuousness that must be coached out of his game. His second of two pick-sixes against the Patriots was totally irresponsible, seemingly chucked out of frustration. "Horrendous," says Christensen. "No explanation for it."

But rewatch the Miami game. The Dolphins entered that early November meeting ranked first in the league in third-down defense, and Luck, in his eighth NFL game, converted on third-and-12, -14, -20, -10, -16 and -11. Ask Luck for a play that he's proud of in 2012 and he'll cite that last one: third-and-11 at his own five with 11:48 to play in a 20–20 game. Indy had two wideouts to the right, one to the left, and tight end Dwayne Allen lined up just off right tackle. At the snap only three Dolphins rushed, which left Luck standing in the end zone with seven men, including Allen and running back Vick Ballard, in protection.

Seven blocking three: Big, big waste of manpower. But after stoning defensive end Cameron Wake, Allen knew to release him to the tackle and drift into the flat. Meanwhile, Luck looked downfield at two curl routes and an out pattern—all covered. "Critical juncture of the game, third and somewhat long," says Luck. "You hesitate throwing the ball into the flat on third-and long because if he gets tackled he's short, but I felt the defender was soft on that side, so I got it out to him."

Allen split two defenders at the first-down spot and dived ahead. Gain of 20. Why'd Luck like it? Because he didn't force the ball to a covered receiver. And with eight first-year Colts in the game, they all had to know what to do at a vital time, and they did it.

More impressive was another play later in that drive, on second-and-seven. All week long Indy's offensive staff had guessed at what new Miami defensive coordinator Kevin Coyle would do to pressure Luck, and they settled on studying the blitzes of his mentor in Cincinnati, defensive coordinator Mike Zimmer, because Coyle had used familiar schemes in much of the first half of the season. Zimmer liked A gap blitzes, and the Colts prepared for both A gaps to be rushed.

But they noticed one tweak. When the Dolphins blitzed the A gap, they also occasionally blitzed a corner, leaving the wideout on the right (usually Reggie Wayne's spot for the Colts) uncovered momentarily. "If that happens," Arians told Luck, "just know this: That corner has seven steps to get to you. You've got maybe three steps to release. And they'll probably send a linebacker over to cover Reggie."

Back to the play: Miami put linebackers Kevin Burnett and Karlos Dansby in the A gaps, and as Luck moved Ballard into protection, Burnett and Dansby backed off. But at the snap, safety Jimmy Wilson blitzed from Luck's right side, and Dansby sprinted over to latch onto Wayne, the hot read, just as Arians had warned. Luck never had time to seriously consider any receiver to his left, and he figured that if he threw quickly to Wayne, Dansby would be there in time. So he lasered a throw to Allen, uncovered for a second up the right seam, just off the line. Gain of 20. Total veteran stuff, and it led to the game-winning field goal.

Luck has a six-year-old flip phone, the same one he had at Stanford. He's not on Twitter and doesn't immerse himself 24/7 in social media. "I'm no Luddite," he says, "but staying unconnected . . . it's a way for me to get away from things. There's a lot in this business you don't need to know."

Luck's a voracious reader but avoids heavy stuff during the season. On his night table now: *A Short History of Nearly Everything*, by humorist Bill Bryson. "I can pick it up for 15 minutes, get something fun out of it, then put it down and go to sleep," he says.

He didn't want to have dinner with a visiting SI writer, didn't want to have his photo taken. As at Stanford, it's clear Luck doesn't want to draw attention to himself in a sport in which the quarterback is already so magnified to the public eye. ∎

way. But this team is so young—when Luck peers into the huddle, he sees as many as six rookies—that his leadership has seemed natural. No one batted an eye when, in his first minicamp following the draft, Luck snapped, "Get your asses going! We gotta win this practice!"

It's taken a village to contribute to Luck's rookie success, and that village includes Pagano, even in absentia. "Coach Pagano started the first week of the season with a great Friday-morning quarterbacks meeting," says Luck. "He'd walk us through 10 or 15 plays of the opposing defense. I learned a lot. Then, with the leukemia, I figured, 'I guess we're not doing our meetings anymore.' But that first Friday I got eight text messages from him—looks, indicators and things to watch for."

Luck's results so far? Mixed. Asked after Week 9 what rookie midterm grade he'd give himself, he said, "C. Average." A bit harsh perhaps given the Colts' 5–3 record at the time, but the stats suggest the grade should actually be lower. He's 29th in the league in passer rating at 76.7, only slightly better than the Jets' Mark Sanchez. And if Indy fails to make the playoffs, Luck will likely look back in disgust on his three interceptions and one lost fumble in a 59–24 loss to the Patriots on Nov. 18.

On the other hand, Luck is on pace to throw for more yards, 4,662, than Manning did in all but one of his 13 seasons with the Colts.

So what's the fair assessment of Luck's play? Several factors balance out that poor passer rating. One: His 10.27-yard average pass length (how far downfield his typical pass was touched by a receiver) is far and away the highest in the league—2.07 yards longer than Manning's. Someone

MATTHEW STAFFORD He reached his 50th career game with 14,331 passing yards, almost 500 more than the mark set by Kurt Warner.

After throwing for 422 yards, an NFL record for a rookie debut, in a 28–21 loss at Arizona, Newton had 432 against the Packers. His total of 854 passing yards in his first two games is the most ever. But he also had four interceptions. He was good. He was bad. And he lost.

—TIM LAYDEN, SI, *September 26, 2011*

CAM NEWTON After two losing seasons, the 6' 6", 260-pound Newton showed new maturity in 2013 while leading the Panthers to a 12-4 record and the playoffs.

"God put me here for a reason," Wilson says, "and I cherish that for the African-American community. I cherish it for all the kids who've been told they can't do something—whether you're white, black, Asian, Hispanic— because I'm 5' 11". Everyone told me I couldn't."

—S.L. PRICE, SI, February 10, 2014

RUSSELL WILSON The Seahawks took a chance on an undersized QB and he rewarded them with a mobile threat, few mistakes and the franchise's first title.

Photograph by Al Tielemans

ACKNOWLEDGMENTS

THIS BOOK WOULD NEVER have been possible without the decades of contributions from the writers, editors, photographers and researchers who created the rich SI archive of quarterback lore that informed and inspired us. But of all those staffers, we pay special tribute to Paul Zimmerman. Dr. Z covered the NFL for SI with passionate zeal for 29 years, until a stroke incapacitated him in 2008, and his contemporaneous reporting on the quarterbacks of his time was invaluable to us. Our thanks also go out to all the MMQB.com crew members, especially Peter King, for their help and guidance. We are grateful for the assistance of Geoff Michaud, Dan Larkin and the rest of the SI Premedia Group as well as Karen Meneghin, Karen Carpenter, Prem Kalliat, Joe Felice, George Amores and Will Welt. And a final note of thanks to Time Inc. Sports Group editor Paul Fichtenbaum and SI managing editor Chris Stone for their support of this project.

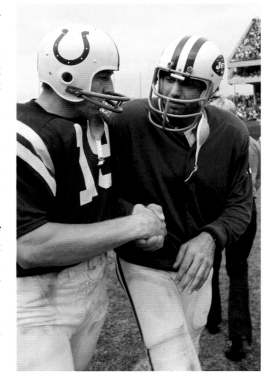

PHOTO CREDITS

FRONT COVER: AP (George Blanda), Robert Beck (Peyton Manning, Alex Smith), Bettmann/Corbis (Jack Kemp), John Biever (Dan Marino, Kurt Warner, Russell Wilson), Simon Bruty (Eli Manning), Andy Hayt (Joe Montana), Walter Iooss Jr. (Ken Anderson, Bert Jones, Daryle Lamonica, Don Meredith, Joe Namath), Heinz Kluetmeier (Brett Favre, Greg Landry), David E. Klutho (Colin Kaepernick, Matthew Stafford), Neil Leifer (Terry Bradshaw, Joe Kapp, Earl Morrall, Frank Ryan, Fran Tarkenton, Y.A. Tittle, Johnny Unitas), Richard Mackson (Phil Simms), Peter Read Miller (Troy Aikman, Randall Cunningham, John Elway), Michael J. Minardi (Warren Moon), Ronald C. Modra (Dan Fouts, Joe Theismann), Patrick Murphy-Racey (Ryan Leaf), Darryl Norenberg/USA TODAY Sports (Jim Hart), Evan Peskin (Otto Graham), Mickey Pfleger (Rick Mirer), Robert Rogers (Steve Young), Bob Rosato (Tom Brady), Carlos M. Saavedra (Nick Foles), Damian Strohmeyer (Jeff George), Al Tielemans (Jay Cutler, Matt Ryan), Tony Tomsic/Getty Images (Ken Stabler), Fred Vuich (Kordell Stewart), Jerry Wachter (Doug Williams).

BACK COVER: Robert Beck (Donovan McNabb), Bettmann/Corbis (Sid Luckman), John Biever (Jim Kelly, Andrew Luck, Phillip Rivers), Simon Bruty (Robert Griffin III), Tom Dahlin (Daunte Culpepper), Nate Fine (Sonny Jurgensen), John Iacono (Jim McMahon, Joe Montana), Walter Iooss Jr. (Drew Brees, Roger Staubach), Heinz Kluetmeier (Brad Johnson), David E. Klutho (Sam Bradford), Neil Leifer (Len Dawson, Bob Griese, Billy Kilmer, Bart Starr), Long Photography, Inc. (John Brodie), John W. McDonough (Doug Flutie, Cam Newton), Manny Millan (Jim Plunkett), Peter Read Miller (Peyton Manning), Marvin E. Newman (Eddie LeBaron), Bob Rosato (Tony Romo), Al Tielemans (Ben Roethlisberger, Tom Brady, Joe Flacco, Steve McNair, Aaron Rodgers, Michael Vick), Jerry Wachter (Bernie Kosar).

ADDITIONAL CREDITS: Page 18 (from top): Hank Walker/Time Life Pictures/Getty Images, Fred Lyon, Neil Leifer; Page 19 (from top): Walter Iooss Jr., John Iacono, Walter Iooss Jr.; Page 20: (from top): Walter Iooss Jr, John W. McDonough, Simon Bruty; Page 21 (from top): Walter Iooss

Jr., Michael O'Neill, John W. McDonough; Page 170 (left to right, from top): Al Messerschmidt/Getty Images, AP, Scott Boehm/AP, Peter Brouillet, Kevin C. Cox/Getty Images, Diamond Images/Getty Images, Rob Carr/Getty Images; Page 171 (left column, from top): Chuck Cook/USA TODAY Sports, David E. Klutho, Courtesy of Fox Sports, ©Rolling Stone LLC 1986 (McMahon); Page 172 (clockwise from left): Mike Segar/Reuters, Allan Grant/Time Life Pictures/Getty Images, Jonathan Ernst/Reuters; Page 173 (clockwise from left): AP, Walter Iooss Jr., Lester Cohen/Wireimage, S. Granitz/Wireimage; Page 176 (left to right, from top): David Duprey/AP, Courtesy of Kraft/AP, Courtesy of State Farm, ©2000 America's Dairy Farmers and Milk Processors; Page 177 (left to right, from top): AP, no credit, Allen Green, Ray Howard/AP, Victor Mikus, Movie Still Archives, AP, Bettmann/Corbis, AP, Time Life Pictures/Getty Images; Page 180 (clockwise from top left): Dana Edelson/NBC/NBCU Photo Bank/Getty Images (2), R.M. Lewis Jr./NBC/NBCU Photo Bank/Getty Images, Dana Edelson/NBC/NBCU Photo Bank/Getty Images, NBC/NBCU Photo Bank/Getty Images; Page 181 (left to right, from top): Alessandro Trovati/AP, Matthew West/Boston Herald/AP, Tim Rasmussen/The Denver Post/Getty Images, Marcio Sanchez/AP, Ron Chenoy/USA TODAY Sports, Doug Pensinger/Getty Images, Joe Amon/The Denver Post/Getty Images, Tim Rasmussen/The Denver Post/Getty Images, Bob Brown/Richmond Times-Dispatch/AP; Page 182 (left to right, from top): Everett Collection (2), Warner Bros./Photofest, Paramount Pictures/Photofest (2), Paramount Pictures/Everett Collection, Warner Bros./Everett Collection, Disney/Photofest; Page 183: Paramount Pictures/Photofest; Page 224 (left to right, from top): Tony Tomsic, Walter Iooss Jr. (2), Neil Leifer; Page 225 (left to right, from top): Walter Iooss Jr., Neil Leifer (2), Walter Iooss Jr.; Page 226 (left to right, from top): Heinz Kluetmeier, Neil Leifer (2), John Iacono; Page 227 (left to right, from top): Heinz Kluetmeier, Walter Iooss Jr., Manny Millan, Andy Hayt.; Page 230 (left to right, from top): Ronald C. Modra, Heinz Kluetmeier, Andy Hayt, John Iacono; Page 231 (left to right, from top): Andy Hayt, Jerry Wachter, Richard Mackson, John W. McDonough; Page 232 (left to right, from top): Richard Mackson, John Iacono, Damian Strohmeyer, Jim Gund; Page 233 (left to right, from top): Robert Rogers, Damian Strohmeyer, John Biever, Timothy A. Clary/AFP/Getty Images; Page 234 (left to right, from top): Bob Rosato, Peter Read Miller, John W. McDonough, David E. Klutho; Page 235 (left to right, from top): Heinz Kluetmeier, Al Tielemans, John W. McDonough, Al Tielemans; Page 238 (left to right, from top): Al Tielemans, Robert Beck, Bob Rosato, Al Tielemans; Page 239 (left to right, from top): Al Tielemans, Bill Frakes, Al Tielemans, John Biever; Endpapers: David N. Berkwitz (artifact courtesy of Pro Football Hall of Fame).

TIME INC. BOOKS PUBLISHER Margot Schupf ASSOCIATE PUBLISHER Allison Devlin VICE PRESIDENT, FINANCE Terri Lombardi EXECUTIVE DIRECTOR, MARKETING SERVICES Carol Pittard EXECUTIVE DIRECTOR, BUSINESS DEVELOPMENT Suzanne Albert EXECUTIVE PUBLISHING DIRECTOR Megan Pearlman ASSOCIATE DIRECTOR OF PUBLICITY Courtney Greenhalgh ASSISTANT GENERAL COUNSEL Simone Procas ASSISTANT DIRECTOR, SPECIAL SALES Ilene Schreider ASSISTANT DIRECTOR, PRODUCTION Susan Chodakiewicz ASSOCIATE PREPRESS MANAGER Alex Voznesenskiy EDITORIAL DIRECTOR Stephen Koepp

Johnny Unitas (left) and Joe Namath, forever linked by their Super Bowl III showdown, shared a handshake before facing off again in 1972. | *Photograph by Neil Leifer*